The Catholic Priest in the United States:

Psychological Investigations

Eugene C. Kennedy, M.M., Ph.D.
Professor of Psychology
Loyola University of Chicago

Victor J. Heckler, Ph.D.
Research Associate in Psychology
Loyola University of Chicago

1972
Publications Office
United States Catholic Conference
1312 Massachusetts Avenue, N.W.
Washington, D.C. 20005

PREFACE

In April, 1967, the Catholic Bishops of the United States at their meeting in Chicago voted to conduct an extensive study of the life and ministry of the American priest. The study was organized under the Committee on Pastoral Research and Practices of the National Conference of Catholic Bishops. In the fall of that year subcommittees under the chairmanship of Cardinal John Krol were formed on each of seven topics of concern. Collectively these subcommittees were constituted as the *ad hoc* committee on the ministry and life of the American priest. The committee was composed of bishops and priests. Father Eugene C. Kennedy, M.M., Ph.D., was named to head the subcommittee on psychology.

The initial group of psychological consultants was composed of James P. O'Connor, Ph.D.; Frank J. Kobler, Ph.D.; Father Charles A. Curran, Ph.D.; Paul F. D'Arcy, Ph.D.; Sister Sara C. Charles, M.D.; Ronald E. Walker, Ph.D.; and Monsignor John Gorman. After lengthy meetings they recommended that research to incorporate in-depth interviewing of priests be designed and carried out in order to achieve the goals outlined by the bishops. These consultants suggested more extensive preparatory consultation with psychiatrists and psychologists who had had experience in working with priests.

This further consultation was carried out during the spring of 1968. The following are among the specialists who were contacted and with whom the plan and scope of the research was discussed:

> Bartemeier, Leo H., M.D., The Seton Institute, Baltimore, Maryland
> Benkert, Marianne, M.D., Private Practice, Baltimore, Maryland
> Bier, Rev. William C., S.J., Ph.D., Fordham University
> Brennan, Edward N., M.D.
> Caldwell, Rev. Joseph, S.J., Loyola University, Los Angeles, California
> Coulson, William R., Ph.D., Center for the Study of the Person, La Jolla, California
> Coville, Walter J., Ph.D., St. Vincent's Hospital, New York City
> Cristantiello, Phillip, Ph.D., New York City

Dondero, Austin, Ph.D., LaSalle College, Philadelphia, Pa.

Flanagan, George, Ph.D., Iona Institute, New Rochelle, New York

Gill, Rev. James, S.J., M.D., Harvard University, Boston, Mass.

Hall, Douglas T., Ph.D., Yale University, New Haven, Connecticut

Hiltner, Seward, Ph.D., Princeton University, Princeton, New Jersey

Hunt, William, Ph.D., Loyola University, Chicago, Illinois

Junk, Ivan, M.D., Private Practice, Baltimore, Maryland

Khlentzos, Michael, M.D., McCauley Institute, St. Mary's Hospital, San Francisco, California

Lynch, Thomas, M.D., Seton Institute, Baltimore, Maryland

McCall, Rev. John, S.J., Ph.D., Boston College, Boston, Mass.

McCarthy, Thomas N., Ph.D., LaSalle College, Philadelphia, Pa.

McCawley, Austin, M.D., St. Vincent's Hospital of Westchester, N.Y.

McNellis, Desmond, M.D., The Seton Institute, Baltimore, Maryland

Mills, Edgar W., Director, Ministry Studies Board, National Council of the Churches of Christ, Washington, D.C.

Murray, Rev. John B., C.M., Ph.D., St. John's College, Queens, N.Y.

Ouellette, Rev. Henry P., Ph.D., Emmanuel College, Boston, Mass.

Schneider, Benjamin, Ph.D., Yale University, New Haven, Connecticut

Tageson, William, Ph.D., Notre Dame University, Notre Dame, Indiana

Thomas, Rev. Leo, O.P., The Menninger Foundation, Topeka, Kansas

Weber, Carlo, Ph.D., Private Practice

Young, Mary F., M.D., Private Practice, Miami, Florida

During the winter of 1969 the permanent staff of the study was established at Loyola University of Chicago. This staff was comprised of the following men: Father Eugene C. Kennedy, M.M., Ph.D., Principal Investigator; Victor J. Heckler, Ph.D., Project Director; Frank J. Kobler, Ph.D., Administrative Council Member; Ronald E. Walker, Ph.D., Administrative Council Member.

In the spring and summer of 1969 a staff of psychologists who were to be interviewers in the study was developed. The following men served in that capacity: Stanley J. Cabanski, Ph.D.; Richard G. Doiron, Ph.D.; Edward D. Doyle, Ph.D.; Father Gerard Egan, Ph.D.; Eugene T. Grembowicz, Ph.D.; Frank J. Macchitelli, Ph.D.; Gerald J. Mozdierz, Ph.D.;

Basil E. Najjar, Ph.D.; Ralph M. Mesenbrink, Ph.D.; Joseph V. Rizzo, Ph.D.; and Edward P. Sheridan, Ph.D.

Bishop Joseph L. Bernardin served for the duration of the study as the representative of the United States Catholic Conference to Loyola University of Chicago. Archbishop John Carberry and Bishop Ernest Primeau functioned at different times as Episcopal Coordinators of the study.

FOREWORD

This report was prepared specifically for the American Bishops who commissioned it. Its form is neither that of a strictly scientific report nor that of a popularized treatment and this must be kept in mind while reading it. The research team sought to explain certain psychological constructs while it simultaneously used them to develop an understanding of the priests of the United States. This necessitated a certain style and pattern of development appropriate to a serious non-scientific audience.

CONTENTS

INDEX OF TABLES

INDEX OF FIGURES

The Catholic Priest in the United States:

Psychological Investigations

CHAPTER I

AN OVERVIEW OF THE FINDINGS

An overview of the results of the present psychological investigation of American priests can be summarized in a sentence which sounds simple but which expresses complex truths: *The priests of the United States are ordinary men.* Many of their conflicts and challenges arise precisely because they are ordinary men who may have to live as though they were not ordinary at all. Perhaps no group of men has such high expectations placed on it by the Church, society, themselves and even their closest personal associates. Psychoanalyst Margaretta K. Bowers (1963) has written that "all through the ages the clergy have suffered from the insurmountable contrast between their very real humanity and the transcendent requirements of their symbolic representation as *the priest,* the Incarnate Christ [p. 9]." The expectations made on the personal life of the priest have shaped his education, his style of living, and his mode of relationship to others. But priests are ordinary men and they can only react to this demanding environment with their ordinary human powers. The results of the psychological investigation are in no sense alarming. Priests do not emerge as seriously disturbed, rebellious, or atypical individuals. They are rather human beings with certain limitations, many of which have not been sufficiently appreciated because of the "great expectations" they are charged with fulfilling. Priests are men, and while this may seem a simple-minded observation, a deepened sensitivity to the limits as well as the possibilities of the human condition is indispensable for a true understanding of the ministry and life of American priests.

Speaking in summary terms again, American priests are bright and good men who do not as a group suffer from major psychological problems. Obviously a cross-sectional look at priests who are actively functioning does not allow an investigation of those subjects who may be psychiatrically hospitalized at the time of the inquiry. A few of the subjects had, at one time or another, been hospitalized for psychiatric reasons; others had sought psychotherapy for themselves on an individual or group basis. The men who have had these experiences, however, constitute a small percentage of the priests of the United States. This is an index of their general health and a sign of their similarity to other men in the population. There is no way, in other words, that the priest population can be described as psychologically sick. The developmental problems of priests, which we will discuss later, are significant but they cannot be appropriately described in psychopathological categories.

American priests are equal to most of the demands that are made on them by the Church and by their people. This is not to characterize these demands as overwhelming; it is to note that priests can and do perform without undue stress the services which are required of them. There is no breakdown, then, in the function which they perform in society in general. This it not to comment on the varying quality of the work which these men may perform. As in any profession or occupation, this is as different as the individual priests are from each other. It is, however, to note that priests meet their general professional responsibilities in acceptable fashion. We may reflect on this in another way. American priests, as a class, do not stand out on either end of the continuum of job performance. There are few who fail to meet the basic demands of what is expected of them as clergymen just as there are few who are outstanding or exceptional examples of professional religious functioning. They carry out the duties which are part of their lives, in other words, pretty much the way most other professional people do, without unusual comment or notoriety.

In many ways priests reflect the problems of the general population. While we will discuss the particular difficulties which many priests have because of lack of full personal growth, these do not seem far different from the problems which many of their contemporary fellow Americans experience. Priests probably stand up psychologically, according to any overall judgment, as well as any other professional group. It is important to remember, however, that we have little data about other professional persons because so few have permitted, encouraged, or cooperated with such in-depth research. Indeed, as the investigation of the American priesthood proceeded at Loyola, it was learned that the American Bar Association, while interested in a study of its members, was unwilling to subject them to the same kind of intense scrutiny which constituted the essential part of this study. What we know of some other professions, however, does suggest that the priests of the United States would not suffer terribly in comparison. This is, it would seem, a function of the common humanity of persons across all the professions rather than of the special nature of any particular profession. While interests, motivations, and the nature of work may differ, there is a common core of personality which overlaps most of the professions, reflecting the truth of psychiatrist Harry Stack Sullivan's famous phrase, "We are much more simply human than anything else."

The priesthood is not reduced in any psychological or philosophical sense by observing the ordinary character of American priests and thereby modifying the expectations made on individual persons who are priests. They are not supermen. But this is not because they have chosen the priesthood rather than some other walk of life; it is because they are men. The profession of the priesthood, if it can so be described for the purpose of this discussion, has long been surrounded with assertions and traditions which have set the priest apart and made him, in effect, an extraordinary personage in the eyes of the Church and its human communities. This is reflected in the way the priesthood has been written about, the social reinforcement of the priesthood by the Catholic population, and also by its share in the general esteem accorded to all clergymen. In the eyes of Catholics, priests have had very special qualities. This has notably affected the conditions of recruitment, training, and the living and working experience of priests themselves. They have been encouraged to look on themselves as separate, called to a very high vocation of service, and asked to transform their own personalities into that of Jesus Christ Himself. Catholics are so familiar with this kind of language that one must step back for a moment and reflect on the powerful effects of these expectations and attitudes on the way priests have looked at themselves and their roles within the Church. Perhaps this is illustrated somewhat dramatically but nonetheless, accurately in the example chosen by Dr. Bowers to underscore the same point. She cites the following reflections from Catherine de Hueck (1950):

> For a priest is a miracle of God's love to us; a man who, through his sacrament of ordination becomes *another Christ* with powers that beggar human imagination . . . nothing can be greater in this world of ours than a priest. Nothing but God Himself.
>
> A priest is a holy man because he walks before the Face of the All Holy.
>
> A priest understands all things.
>
> A priest forgives all things.
>
> A priest is a man who lives to serve.

A priest is a man who has crucified himself, so that he too
may be lifted up and draw all things to Christ.
A priest is a symbol of the Word Made Flesh.
A priest is the naked sword of God's justice.
A priest is the hand of God's mercy.
A priest is the reflection of God's love. He teaches God to us
. . . he brings God to us . . . he represents God to us
[pp. 85–87].

As Bowers notes: "This statement on the nature of the priesthood,
though put in exalted terms, reflects in a very real sense the clergymen's
ideal self-image, and at the same time intimates the staggering demands
on his heart and conscience if he is to fulfill it." It may well be observed
that this is precisely the attitude which one should have toward the
priesthood, that this traditional style captures the essential separateness
and dignity of this occupational choice. That may well be the truth, but
the psychologist as such cannot pass judgment on theological realities.
He can only look at the psychological truth as it emerges in the individual
persons into whose lives he is privileged to look. Presumably, however,
theological realities manifest themselves in the psychological realities of
priests' lives. The psychologist must conclude that the priests of the
United States, marked largely by sincerity and good will in trying to
meet the expectations of their role as priests, cannot shatter or transcend
the bonds of their own humanity in the process. In other words, priests
remain limited human beings under strong pressures to be more than
this on a fulltime basis. One need not destroy an ideal to recognize that
this is extremely difficult for even exceptional men; it is understandably
impossible for ordinary persons to exceed the limitations of their own
personalities. In fact, the priests of the United States do not transcend
their personal limitations in their professional functioning.

It is important to put the reality of their psychological "ordinariness"
into focus if we are to understand the ministry and life of American
priests. They do not demonstrate any exemptions from what we understand as the ordinary laws of psychological growth. Nothing makes up
for the human experiences which they may have missed or which, for
one reason or another in their personal histories, may have been distorted for them. There is, in other words, and despite the other theological claims and powerful wishes of the Catholic community itself, no
special psychology for priests.

Unless we can accept the fact that priests are psychologically similar
to the general population of men, it may be difficult to understand one

of the major findings of this research. A large proportion of the priests in this cross-sectional sample has not developed to full maturity. Although we do not wish to make statements about proportions as though we could project these estimates onto the entire population of priests, the careful method of sampling employed in this study indicates that successive samples drawn with the same care would yield the same results as those which have come from the interviews with this group of men. In other words, if one were to draw successive samples until the entire population of American priests had been interviewed, the results would not appreciably change. A large proportion of priests would emerge as underdeveloped persons. This means that these priests have reached a level of overall personal growth that is not equal to that which is expected of them at their age and in view of their careful selection and lengthy training. This is a major significant finding of this research. These psychologically underdeveloped priests probably reflect the fact that a great many American males are also underdeveloped. You do not have to be a priest in order to have this growth difficulty. In other words, in this regard the priesthood tells us something about normals and their developmental problems just as surely as it tells us about the men who are specifically priests.

The difficulty, of course, is that the population of priests is carefully selected and supervised during a long training period. One would presume with this care, psychological underdevelopment would have been noticed and would have been remedied. In fact, however, it may be that the selection and training process tended to mask rather than reveal the lack of development in many of the candidates for the priesthood. It did, after all, reward conformity, a certain passivity to regulations and authority, as well as a willingness to stay away from many normal developmental experiences such as dating and a normal social life. Recruitment and training for the priesthood have not, in any case, eliminated the difficulty of finding so many psychologically underdeveloped persons functioning within the profession. Were we to inspect the general population, even without sophisticated psychological data, one could see many signs of widespread underdevelopment in the American male population. The unobtrusive measures on divorce, stress in marriages, the almost epic interest in psychological group experiences to expand personal sensitivity; all these tell us that men in general have real difficulties with psychological growth. Immaturity in personal development is manifest in subtle statistics, such as the fact that over six million buy and read *Playboy* Magazine, a publication designed, according to social commentators, for the immature and undeveloped personality. So too the wide-spread middle-class, white-collar interest in pornography also points to a lack of full personal development in a great many Americans. To say that priests have psychological difficulties because they are not fully developed is to speak about them as typical members of the American male community.

This is not to say that most priests, or American men for that matter, are sick. This medical notion of sickness is not entirely appropriate in speaking of the psychological difficulties which indicate immature personal development. *Sickness* is not the correct concept to describe problems which are related to inadequate social and/or educational experiences. People who are immature may not need medical or psychological treatment as much as they do need a broader and richer experience of life itself. We shall discuss some of the characteristics of the priests of the United States and the way that this lack of personal development is manifested in their lives.

First of all, the problems of underdeveloped priests are not cognitive in nature. Priests do not lack knowledge nor are they defective in their capacity to understand or reason. The problems of underdeveloped priests are emotional in character. They reflect a lack of proper integration of their emotional and intellectual growth. Underdeveloped men have not passed through all the stages of growth which lead to what is recognized as adult and mature behavior. They look like adults but, on the inside, they still struggle with the challenges of a previous level of development. The underdeveloped have not successfully passed through adolescence.

The priests of the United States use high order defenses to handle the problems of psychological underdevelopment. They utilize, for example, intellectualization with obsessive features in order to adjust to their lack of growth. As defenses go, intellectualization is a good one. It is much better, in other words, than some regressive or erratic pattern of behavior because it reflects a certain measure of intelligence and psychological resourcefulness. It also indicates that instead of moving forward and dealing with the problems of growth, priests who are underdeveloped tend, if we can extend the analogy, to move sideways through multiple adjustments to their lack of growth. They do not confront their lack of growth or deal with it directly but they are adept at smoothing it over through their skilled use of this intellectual defense. This enables them to think about life while it excuses them from having to feel the conflict which they might experience if they were not so skilled at employing this defense. This intellectual defense enables underdeveloped priests to impose a consistency on their view of themselves even when their understanding of themselves really does not match what they are like in reality. They are good, in other words, at not looking closely at the gaps between what they are really like and what they perceive themselves to be like. The use of such defenses, of course, exacts a price from them. It makes it more difficult for the underdeveloped person to grow further and it also imposes limits on his capacity to enter into and to enjoy life in an adult way.

How does this lack of personal development manifest itself? The chief area in which the underdeveloped priests manifest their lack of psychological growth is in their relationships with other persons. These relationships are ordinarily distant, highly stylized, and frequently unrewarding for the priest and for the other person. Underdeveloped priests report their interpersonal relationships as difficult, even though they like people and, at a deep level of their personality, would like to be closer to them. There is a certain pain involved for them in this conflict between wanting the psychological experiences of being close to people and yet finding it awkward and difficult to get themselves into close relationships with others. Some may have the impression that the priest has a host of intimate friends. This is true of some priests. We speak here of that segment of underdeveloped priests, however, who reveal in depth interviews that they have few close friends. There is quite a difference between revealing one's isolation and fears about relationships in a lengthy interview and making the surface claim of many friends. Beneath the surface one finds extensive interpersonal uneasiness. This is reflected in the underdeveloped priests' description of their problems in getting through to people in the context of their priestly functioning. Underdeveloped priests are genuinely uneasy about intimacy. Intimacy is here used as it is employed in the developmental scheme of Erikson (1963). It refers to responsible closeness with other persons, one of the most important challenges of adult life, and one that can only be handled by a person who has worked through the adolescent challenge of securing his own identity. Most of the underdeveloped priests have not worked through these problems, and they do experience difficulty with their own personal identity; they are, therefore, uneasy in handling psychological intimacy. They may report many acquaintances. Acquaintances are not the same as friends. It is indeed a moving experience to sense the lack of depth in the human relationships of many priests. What these men say about themselves over and over is that there are few people to whom they are close, few people who know them well, indeed, few people who have enabled them to express themselves as fully as they did during the interview conducted for the study. Psychologists have long been aware of the fact of social desirability which affects the way people respond to questions. This tendency to say the things that make a person sound normal or like most others explains why priests may report many acquaintances in one moment and then admit few friends in the next.

Underdeveloped priests experience difficulty at a focal point of their priesthood because their relationships with others constitute such a substantial part of their day and, therefore, of their basic life and occupational experience. They know difficulty and discomfort in the very area which should be a deep source of personal and work satisfaction. For a more rewarding sense of pastoral achievement they should feel confident and at ease in their dealings with other people. The opposite seems to be more characteristic with feelings of fear, unsureness, and lack of self-confidence dominant in their personal relationships. Some priests feel that on principle they should remain at a distance from other people. This is a good example of the use of an intellectual defense. This asserted principle provides a socially acceptable and inwardly rewarding good reason, in other words, for not solving the problems of intimacy. But the person, whether he is a priest or not, who has not solved the problem of intimacy has not reached maturity either. The individual who is not sure of his identity and who experiences uneasiness in his personal relationships and work experiences cannot enter very deeply into life.

In underdeveloped priests there are evidences of passivity, exaggerated docility, and a tendency to identify themselves through the role of the priesthood rather than through their own personalities. This may be the outgrowth of their seminary training which so emphasized the function of the priesthood and which systematically trained them not to trust or place confidence in their own powers. It has been pointed out that a certain theological and scriptural interpretation of traditional Catholic teachings tended to diminish the value and importance of personal identity especially in the work of clergymen. They were to minimize the possibility of their own contribution to any work they might do, feeling that this work was validated by their cooperation with God's will and through the manifestation of His power rather than through the exercise of God's help. They mistrust themselves, feel unworthy, and frequently hold back from using their full capacities. This lack of development is reinforced by aspects of their training and by some of the principles by which they choose to live. They perform adequately, as was noted previously, but this is not the same as performing with a sense of or an aspiration toward excellence.

There are many other ways in which this lack of personal development is manifested in underdeveloped priests. Perhaps chief among these is the fact that so many of the underdeveloped have not achieved an integrated psychosexual identity. For whatever reasons, these priests have not resolved the problems which are ordinarily worked through during the time of adolescence. Sexual feelings are a source of conflict and difficulty and much energy goes into suppressing them or the effort to distract themselves from them. They find it difficult to place sexuality into an easy and manageable perspective in their lives. Sexuality is, in other words, non-integrated in the lives of underdeveloped priests and many of them function at a pre-adolescent or adolescent level of psychosexual growth. This uncertainty about their sexuality affects their sense of personal identity and makes it difficult for them to accept and deal with the challenge of intimacy. This uneasiness concerning sexuality is reinforced by the guilt which has been culturally associated with sexuality. This is especially so because of the underdeveloped priests' lack of instruction or emotional understanding of the meaning of sexuality in their own lives. Most report that their education about sexual development was negative or non-existent; many report no normal developmental social experience. Most of them use strong psychological controls so that their public behavior will in no way stray out of bounds. These controls, however, drain away an inordinate amount of energy and time in these priests' lives. To put it simply, sex takes more time and effort to handle and control, and is productive of more anguish than it should be in any adult life. This excessive concern and uneasiness does not produce growth. Frequently the underdeveloped rationalize continued autoerotic problems as necessary outlets for their sexual energies. This is a painful area for underdeveloped priests.

It is surprising to find in this group of men a general inability to articulate a deep level of personal religious faith. What is presumed to be central in their lives is found to be peripheral and frequently superficial. Underdeveloped priests have not questioned or worked through for themselves an integrated and sustaining theology or philosophy of life in depth. They would not, in most cases, bring up the subject of religious faith if it were not suggested by the interviewer himself. Indeed, one of the general reactions of the interviewers was surprise at the absence of the spontaneous discussion of faith on the part of the priests whom they interviewed. A lack of depth in faith goes along with an underdeveloped personality and a general tendency towards shallow living. It is also clear that the priesthood, howsoever it may be surrounded by religious ideals and presumed theological motivations, frequently meets the needs of underdeveloped priests in a very detailed way. In other words, the vocation to the priesthood frequently does more for the underdeveloped individual than the individual does for it. It enables the underdeveloped priest to maintain a position of prestige and security and to enjoy protection from testing his own powers against the competition of the world. The priesthood for many of these underdeveloped men is a vocational choice which allows them to continue in life without really needing to develop. It offers them a setting in which they can survive without growing.

This combination of factors, personal immaturity, a poorly realized religious faith, and the protective function of the priesthood role for the underdeveloped, affects markedly their capacity to implement religious ideals in their lives. We speak here of the underdeveloped priests, although, for proper perspective, it is important to remember that developed priests do, in fact, live their religious ideal authentically. The number of well-developed men is not great. However, the priests who are described as developing are dealing in a progressively more realistic manner with their religious principles and practices. The maldeveloped priests, again a small number, have major and relatively unresponsive psychological problems in dealing with their religious convictions. The underdeveloped have difficulties, for which they frequently blame themselves, which are, in a real sense, perfectly predictable and understandable given the fact that they are ordinary men. In other words, their failure to realize fully the proposed meaning of celibacy in their lives is not an indictment of them or their good will; it reflects the difficulties any group of average men would have if they had to live in the same circumstances. It is important to understand this clearly because the danger of distortion here is great. The underdeveloped practice celibacy exactly the way any ordinary group of well-educated but personally immature men would. Their difficulties are precisely those you would expect if you took a group of young men, sent them to special schools, virtually eliminated their contact with women, and then put them to work in circumstances that continued to reinforce all-male living in a socially restricted public religious role. Any group of men would find it difficult to make celibacy a vital and integrating force in their lives if they had this educational experience. So it is with the underdeveloped priests, few of whom violate their vow of celibacy, but who adjust to it rather than live it with much vitality. Celibacy for underdeveloped priests means that they are not married; it does not reflect a higher development of religiously motivated dedication.

On the contrary, celibacy, which most of them maintain, as has been noted, through adjustment, creates a situation which makes it genuinely difficult for them to continue their development. So much energy goes into adjusting to celibacy, so much effort into dealing with basically non-integrated sexuality, that these men could hardly be described as more free to do their priestly work because of celibacy. As a condition of life, celibacy tends to reinforce the very aspects of these men which need development if they are to be more mature as individuals. It is also suggested that it is the lack of overall personal maturity which prevents these men from deepening their own religious faith.

The problematic situation of celibacy probably explains the general attitudes toward celibacy found in the depth interviews as well as in the sociological questionnaire. The majority of priests favor making celibacy a true option for the clergy. At the same time the majority of priests would not marry if the celibacy law were changed in their lifetime. One senses their willingness to continue in the present situation with the simultaneous realization that there should be greater practical freedom in regard to the election of celibacy as a condition of clerical life. Many of these men seem to realize that marriage is not the automatic answer to their own problems; indeed, it is clear that many of the underdeveloped priests know that they would not be ready for marriage until they were more fully grown as persons. Some feel that they are too old or too set in their ways to marry. In any case they share a conviction that, no matter what they would personally do, celibacy should be made optional. This conviction also obtains among the most developed priests who have integrated celibacy in a meaningful and religiously motivated manner in their lives. Although not all of them would marry, they strongly favor making celibacy optional. As a matter of fact, some of those priests most resistant to a change in the celibacy law are those who are most threatened by possible contact with women. Their rejection of the possibility of optional celibacy expresses their own desire to preserve it because it is such a functional facet of their own hesitant adjustment to life. It is quite remarkable that most of the priests who do make celibacy a well-rounded value in their lives are not only unthreatened by a possible modification of the law but are, in fact, strongly in favor of a change to optional celibacy.

It seems clear that, were the law of celibacy modified to allow greater practical freedom of choice, most priests would approve and some would immediately marry. The majority would, however, remain as they are. This suggests that the real psychological issue, even when it is not identified consciously as such, is greater freedom rather than the question of celibacy itself. The priests of the United States are not, as they are sometimes popularly pictured, restlessly waiting to marry. They do want the freedom to choose or not choose celibacy, however, and this development might vitalize rather than destroy this traditional condition of service. Freedom, of course, concerns much broader issues than just celibacy and has many implications for the fuller development of American priests.

From the depth interviews it seems clear that most of these men did not feel psychologically free about the question of celibacy when the time came for them to make the decision during their seminary training. This is also understandable from a psychological point of view. The point of choice for these men came near the end of a long and secluded seminary training during which, it now seems clear, the conditions of removal from the world, strict discipline, and the reduction of social contacts, arrested the development, to one degree or another, of the seminarians. This result, as has been noted, is exactly what would be expected with ordinary men. Nothing in the atmosphere of the training successfully supplanted the growth that simply did not take place because of these restrictive psychological conditions. These men did not, in fact, know themselves as well as a man making this major kind of commitment might well be expected to. Indeed, men who have integrated celibacy in their lives in a successful way frequently report that this was the outcome of self-search and growth only after they had been ordained to the priesthood. The fact that so many men, across all the classifications, feel that they were not completely free at the time of choice in the seminary may explain why they want celibacy to be made more truly optional at this time.

There is little indication that American priests would exercise freedom in any impulsive or destructive way. Most of them want to do their best and they would not flout the laws of God or the Church if they were given a wider range of options. Indeed, they might, as a group, develop a more mature concept of authority than they now have. They are not men about whom one would have to be afraid if greater freedom were allowed to them. The developed men would hardly change their present mode of living and working, because they live very responsibly already. The maldeveloped have lost so much inner freedom that an increase of it in their life or work situations would mean little. The developing priests would use greater freedom to pursue their own understanding of themselves; they might seek wider forms of life experience but not in any over-sensationalized way; they would merely broaden their social and occupational horizons, such as any growing persons do.

The underdeveloped priests are not a group that would abuse greater freedom either. In fact, the problem might be to get them to use it responsibly, to accept, in other words, the consequences of their own decisions and programs. The underdeveloped American priests have not resolved their feelings toward authority, largely because this is a developmental task which they have not really worked through yet. Many tend to have ambivalent attitudes toward authority, wanting its protection and direction on the one hand while they resent it and use it as a handy device with which to externalize their own problems on the other. This is not a remarkable finding; again, it is predictable behavior in men who have been educated to docility in a profession which has always emphasized the role and dignity of authority. The remarkable discovery of this study is that authority seems to impinge so little on the day-to-day activities of these priests. They perceive their lives as circumscribed by authority, but authority, in the person of a living and controlling authority figure, does not enter their lives often in a practical way. It is true that in some parish settings the pastor operates in an authoritarian manner but his domination ordinarily does not go beyond a fraction of the priests' activities; there are many parish situations where the pastor operates in a very different manner. The point is that most of the underdeveloped priests are not sure what they really feel about authority. In this they may reflect a broader American problem, but, in any case, they are not totally consistent in their attitudes. This may spring from the psychological sources of their own personalities; their ambivalence about earlier authorities in their lives, their need for approval, and their consequent tendency to some passivity toward authority. Whatever the case, they do not evince a completely integrated attitude toward authority in their adult lives.

They find it easy to describe their problems in terms of authority but this is a common strategy for all men who would prefer to do this than recognize their own limitations. There is little evidence, however, to suggest that, were all the authorities in their lives suddenly to transform themselves according to their wishes, they would find their problems solved. The underdeveloped priests do not, in general, display a well thought out or consistent pattern of responses to authority. They may speak about changing it but they would feel very uneasy if they did not have its approval. They may perceive it as personally oppressive and yet, for all practical purposes, ignore it in their own lives. In fact, in the day-to-day transactions of their lives, it seems clear that these priests do pretty much what they want to do within the general limits of the profession. They have a practical flexibility of scheduling which is not available to many professional people. When regulations get in their way they frequently display real ingenuity in circumventing them.

Authority is not the practical problem in everyday living that one might have anticipated. This may be a function of the way authority is exercised, but it is also a function of the lack of development in many of these men. They are freer than they would like to admit to perform their professional service; authority seldom personally intervenes in their lives; their own ambivalent attitudes toward authority make them inconsistent in their feelings about it as they waver from dependence to independence in relationship to it. Authority, if it is a major problem, may be such because it does not seem to be a fully realized value on the part of those who exercise it or those who are subject to it. There is some evidence to suggest that priests are becoming increasingly indifferent to it.

In summary, the ordinary men who are American priests are bright, able, and dedicated. A large number of them are underdeveloped as persons with a consequent lack of fully realized religious and human values in their lives. They are not sick; they are not fully grown. They seem to need a broader, deeper, and genuinely freer experience of life to overcome this lack of development. There seem to be minimal risks in increasing the active options in their lives and, therefore, increasing the areas in which they must become more fully responsible for themselves and their work. The priests of the United States are clearly adequate in their function; they could be far more effective personally and professionally if they were helped to achieve greater human and religious maturity. The basic therapy for this kind of problem is the opportunity and encouragement for a deeper and freer participation in life itself.

CHAPTER II

THEORETICAL BACKGROUND

"Books must follow sciences," Sir Francis Bacon wrote, "and not science books." This book follows upon the methods of social science which enable us to face and understand in a systematic way the complex nature of reality. No truth in our experience is more complex than that about human beings, whose separate life histories, varied environments, and many-faced motives make the use of generalizations a difficult game indeed. There are many approaches to the reality of man: the poet, the novelist, the biographer, even the politician can give a sharp and workable insight into human behavior. Science, however, cannot settle for lyrical impressions or individual intuitions about man, though it cannot totally ignore them either. The method of science attempts to put order into the gathering, the naming, and the interpretation of information about persons or events under study.

Science's disciplined path to understanding commits an individual to an openness to all aspects of the truth as well as to a keen and reflective sensitivity to the many factors which may affect the observation, measurement, and interpretation of data. These factors may be obvious or subtle; they may reside in the subjects, the investigators, or just the times themselves. They must, however, be controlled if an objective exploration of the truth is to take place. The methods of science correct our tendency to find faults instead of facts. They demand that we examine and take account of our own prejudices or unconscious inclinations so that these will not bend the findings to plead a special case one way or the other. The social scientist seeks to discover rather than to make the truth.

The investigation of the ministry and life of the American priests has offered both a challenge and an opportunity to social scientists. The challenge consists in developing and carrying out careful and thorough observational designs to secure reliable information about a group of men who have been the subjects of endless speculation. The opportunity lies in putting together a picture of the American priest that is fair, accurate, and full bodied enough to serve as the basis for future decisions and recommendations about priests' lives and work. The opportunity is enhanced by the interrelation of two social science approaches, those of sociology and psychology, on this particular project. Seldom have psychologists and sociologists been able to work as closely in developing their research designs and in carrying them out as they have during the investigation of the life and ministry of the American priest. This cooperation has guaranteed a better grasp of the reality under study because the two approaches, with their common language but differing research traditions, have insured a multi-dimensional picture of the American priest. While sociology provides an extensive view, psychology offers an intensive set of measures. Taken together these provide breadth and depth at the same time. The combination of social scientific approaches allows one to approach more closely and confidently the reality under study. The advantage resembles that which is ours when we have a three-dimensional globe rather than just a flat surface projection of the map of the world. The more you can inspect the reality from different angles, the more surely you can define the subjects in time and space.

Social science carries out its tasks publicly, making its methods and techniques clear so that others can repeat the inquiry if they so choose. Social science also builds on the inferential skills of the specialists who are engaged in carrying it out. This provides the disciplined judgment that comes from a combination of education and experience with the methods of science and the realities of human behavior. The methodology of science demands consultation, planning and a careful carrying through of the design appropriate to the subject under study. This is exemplified in the present investigation which began with an extensive review of the literature and wide consultation with other psychologists, psychiatrists, bishops, religious superiors, and seminary educators across the United States. Thus, the framework of the research design has been worked out on the foundation of broad consultation. The basic question facing the psychologists was, "What are the priests of the United States like as men?" The task was to understand American priests as human beings with as much objectivity and depth as possible. A review of the previous psychological research on the American Catholic clergy, which is presented elsewhere in this volume, indicates that most of the earlier research was done through psychological testing. The motivation for much of this research was the development of satisfactory scales for screening candidates for the seminary and the priesthood. Very little scientific investigation was done on the basis of direct observation of priests or seminarians. Direct observation, however, is a basic attitude of science and it was a stance which was implemented on the present research. Rather than using psychological test instruments, the clinical psychological approach implemented in this study was based on first-hand and extensive experience with the priest subjects. The in-depth interview, a particular specialty of clinical psychology and psychiatry, offers an advantage to both the interviewer and the subject interviewed. It enables the interviewer to proceed systematically through the important developmental experiences of the individual interviewed even as it allows the latter to explain and express himself in a full manner which is difficult in any other format. The clinical interview, then, far from being merely a probing device, is respectful of the individual because it focuses on him alone and allows him the fullest possible opportunity to express himself and his motivations. It is not surprising that many of the priests interviewed clearly expressed a gratitude for the opportunity to describe themselves with such systematic thoroughness.

Once the task of providing an understanding of the persons who were priests was clear, a series of rational decisions to implement plans for research was made. These centered on the nature of the clinical interview and other instruments to be employed, the professional persons who would serve as interviewers, the composition of the research staff, and the detailed planning of the research procedures themselves. Each one of these rational decisions, of course, eliminated certain alternatives which had to be considered for those planning the investigation itself. Each decision flowed consistently from the previous decision, and all aimed at achieving the objective of the study: *to allow the priests of the United States to speak for themselves, and to help them articulate what they themselves cannot fully express about their life and their ministry, to understand, at as deep a level as possible, and in language as clear as possible, what kind of men American priests are.*

The setting for the research, Loyola University of Chicago, has a long history of active research on the priesthood and seminary life. The Core Research Council, responsible for the experimental design, planned a thorough pilot study to refine the specific nature of the clinical interview which would be carried out and to allow for the selection, from a group of Ph.D. psychologists, those interviewers who demonstrated superior capacity for carrying out the clinical interviews with professional skill and human sensitivity. The pilot study, carried out in June and July of 1969, also led to a clarification of the objectives of the research as well as to a modification of the interview procedure to insure that it would attain these objectives as well as possible. Other similar measures were also built into the research after evaluation of the pilot study itself.

Perhaps the most important decision made at this time was the choice of a developmental framework for understanding and interpreting the lives of American priests. A word of explanation is in order. When one speaks of the developmental framework, one is choosing to speak of the subjects in terms of health rather than in terms of sickness. In other words, instead of choosing a system of psychiatric classifications, or emphasizing a diagnostic method that would lead to an emphasis on possible pathological features of the population, the interview was designed as a vehicle for understanding a normal group of men in the language of growth and development. This flowed from the basic understanding that the subjects of the research were normally functioning individuals who would best be understood in a positive rather than a potentially negative language. To speak about healthy people in the language of illness is bound to be misleading. While the researchers recognize that certain features of illness would inevitably present themselves across a large number of interviews, it was felt that this would be no greater than in any comparable group of normal male subjects. To follow the individual's life history according to developmental stages also made good sense in working out the format of the interview itself. It provided what the researchers wanted to understand — information in depth about the persons who are priests — and did so in an orderly yet comprehensive form. The same kind of constructs guided the development of the other psychological instruments, such as the sentence completion test, and also provided the framework, at least in part, for the development of the sociological survey questionnaire.

Every framework has scientific roots in the writings and theories of the men who have offered the most helpful and influential understandings of the person. The model chosen for this study was that offered by the Harvard psychoanalyst Erik Erikson. Erikson has provided a multi-stage schema of what he describes as man's psychosocial development. Employing this framework allows the investigators to tap the sources and expression of the individual's self-development and provides the possibility for understanding the positive unfolding of the personality and the factors which affect this at each of the stages of development. There are advantages to this positive orientation besides the obvious one of avoiding psychopathological classifications. If you view an individual in the context of his overall personal growth, there is much less likelihood that you will distort any one aspect of personality in the process. The very method encourages the investigator to put the various dimensions of personality into proper perspective and into healthy relationship with one another. A fuller, more detailed understanding of the persons who are American priests, therefore, emerges.

To employ such a model of human development also allows us to understand the problems that an individual has in growing to his full maturity. Frequently a man's problems are related to his difficulty or his failure to work through a particular stage in his growth and development. When we can understand all the factors in his family and in his environment which have played upon him at this stage we can understand far more clearly why he has never gotten beyond this particular phase of his growth. A man can, in other words, get stalled at a certain point along the way. When he fails to work himself through this period, he develops certain patterns which shape all his later behavior. It is possible for his actions, his way of relating to others, to tell us something about the nature of and reasons for his lack of development. Men have always commented on this, using an innate yardstick of development to measure their fellows. They do it when they speak of adults whose behavior does not match the kind of maturity expected of them. Remarks like "he's a crybaby" or "he acts so childish" accurately describes the man who is old enough to be more grown up but whose inner development had not gotten beyond a very early and self-centered stage of life. The person who does not grow fully, in other words, develops what psychiatrist Theodore Lidz calls "dominant themes" of behavior which flow from the level of growth at which his development has stopped. As Lidz (1968) notes: "Sometimes the dominant theme results from an early childhood fixation and reiterates itself, unable to develop and lead onward, remaining in the same groove like a needle on a flawed phonograph record. The basic themes are more readily detected in emotionally disturbed persons because they are more set, more clearly repetitive, and perhaps more familiar to the practiced ear that has heard similar themes so often before. Still, repetitive ways of acting and relating occur in all lives. The meaning of an episode in life can be grasped properly only through understanding how it furthers, impedes, or disrupts essential themes (p. 510)."

The employment of a model of positive development allows us to understand man's forward motion and to see where this can be slowed down and to understand the reasons why. It can often help us to understand the most helpful corrective measures to allow a person to begin to grow again. It avoids the somewhat negative psychopathological categories that make these people sound as though they were suffering from a sickness rather than a problem of development. A developmental scale, then, is most appropriate for the study of a normal population. For these many advantages Erikson's framework was chosen as the basis for designing the interview and interpreting the results. Before one can pass on to the actual research itself, it is necessary to review Erikson's work so that the reader can understand the ideas and language of psychological development in which this report is written.

Erikson (1963) describes eight stages of psychosocial development and he employs literary as well as scientific terms to give us an understanding of them. For Erikson, man is capable of growth throughout the entire life cycle. This growth is related at each stage to the important persons in the growing person's life. Erikson also describes specific crises which the individual must meet and work through at each stage in order to achieve the human values and characteristics which he needs to proceed to the next stage of development. We will review these briefly here, noting the conditions, typical crises, and important issues involved in each stage of development.

Stage 1:   The first year of life

During this year the most significant other person in the child's life is the mother or, if she is absent, whoever takes her place. The way this person relates to the child will determine in many ways the child's whole attitude of trust or mistrust of the world around him. This is not to exclude the possibilities of modifications of the child's attitude by a later experience, but it does highlight the fundamental nature of the learning which takes place at this stage. What do we mean by trust in this context? It may be defined as a deeply engrained conviction that one's needs, material and emotional, will be satisfied; that the world and people in it are basically good, abundant in their supplies, and well meaning. It goes beyond this, however, to imply a personal feeling of being all right oneself, and of being considered all right by other significant people; the feeling that one can handle the world and deal with oneself confidently, feeling at home in one's own body; a confident feeling that makes sense and copes with requirements and even frustrations from the outside.

Basic mistrust may be thought of as a sense of living precariously, of feeling that good things never last, that one does not know if one's needs will be satisfied tomorrow and rather doubts that they will be. For the person plagued with basic mistrust the world is full of hidden dangers and people who are out to get or to exploit him. He also experiences himself as bad and empty, as incapable of handling life, and as doomed to experience failure and injury. The world for the person who does not learn basic trust is unsafe, unpredictable, threatening and cold.

Failure of trust and fear are obviously infectious diseases at this stage of growth and more than a little damage has been done to children by elders who have failed to teach them the meaning of trust at this level. The infant's fundamental experience of the world and other persons as trustworthy or not strongly shapes, for good or for ill, enduring attitudes that he will bring into all other later life relationships. This first stance of trust or mistrust profoundly affects the person's ability to express himself as a human being in a healthy and appropriate manner. It is clear that this stage is of profound importance if the individual is to continue growing at all.

Stage 2: Through the second year

The child has at this stage developed enough to control its own movements and with this mastery of himself a whole new sense of individuality awakens. His sense of autonomy, of what we can call self-control and will power develops in the context of his relationship with both parents. If the child is mishandled (not allowed to do what he can do) or overprotected, he may be dominated by a sense of shame or doubt instead of a healthy sense of autonomy. Much that is essential for impulse control is learned at this level. The do's and don't's of later life may not mean much to an individual who has never been able to take control of himself at this stage of growth.

Autonomy requires this self-control: that one is capable of being and may be the originator of one's own actions, that the individual has a will of his own and can exercise it, that he can be in control and experience a consequent sense of pride and healthy independence. Shame and doubt, these are the feelings that the individual may be plagued with if he does not work through this growth stage successfully (being easily exposed as powerless, incapable, weak, and somehow bad). The individual's plans and actions are surrounded by doubts concerning their worthwhileness. Self-consciousness and a lack of self-confidence are present as well as or an inability to make up one's own mind about things.

Stage 3: From three to six

The child, now related to the basic family, is in control of many of his actions at this stage. The outcome of this challenge is the achievement of a sense of healthy initiative which will animate his attitude of direction and purpose in life. The child, probing his environment, must be taken seriously or he may find that a sense of guilt outweighs any initiative toward life. In other words, at this stage he will be freed to move forward confidently, or he may be burdened by a confining sense of guilt. Initiative here refers to some sign of ambition, to some drive to accomplish, a tendency to solve problems directly and to enjoy it. It also refers to an active, curious exploration of life.

Guilt, on the other hand, drains enjoyment out of acts of making and achieving. It also plagues the individual because of the aggressive components involved in active competition. There is excessive guilt as manifest in self-restriction, over-conscientiousness in planning enterprises and a kind of paralysis of action.

Stage 4:   From six to puberty

The child moves into a wider arena of life at this period; the neighborhood and the school are new worlds for him. He achieves a level of intellectual development that allows him to see his environment, with its gains and tasks, in a more comprehending way. Now he must develop a sense of industry, a feeling that he can make things, and that he can participate with others in a competitive and cooperative manner. Failing in this, he will experience a pervasive sense of inferiority.

Industry here refers to any active orientation toward producing things which enable the individual to win recognition; to the absorption in the productive situation and the determined striving toward the completion of things; it is what people describe in the old phrase "stick-to-it-iveness." The individual gets his first sense of wanting to be useful and to achieve useful things and so he achieves skills which he practices and values highly, and he shows a real interest in learning how things are done according to the generally accepted skills and rules of his own culture.

Inferiority, however, refers to one's losing faith in one's own tools and skills. This leads to a feeling of being unable to be like others and of being doomed to mediocrity or to some kind of crippled and isolated state.

Stage 5:   Adolescence

One hardly needs to describe the dynamic quality of the growing individual's life experience at this stage. During this time the person draws together the strands of his life experience to form his own identity. Either he develops a sense of his unique personhood or he experiences confusion because of the diffused quality of his self-understanding at this time. The person's peer groups and the leadership figures in his world become important to him. At this time he begins to deal with profound human values, values that touch on the way he presents himself to the world and to other persons. It is at this stage that he must develop a sense of fidelity and devotion to others.

Identity, a familiar word in our culture, refers here to a sense of inner sameness and continuity in time, that one fits together, is at home in his own body and knows where he is going. It flows from a good integration between inner drives and wishes and a man's social conditions, especially in terms of work, sex, relationship to one's fellows and to the community. Without a sense of identity a man finds it difficult to relate to himself or to another person in any kind of enduring way.

Identity diffusion refers to a feeling that one's appearance and one's being do not really fit together. The individual may have doubts concerning his sexual identity and evidence an inability to choose a career because of conflicting interests and doubts. In the same way he may not be able to relate to others as equal partners or to compete with them. Again there is a feeling of emptiness, a lack of a coherent philosophy of life and of a goal for one's existence. No commitments are made and a state of paralysis with regard to the making of choices exists.

Stage 6: Early adult

Here a young person takes his identity and tests it in relationship to others in a deeper way than he has done before. He must learn the meaning of intimacy as he moves either closer to others in friendship and love, or away from them in some kind of isolation. At this stage the meaning of love as a lasting value and motivation comes into his life as he faces the experience of losing and finding himself in relationship with another.

Intimacy refers to something more than sexual intimacy although it includes this. It refers, for example, to the ability to share mutual trust and to regulate, as Erikson notes, with another life's "cycles of work, procreation and recreation." It includes the ability to face what is called ego-loss with others as well as within one's self. And this is a very important experience for any creative person. Isolation, on the other hand, refers to a sense of having to remain alone, of being self-absorbed, or being afraid of ego-loss. Social relationships remain formal or they do not get very far at all. The isolated person is, of course, the lonely person.

Stage 7: Young and middle adult

Here the individual has joined himself in love with another for the mature tasks of building a family and passing life and growth on to others. The individual either becomes truly generative in the sense that he has an active and genuine concern for the generations which are to follow, for the consequences, in other words, of his work and love, or he turns away in self-absorption, letting the meaning of life pass him by.

Generativity implies a deeply sensed interest and involvement in establishing and guiding the next generation. When the individual does not have direct parental responsibilities, healthy generativity is reflected in concerns of an altruistic and creative quality.

Stagnation is the absence of such rich generative involvement. It may result in an obsessive need for a pseudo-intimacy, in self-indulgence, and will show up in a personal sense of impoverishment and lack of genuine purpose.

Stage 8:   Later adult

At this level, an individual puts his life together in some reflective way. His major achievements are behind him and now he must sum it all up, viewing it with a sense of integrity or, if there have been major flaws, with a possible sense of despair. In other words, these are the experiences of a man who has finished his work in life and done it with as much commitment to the truth about himself and others as he could muster. It is a stage of wisdom for the person who has dealt with life constructively and who has attempted to grow and to express that growth in creative relationships with other persons. When these efforts are lacking, the person may be overwhelmed with a sense of despair, at having failed, at having missed the point of it all and of having no time now to do anything about it. All the chances for growth are over with and there is only a black uneasiness left in this individual's soul.

These are the stages and the important features of psychological development as viewed by Erik Erikson. They served as the basis for the interview experience itself, and have also provided the researchers with the framework in which to write about the subjects under investigation. After a thorough study of the clinical reports, and on the basis of extensive professional experience with the subjects under investigation, the research council chose an abbreviated version of the Eriksonian model in which to describe the American priests. This uses the same growth terminology while collapsing certain of the life stages within broader categories. The following chapters will describe these classifications and illustrate with case histories the growth problems or achievements of the priests who fit into them. In other words, the four stages actually present us with four types of priests, that is to say, four groups whose dominant life themes and patterns of adjustment place them, in the judgment of clinical experts, into one or the other section of the continuum of growth which is appropriate for normal persons. This is not to say that the categories are exact or exclusive of one another nor that they do not have a certain measure of overlap. They represent a growth line toward maturity and priests, like every other group of human beings, tend to cluster, according to developmental problems, at certain points along that line. An understanding of these points enables us to see the reasons for the growth problems and a typical fashion in which the subjects of the inquiry deal with them. It also provides a basis for understanding better ways to deal with these problems and to work through the difficulties of growth in which they are evidenced. These are dynamic categories, not frozen pictures of men who are locked in position for all time. This is what living, functioning, priests are like in terms of the kind of growth they have achieved.

CHAPTER III

METHODOLOGY

As noted in Theoretical Background (Chapter II), out of the early seminars which took place during the spring of 1969 arose the conviction that a highly personalized method was needed. As one consultant put it, the priests who volunteer for the interview should experience the interview as a "highly dignified approach to me as a person." Only under such conditions would a man reveal his most salient personal characteristics, the dynamic significance of his past experience, his belief and motivational systems, and his life-giving satisfactions as well as his disillusions. Then followed a series of discussions with the aim of fashioning a plan which could carry this conviction into action.

Personnel

A pivotal decision which affected virtually all later decisions was the choice of professional clinical psychologists as interviewers instead of, for example, students or survey technicians. Clinical psychologists were chosen for several reasons. They have experience in dealing with people in close relationships, have highly developed interview skills, and have been trained to be aware of potential sources of bias inherent in an interview situation and perhaps arising out of their own personalities. They are knowledgeable of personality dynamics and are skilled in communicating their knowledge in a clear and integrated fashion. That is, an integral part of their training and practice is the writing of psychological evaluations of individual persons. In addition, they appreciate the need for the rigor involved in psychological research.

The recruitment, screening, and specialized training of the psychologists who served as interviewers was a careful and costly process. An early decision was that all the psychologists should be at the Ph.D. level. Further, it was decided that only graduates of the Clinical Division of the Psychology Department of Loyola University of Chicago would be asked to serve. This latter decision was made for two reasons. First,

29

having had academic training at Loyola helped to insure that the psychologists had knowledge of and empathy toward Catholic values. Such characteristics obviously were to be of no small importance in a study of the priesthood. Second, their personal maturity, stature, and sense of professional responsibility were known to the Director of Clinical Training at Loyola who served as a senior consultant to the study.

Those psychologists who were so screened and were willing to seriously consider service as interviewers attended training seminars where the purposes and techniques of the study were described and illustrated. Further, they participated in a pilot study (Appendix B) where they practiced the techniques of interviewing and writing of evaluations designed for this study. This training phase was a mutual one. That is, not only did the potential interviewers learn the proposed techniques, they also criticized and refined them.

The training phase resulted in a core of 12 interviewers who established a mutually satisfactory relationship with the administrators of this study. All are members in good standing of the American Psychological Association. Their average was 35.5 (SD = 7.01) years. They had an average of 5.5 (SD = 4.97) years of professional experience beyond the attainment of the Ph.D. Five interviewers had as their major professional affiliation a college or university; five, a mental health setting; two, private practice.

The Interview

Once the decision to employ the professional clinical psychologists as interviewers was made, it followed that the interview technique which would be designed for the field work should allow for a good measure of latitude in its application at the discretion of the interviewer. Hence, the interview manual (Appendix C) which was eventually constructed was to be used as a set of guidelines, rather than a series of preset questions. Of course, such a format also allowed the priest to express himself more fully and freely.

The content of the interview arose out of a search of literature on psychological interviewing, research interviewing, research on the priesthood generated by the behavioral sciences, and the current sources of concern to priests as described in popular publications. Further, and perhaps more influential, sources of content were consultations with colleagues among the clergy and hierarchy and in the disciplines of sociology, psychiatry, and psychology.

Listed below is a brief description of the salient features of the major areas covered in the interview and the rationale for including them:

1. *Family Life and Relationships.* The development of personality is strongly affected by an individual's family experiences. It is necessary to understand the full dimension of the priest's relationships to his parents, his brothers and sisters, and to other significant persons, such as relatives and friends, who played a role in his development. It is especially important to sense the emotional meaning of these relationships to each individual priest. In the same way, one must understand the kind of values that permeated family life as well as any important change which may have taken place in the priest's family.

2. *Other Developmental Experiences.* This includes the general health of the individual as well as his career in schools and his relationships with his age-mates. Here again, it is not just information that is important, but the psychological aspects of these experiences which must be understood.

3. *Psychosexual Development.* While it is obvious that this is influenced strongly by his early experiences and must be treated with sensitivity, it is nonetheless essential to grasp the course of the individual's development as a human being. Psychosexual development means exactly that. It refers to the overall growth and development of the individual as a man and the quality of his self-identification as a man. Here again, the emotional meaning of his social experiences is significant to an understanding of the priest as a fully developed person.

4. *Self-Concept.* It is vital to ascertain the image which each individual priest has of himself because it is in terms of his self-image that he places himself in relationship to God and to all other persons in his life. The picture he has of himself and the attitudes he has about himself are vital aspects of a thorough understanding of the priest as a man.

5. *Development of Vocation.* This is clearly related to many of the areas already mentioned, but it is important to grasp as clearly as possible the factors which influenced his choice of the priesthood. These include his family experience, his religious experience, and his growth experience in understanding his vocation as he proceeded through school and the seminary. Important points of decision and the factors that affected these must also be explored. His present understanding and growth in his vocation are also to be understood if a complete picture of the person is to be had.

6. *Interpersonal Relationships.* A careful examination of these is important because they so significantly affect and express the personality

of the individual priest. The nature of his relationships with family friends, parishioners, and fellow-priests must be examined if a true understanding of the man is to emerge. Here again, it is not information as much as an appreciation for the psychological significance of his relationships that must be obtained. It is also here that the priest's ability to relate to authority is examined. This will necessarily include an understanding of his own use of authority in relationship with others.

7. *Faith.* While this dimension is considered in examining all aspects of the priest's life, it is important to examine the quality of the life of his faith in some detail. The basic values and beliefs by which he lives, the strength of his commitment in faith, the means he uses to deepen his faith and his understanding and appreciation of the Church are all highly significant.

8. *Priesthood.* While this may be distinguished topically, it is closely related to any understanding of the priest's religious life. There are, however, specific questions connected with his understanding and appreciation of the priesthood which must be investigated in some detail. These include his perception of the priesthood, his attitude towards it, and the manner in which he exercises the priesthood at the present time.

9. *Celibacy.* This topic is hardly separable from the context of the priest's overall understanding of himself, his faith commitment, and his attitude toward his vocation. Here again, however, an understanding of his appreciation of celibacy and the manner of his celibate life must be established. Only if one has a sensitive grasp of the meaning of celibacy as a value in the priest's life can any real understanding of the individual emerge.

10. *The Future.* Always significant in man's life is his way of looking forward in his life, his plans for future work, and his hopes of further growth and development.

The Evaluation

After the interview format was established, a technique for evaluating the material obtained in the interview was developed. The technique, which underwent revisions as a result of the pilot study, relies heavily upon the inferences made by the interviewers. In its final form (Appendix D), it consists of the following eight major areas:

1. *Interview Process.* Here the psychologist writes a description of the priest's physical presence, and the manner in which he behaved during the interview: anxious or relaxed, passive and submissive or active and controlling, and so on. In addition, he describes how he himself felt

towards the priest and how he believes the priest felt about the interview and toward him.

2. *Development.* In this section the psychologist describes the priest's parents and other significant adults in his life and indicates the nature of the emotional relationships of these figures to the priest and among themselves. Also are described the relationships of the priest to his siblings, friends, and general cultural circumstances. Events which had special impact on the course of his development are noted.

3. *Functioning.* The psychologist then addresses himself to the functioning of the priest in the six areas listed below. He communicates his understanding by writing five interpretive statements in each area. He then ranks each statement twice; once for its salience in describing the priest and again for his degree of confidence in making the statement. The six areas are the following:

a. *Interpersonal Relations.* This section communicates the typical way the priest interacts with others, whom he feels most comfortable with, the degree of closeness with others, and so on.

b. *Psychosexual Maturity.* Here is described the level of psychosexual maturity the priest has achieved, what impact sexuality has on his life, how sexuality is linked to his vocation, etc.

c. *Self-perception.* The psychologist lists what the priest feels are his most important characteristics, his strengths, his weaknesses.

d. *Job-satisfaction.* Here are described the satisfying and frustrating elements of the priest's work life.

e. *Church, Faith, Religion.* The psychologist attempts to capture the stance the priest takes toward the Church, its leaders and organization, the nature of his beliefs and religious practices.

f. *Priesthood.* Here is described the personal meaning of the man's vocation, not so much how it should be, but how it is actually lived.

4. *Report.* The psychologist ties all the preceding sections together in an integrated way, giving a comprehensive sketch of the way in which the priest's background, personality, and vocation interact.

5. *Future Outlook.* The psychologist makes tentative predictions about the priest's future: his vocational commitment, further personal growth, best assignments, possible need for treatment, etc.

6. *Psychosocial Modalities.* The psychologist makes judgments about the priest within the framework of Erik Erikson's theory of development (adapted from Prelinger and Zimet, 1964), for example, along the identity vs. identity-diffusion dimension.

7. *Diagnosis.* If a psychodiagnostic label is warranted, it is entered here.

8. *Scale of Adjustment.* The psychologist locates the overall adjustment (personal integration, occupational adaptation, and mental health) of the priest on a twelve-point scale used in other studies of normal persons.

Other Instruments

In addition to their participation in the personal interview, the subjects were asked to fill out several psychological tests. There were four basic tests: Loyola Sentence Completion Blank for Clergymen (Sheehan, 1971), Self-Anchoring Rating Scale of Maturity of Faith (adapted from Strunk, 1967), and Identity Scale (Henry and Sims, 1968), and Personal Orientation Inventory (Shostrom, 1966).

1. *Loyola Sentence Completion Blank for Clergymen (LSCBC).* The rationale, development, and the complete description of the LSCBC designed for the present study can be found in Appendices B and E. Briefly, the LSCBC is one of a variety of similar tests, all of which present the respondent with a series of sentences which have a beginning only. The respondent completes each of these "stems" in his own words. The LSCBC consists of 72 such stems. The respondent's completions are scored according to an empirically derived system. The LSCBC yields an overall index of adjustment and six sub-indices in the following realms: interpersonal relations; psychosexual maturity; self-perception; job satisfaction; Church, faith, religion; priesthood. It may be recalled that these are the six areas described by the psychologist in the "Functioning" section of the report.

The scorers of the LSCBC obtained in the present study were four graduate students enrolled in the Clinical Psychology Program at Loyola University of Chicago.

2. *Maturity of Faith Scale (FS).* Psychological tests which measure religious and moral attributes are relatively few in number and often lacking in technical adequacy (Pittel and Mendelsohn, 1966). Few are applicable to the population of priests. Some such tests attempt to infer the strength of the respondent's religious sentiment via the quantity of religious acts he performs. Others assess knowledge of moral principles. In the present study, an attempt was made to assess a qualitative aspect of the respondent's faith via his relatively spontaneous descriptions. The procedure for this assessment was adapted from Strunk (1967). In its final form, the respondent reads the following instructions:

Everybody has some idea of what having a mature faith means. Some people, we say, have a mature faith. Others, we claim, have an immature faith. From your point of view, what are the essential characteristics of the most mature kind of faith? (Take your time in answering; such things aren't easy to put into words.)

The respondent then writes his description. Next, the respondent is asked, "Now, again from your point of view, what are the essential characteristics of the most immature kind of faith? (Again, take your time in answering.)" After he writes this second description the respondent sees a picture of a ladder with 11 rungs and reads:

Below is a picture of a ladder. Suppose we say that at the top of the ladder (step number 10) is the most mature kind of faith you have just described; at the bottom of the ladder (step number 0) is the most immature kind of faith you have described.

1) Where on the ladder do you feel you stand *as you really are?*
   Step Number _____
2) Where on the ladder would you *like* to stand?
   Step Number _____
3) Where on the ladder do you feel your *closest friends* believe you stand?
   Step Number _____
4) Where on the ladder would you say you stood *five years ago?*
   Step Number _____
5) And where do you think you will be on the ladder *five years from now?*
   Step Number _____

A separate pilot study was conducted with this "self-anchoring" scale. Three forms of the test were developed, each form asking subjects to describe one of the following concepts: mature religion, mature religious belief, or mature faith. Each of the 59 priest volunteers anonymously filled out one form. It was the judgment of the authors that the "mature faith" form yielded the richest descriptions. So it was employed in the actual field work.

The quantitative data from the FS provided by the respondent were recorded directly. The qualitative data were subjected to a rating procedure.

The qualitative data were rated along an intrinsic-extrinsic dimension. This dimension as it applies to the religious sentiment has been described and empirically investigated by Gordon Allport (1950, 1968). Allport (1968) described extrinsic religion as "something to *use,* but not to *live."*

It can be used in a variety of egocentric ways: to bolster self-confidence, to improve social status, to defend the self against reality, "and, most importantly, to provide a super-sanction for one's own formula for living (p. 149)." Intrinsic religion is "not primarily a means of handling fear, or a mode of conformity, or an attempted sublimation of sex, or a wish-fulfillment (p. 150)." It is a "comprehensive commitment" which is partly intellectual but primarily motivational. The development of intrinsic religion implies that motives of childhood have been subordinated to an overarching motive. Its development is no different from any other phase of development: they are all subject to arrest. As Allport (1955) put it, "Infantilism in religion results in an arrest due to the immediate needs for comfort or security or self-esteem (p. 97)."

A bipolar rating scale was developed with the intrinsic pole assigned the value one; the extrinsic pole, nine. If for some reason a protocol could not be rated, it was eliminated from analysis. Two judges[1] independently rated the protocols in a different random sequence. A protocol consisted of the priest's description of both mature and immature faith. No other information about the subject was available to the judges.

3. *Identity Scale (IS)*. The IS (Henry and Sims, 1968), measures a concept central to Erik Erikson's (1959, 1963, 1968) theory of personality development, i.e., the identity-identity diffusion dimension. The formation of a person's identity is the major "task" of adolescence. Identity refers to a sense of inner sameness and continuity in time. A person who has achieved a stable sense of identity feels basically that he is of a piece. It is a sense which is derived from an integration between the person's inner drives and societal demands. Only after a person has achieved an acceptable identity can he afford the responsibilities of mature interpersonal relationships. Its opposite, identity diffusion, is marked by doubts about goals, career choice, sexual adequacy, the meaning of one's existence, and values. With so much doubt about one's self, little energy is available for mature relationships with others. Erikson makes it clear that it is a balance between the poles, identity and identity-diffusion, which makes for a healthy person. That is, just as identity diffusion results in a doubtful conflicted person, an overly strong or prematurely adopted sense of identity results in an overly rigid person.

Although all eight of Erikson's stages constituted sources of items for the scale, their selection depended upon their relationship to the identity-

1. Orlo Strunk, Jr., Ph.D., Professor of Psychology of Religion at Boston University, and Michael O'Brien, C.S.V., Ph.D., Professor of Psychology at Loyola University of Chicago.

identity diffusion dimension. As noted by Erikson (1959), the derivatives or precursors of the psychosocial modality defining each stage ". . . are part and parcel of the struggle for identity."

The respondent is presented with the 56 pairs of words and is required to choose a position on a seven-point (point four eliminated) scale which most closely describes himself (Appendix E). In scoring the test, the items are grouped into factor-analytically derived scales. A description of the scales as applied to males is as follows (adapted from Sims, 1962, pp. 26–32):

Factor I: Identity

The factor accounting for the greatest amount of variance, i.e., most meaningful, is interpreted to be the best measure of Identity-Identity Diffusion. Four clearly identifiable elements, each important in Eriksonian theory, are found within its item pairs. These components of identity are:

Ia. *Ego-Career* (occupational commitment vs. career diffusion)

Ib. *Ego-Group* (sense of group membership vs. sense of isolation)

Ic. *Ego-Self* (positive evaluation of self vs. self-abasement)

Id. *Ego-Affect* (positive affectual experience vs. negative affectual experience)

Taken together these elements form an operational definition of identity (and of identity diffusion) congruent with Erikson's conceptual formulations.

Factor II: Expressivity and Comfort within a Social Context

Factor II is defined as measuring comfort and expressivity within a social context. The meaning of "social context" refers more to a person-to-group, than person-to-person relationship. Thus, the comfort within such contexts follows primarily from a sense of membership or "belongingness," and only secondarily from direct interpersonal involvement. The expressivity and freedom of affect result, in turn, from the comfort and ease experienced in social relationships. The negative pole of the factor continuum indicates discomfort in a social interaction, inhibition of emotional expression, and a sense of isolation.

Factor III: Individualistic Expressivity

In contrast to Factor II, this factor is interpreted as measuring that expressivity and freedom of affect which issues from within the self, rather than from amenable relationships between the individual and his society. There is an impulsive and vigorous quality to this expressivity which, while not necessarily or primarily opposed to societal values, is separated from them. The inverse of the factor shows a constriction of impulsivity, both in feeling and expression, and a belief that a conforming moderation is safest.

Factor IV: Integrity

This factor is interpreted as measuring the current status, or precursory phase, of integrity — that issue which defines Erikson's final stage of development. It reflects a critical but positive acceptance of one's self, of one's fellow man, and of their shared moment in history. There is a belief in the value and joy of life, and a pervading sense of fulfillment. The factor's opposite pole is a sense of frustration regarding who one is, and an anticipatory fear of what one will become.

Factor V: Autonomy Within Social Limits

This factor is defined as measuring the working relationship between self-direction or independence and societal demands. It recognizes that the organization of society necessitates norms of behavior, but that reasonable adherence to them need not prevent individuality or interfere with autonomous functioning. Such norms include a willingness to cooperate with others, trustworthiness and the acknowledgment of time as a necessary dimension for ordered living. The negative pole of this factor reflects recalcitrance, obstructionism, and a "thumb-your-nose" attitude toward society. However, beneath this contemptuous evaluation of societal norms runs an emotional undercurrent of guilt and self-doubt.

Factor VI: Trust

Factor VI is defined as measuring the adult development of what Erikson describes as a sense of basic trust. It denotes a confidence in self and environment and in the relation between them. As a consequence, there is an open and generous approach to interpersonal interaction and a willingness for cooperative effort. Its opposite pole is an assertive suspiciousness and a resultant resistance to what might be a "dangerous" engagement with others.

A further use was made of this test to explain the respondent's ideal self and his experience of the Church. That is, as described above, the priest judges "yourself, as you really are" on the 56 pairs of words. Next, he judges "yourself, as you would like to be." His third judgment is of "the Church, as you experience it." The second and third judgments were not made on all 56 pairs of words due to the length of time required to make the ratings. Only 14 pairs of words were used for the judgments of ideal self and Church. Previous research (Sims, personal communication) has shown that these 14 pairs had the highest factor loadings (that is, provided the most accurate information about the respondent) of all the items. It was anticipated that the similarity between the priest's image of himself and his experience of the Church would be positively related to his satisfaction with the priesthood. It was also anticipated that where a large difference between the priest's self-image and his ideal self-image existed, poor adjustment would be found.

4. *Personal Orientation Inventory (POI)*. The POI was developed by Shostrom (1966) as a measure of positive mental health. The theoretical rationale for the POI was derived from the psychology of self-actualization. In brief, a self-actualized person in comparison with a relatively non-self-actualized person utilizes his talents more fully, uses his time more effectively, functions more autonomously, tends to "live" more in the present, and tends to have a more positive outlook on life and the nature of man. A test which measures such positive aspects of health and growth is more in keeping with theoretical underpinnings of the present study than the most widely used test for psychopathology, the MMPI.

The POI consists of 150 paired items, each pair defining an opposition. The subject selects that member of each pair which is more characteristic of himself. The items are then scored along two major scales and ten sub-scales. Briefly, these are as follows:

    a. Major Scales.

       Time-Competent — "lives" in the present.

       Inner-Directed — independent, self-supportive.

    b. Sub-Scales.

       Self-Actualizing Value — holds values of self-actualizing people.

       Existentiality — flexible in application of values.

       Feeling Reactivity — sensitive to own needs and feelings.

       Spontaneity — freely expresses feelings behaviorally.

       Self-Regard — has high self-worth.

       Self-Acceptance — accepting of self in spite of weaknesses.

       Nature of Man, Constructive — sees man as essentially good.

Synergy — sees opposites of life as meaningfully related.
Acceptance of Aggression — accepts feelings of anger or aggression.
Capacity for Intimate Contact — has warm interpersonal relationships.

Summary of Data Collected

In order to summarize the input of information of the present study, the following outline is provided:

I. The Interview (Approximately two hours in length, tape recorded)
   A. Beginning the Interview (Introduction, use of recording device, etc.)
   B. Developmental History
     1. Family Life and Relationships
     2. Illness and Accident History
     3. School Career
     4. Relationship With Peers
     5. Psychosexual Development
     6. Self-Concept at Present Time
   C. Core Areas of Priesthood
     1. Development of Vocation
     2. Priestly Assignments
     3. Interpersonal Relations
     4. Faith and Church
     5. Priesthood
     6. Celibacy
     7. Future
   D. Termination

II. The Evaluation (Written by interviewer on the basis of information obtained in the interview)
   A. Interview Process (Clinical observation, unscaled)
     1. Behavioral Observations
     2. Affective Tones
   B. Development: Childhood, Adolescence, Adulthood (Clinical inference, unscaled)
     1. Parents and Other Significant Adults
     2. Relationship Between Parents
     3. Siblings, Peers, Group Identifications
     4. Notable Events

C. Functioning (Six sets of five psychodynamic statements; each statement ranked twice within its set: salience and confidence)
1. Interpersonal Relations
2. Psychosexual Maturity
3. Self-Perception
4. Job Satisfaction
5. Church, Faith, Religion
6. Priesthood
D. Report (Psychodynamic summary)
E. Future Outlook (See C above; includes statement concerning probability of leaving priesthood)
F. Psychosocial Modalities
1. Subject's Standing on Each Modality (Five-point rating scale, points defined)
   a. Trust vs. Basic Mistrust
   b. Autonomy vs. Shame and Doubt
   c. Initiative vs. Guilt
   d. Industry vs. Inferiority
   e. Identity vs. Identity Diffusion
   f. Intimacy vs. Isolation
   g. Generativity vs. Stagnation
   h. Ego Integrity vs. Despair
2. Degree of Emphasis on Each Modality (Rank ordering of eight modalities)
G. Diagnosis (Normal/Abnormal, APA nomenclature)
H. Scale of Adjustment (Twelve-point rating scale)

III. Psychological Tests
A. Loyola Sentence Completion Blank for Clergymen
1. Sub-scales
   a. Interpersonal Relations
   b. Psychosexual Maturity
   c. Self-Perception
   d. Job Satisfaction
   e. Church, Faith, Religion
   f. Priesthood
2. Total Score
B. Faith Scale
1. Self-Rating
   a. Real Self
   b. Ideal Self

      c. Social Self
      d. Past Self
      e. Future Self
   2. Clinical judges' rating of respondent's description of mature and immature faith along a continuum of intrinsic-extrinsic faiths
  C. Identity Scale — Self-Rating (56 items)
    1. Identity
      a. Ego-Career
      b. Ego-Group
      c. Ego-Self
      d. Ego-Affect
    2. Expressivity and Comfort Within a Social Context
    3. Individualistic Expressivity
    4. Integrity
    5. Autonomy Within Social Limits
    6. Trust
  D. Identity Scale — Rating of Ideal Self (14 items)
  E. Identity Scale — Rating of Church (14 items)
  F. Personal Orientation Inventory
    1. Major Scales
      a. Time-Competent
      b. Inner Directed
    2. Sub-Scales
      a. Self-Actualizing Value
      b. Existentiality
      c. Feeling Reactivity
      d. Spontaneity
      e. Self-Regard
      f. Self-Acceptance
      g. Nature of Man, Constructive
      h. Synergy
      i. Acceptance of Aggression
      j. Capacity for Intimate Contact

Sampling Methodology

When it came to drawing from the population of American priests a sample of potential subjects for this study, several considerations were kept in mind. First, it was important that the sample be drawn in such a way that it reflects an accurate image of the men who comprise the

American priesthood. That is, that no sub-group (younger vs. older, urban vs. rural, etc.) should be given undue emphasis. Another way of expressing this need is that if another sample of potential subjects were drawn in a similar fashion, the results should not be substantially different. A second consideration was the need for groups which were somewhat special (e.g., Trappists) to be represented in the study. A third consideration was the cost factor. That is, a totally random sampling of individual men would surely present grave problems of travel, time, and expense. A final consideration was the desirability of maintaining parallelism between the present psychological study and the sociological study which was simultaneously conducted at NORC. This sociological study employed a sampling strategy which divided the population of American priests into large groups or "strata" before sampling individuals. These strata, in the main, were size categories of dioceses and religious orders.

After consultations were held with sampling specialists at the Survey Research Center at the University of Michigan and NORC, a sampling strategy was devised in such a way as to give due consideration to each of these needs. A plan was created and executed by Benjamin King, Sampling Director, NORC. A brief description of this design follows.

In order to insure that priests from all size categories would be represented, it was decided that dioceses and religious communities would be stratified according to the number of priests contained within them and then selected as first-stage sampling units or clusters. In the case of religious institutes, in addition to the size strata, two special strata were formed for the Trappists and the United States Foundations.

The size categories for dioceses and religious orders were defined as follows:

Dioceses:
1. Small (1–100 priests)
2. Medium (101–200)
3. Large (201–500)
4. Extra large (501 and above)
Religious Institutes:
1. Extra small (1–20 priests)
2. Small (21–50)
3. Medium (51–135)
4. Large (136 and above)

After they were separated into size strata and the two special strata for the Trappists and the United States Foundations, the dioceses and religious communities were arranged in geographical order according to the four major United States census regions and then sampled within each stratum. Complete lists of priests within the selected units were obtained by written request from contact persons officially designated by bishops and major superiors. Sub-sampling was then performed at the desired rate.

A further word on the relationship between the Loyola sample and the NORC sample is in order. The Loyola sample is in fact a sub-sample of a sub-sample of the NORC sample. That is, a portion of the NORC sample was selected to receive, in addition to the sociological questionnaire, the POI. A portion of these priests was selected to receive, in addition to the sociological questionnaire and the POI, an invitation to participate in the Loyola interview study. Thus, these priests comprise a sub-sample of a sub-sample.

The sampling plan for the present study did not have as its aim the estimation of population parameters. Such an aim would have required a useable number of respondents in the range of 1,200 to 1,500 priests. The technique of the depth interview with its high cost prohibited the attainment of such a figure. Rather, the plan eventually chosen insured that no systematic bias entered into the selection of subjects. Hence, when proportions, average scores, and other statistics are cited in this report, they are not intended to be simple point estimates of population values. Such estimates are possible and, were they to be made, consideration would need be given to the statistical matters of standard error, weighing for stratification, and correction for nonresponse.

The Respondents

A total of 719 priests was selected for participation in the field interviews according to the sampling methodology outlined above. This figure does not include the 60 who were interviewed in the pilot study (Appendix B).

Each of the potential subjects was contacted in either of two ways. The first method was by phone. By and large, the telephoning was limited to the priests in the Chicago area. The second method was by mail. As previously indicated, a letter requesting the priest to participate in the interview study was included in the mailings of the sociological questionnaire from NORC. Potential subjects were provided with a pre-addressed postcard on which they were to indicate their willingness to be interviewed, age, year of ordination, current assignment, and telephone number. Two follow-up mailings were undertaken. The first was included with a follow-up sociological questionnaire. The second was another request to participate in the interview study only. Those subjects who indicated that they did not wish to participate received another letter asking them their reason for refusal and asking them to reconsider.

After a priest indicated that he was willing to be interviewed, specific arrangements were made. In most cases, the priest met with the interviewers in the interviewer's room in a hotel near the priest's residence. In other cases, the psychologist conducted the interview in the priest's residence or place of work. In still other instances, it was necessary for the priest and the interviewers to meet in a location far away from both living quarters. In a very small number of cases, the interview was conducted in the psychologist's private office. As might be inferred, bringing priest and psychologist together at a given date, time and place usually hundreds of miles away was often a very difficult task. The schedules of both were often tight. Hence, travel delays, emergencies or even minor errors resulted in missed appointments. Almost to a man, the priests were understanding of these difficulties and tolerant of the inconveniences caused by them.

Two-hundred and forty priests stated that they were not willing to be interviewed and would not change their intention when requested to do so. One-hundred and eleven men did not respond to the original request or to any of the follow-ups. Ninety-seven priests were eliminated from participation in the study. The most frequent cause for elimination was residence outside the 48 adjoining states. Other less frequent causes included the following: report of having left the active ministry, hospitalization, death, missing many appointments for an interview (two priests), and being an interviewer for the study (one priest). A total of 271 priests completed the psychological interview.

Table 1 describes the 719 potential subjects in terms of status in this study and sampling stratum. As can be seen in Table 1, a disproportionately large number of priests belonging to United States Foundations was eliminated. This primarily is due to residence outside of the 48 adjoining states.

Table 2 describes the 719 potential subjects by status within the study and by diocesan or religious order affiliation. Of the 424 diocesan priests initially selected, 179 (24%) were eventually interviewed. Of the 295 religious order priests initially selected, 92 (31%) were eventually interviewed. The difference in willingness to be interviewed is more striking when one considers the fact that only 25 (6%) of the diocesan priests were eliminated from participation whereas 72 (24%) of the religious order priests were eliminated. Elimination of religious order priests, as

TABLE 1

STATUS OF SUBJECTS WITHIN STUDY ACCORDING
TO SAMPLING STRATA

		Completed	"No"	Non-Respondent	Eliminated	Total in Sample
Diocese	Small	31	28	16	2	77
	Medium	44	28	13	12	97
	Large	53	48	18	3	122
	Extra Large	51	45	24	8	128
Religious Order	Extra Small	7	15	1	0	23
	Small	5	9	4	7	25
	Medium	16	17	9	8	50
	Large	44	35	22	26	127
	Trappists	7	3	1	1	12
	U.S. Foundation	13	12	3	30	58
Total		271	240	111	97	719

noted above, was due primarily to their residence outside the 48 adjoining states.

Table 3 describes the distribution of potential subjects by status within the study and by age grouping. For comparison, the estimated age distribution of all the men who comprise the American priesthood is included. This estimated distribution was obtained as part of the sociological study. The ages of the 32 non-respondents in Table 3 were obtained from the sociological questionnaire. In most cases, this information for the non-respondents was not available.

Inspection of Table 3 suggests that among the priests who were interviewed, there was no gross over- or under-representation of any age group. There does appear to be a slight over-representation of younger priests. In general, the younger the man, the less likely he was to refuse to be interviewed. To a degree, this tendency did not result in gross over-representation of the young. This was due to the greater rate of elimination of those under 46 years of age. Although the data are quite spotty, there is suggestion that the older the priest, the more likely he would not respond to the requests to be interviewed.

To this point, comparisons on the variables of sampling strata, diocesan or religious order affiliation, and chronological age have been drawn

TABLE 2

STATUS OF SUBJECTS WITHIN STUDY ACCORDING TO DIOCESAN OR RELIGIOUS ORDER AFFILIATION

	Completed		No		Non-respondent		Eliminated		Total in Sample		All Active Priests
	n	%	n	%	n	%	n	%	n	%	%
Diocesan	179	66	149	62	71	64	25	26	424	59	55
Religious	92	34	91	38	40	36	72	74	295	41	45
Total	271	100	240	100	111	100	97	100	719	100	100

TABLE 3

STATUS OF SUBJECTS WITHIN SAMPLE ACCORDING TO AGE[a]

Age	Completed		"No"		Non-respondent		Eliminated		All Active Priests
26-35	75	.28	19	.10	3	.09	16	.22	.22
36-45	78	.29	36	.18	4	.12	34	.47	.30
46-55	61	.22	65	.33	10	.31	17	.23	.23
56+	57	.21	79	.40	15	.47	6	.08	.26
Total	271	1.00	199	1.01[b]	32	.99[b]	73	1.00	1.01[b]

[a] No information from 144 priests.
[b] Error due to rounding.

among the men who were actually interviewed and those who were selected but not interviewed. Although these variables are enlightening, they are not as relevant to the theoretical underpinnings of this study as is, for example, personal maturity. Some data relevant to this variable are available. As noted earlier, the POI, a measure of self-actualization, was sent to all 719 potential subjects along with the sociological questionnaire. In many instances the priests who were not interviewed (i.e., did not respond, were eliminated, or refused) did fill out this test. Two variables on this test were chosen for comparative analysis. They are the two major scales of the test, "Time-Competence" and "Inner-Directed." Tables 4 and 5 show the results of the analyses of variance of these two variables across categories of participation in the study. Analysis of variance is a statistical tool which helps one determine whether differences among groups of people on selected variables represent random fluctuations or true differences. This tool is described in more detail in Chapter IX.

TABLE 4

ONE-WAY ANALYSIS OF VARIANCE OF TIME-COMPETENCE OF SUBJECTS WHO WERE ELIMINATED, DID NOT RESPOND, DECLINED TO PARTICIPATE, AND THOSE INTERVIEWED

	Sum of Squares	Degrees of Freedom	Mean Square	F Ratio
Between Groups	4.96	3	1.65	0.21
Within Groups	2942.48	378	7.78	
Total	2947.44	381		

TABLE 5

ONE-WAY ANALYSIS OF VARIANCE OF INNER-DIRECTEDNESS OF SUBJECTS WHO WERE ELIMINATED, DID NOT RESPOND, DECLINED TO PARTICIPATE, AND THOSE INTERVIEWED

	Sum of Squares	Degrees of Freedom	Mean Square	F Ratio
Between Groups	1243.23	3	414.41	3.18*
Within Groups	49285.94	378	130.39	
Total	50529.17	381		

* $p. < .05$.

The analysis of variance summarized in Table 4 indicates that the four categories of men do not differ in the "competent" use of time. However, Table 5 indicates that the groups do differ among themselves on the dimension of inner- as opposed to other-directedness. A high score indicates that the person's values arise out of internal conviction, rather than external demand. Of particular interest is the statistically significant (Scheffé, 1959) comparison (p. $< .05$) between the "No" and the "Completed" groups. That is, those subjects who were interviewed were, on the average, more inner-directed than those who refused to be interviewed. Further, it will be shown (Chapter IX) that this variable is of significance in understanding the levels of personal development found among the clergy.

The geographic dispersion of the interviewed priests is illustrated in Figure 1. Twenty-eight states and the District of Columbia are represented. The smallest number of interviewed subjects in any state is one (New Jersey, New Mexico, Wyoming), the largest is 29 (Illinois).

Analytic Techniques

After the 60 psychological reports obtained in the pilot study and those obtained in the field early in the data collection phase were evaluated, it seemed possible to group the priests into categories which were ordered along a continuum of development. Four major types emerged: Maldeveloped, Underdeveloped, Developing, and Developed. Such a classificatory system was well suited to the purpose of the study, that is, answering the basic question, "What are the priests of the United States like as men?" The focus was on groups of men, not on groups of variables.

Composite personality sketches of men found in each of the four categories were drawn. These sketches served as preliminary definitions of the categories. Next, a sample of 25 reports was read and categorized independently by the authors and two other psychological consultants. The level of agreement among the four raters was good. Disagreements served the purpose of clarifying important issues. For example, one rater used adaptation to vocational demands as a primary factor in his judgments. The other raters used more personal factors, such as depth of emotions and presence of satisfying interpersonal relationships, as primary indices. The matter was discussed and the latter emphases agreed upon.

The next step was the refining of each category into three levels. This resulted in a twelve-point scale of development. The purpose of using

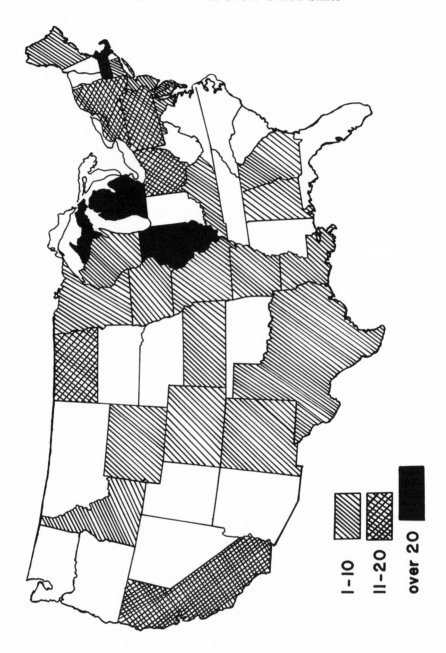

Fig. 1.—Geographical distribution of interviewed subjects.

a twelve-point scale (four major categories with three levels within each category) rather than a four-point scale (four major categories) was to achieve increased utility for further correlational studies.

Next, the authors independently read the 271 reports in their entirety. The sequence in which the reports were read was random and different for each author. They independently assigned a developmental rating on the twelve-point scale to each case and wrote comments about each report.

The value of the Pearson product-moment correlation between the two independent sets of ratings was .76 (p. < .01). Hence, the authors were in substantial agreement at well beyond chance levels. It was decided that the rating system was an adequate means of generating groups of priests for analytic purposes.

The major focus of this report is "clinical" in the sense of individualized. In this light a decision was made to collapse the twelve-point scale into the four-point scale for purposes of analysis. That is, the primary task at hand was the description of groups of priests rather than describing relationships among variables. Table 6 shows the extent of the agreement of the authors' independent ratings collapsed into the four categories.

The sum of the numbers in the diagonal of Table 6 is 209. In other words, the authors agreed on the developmental category of 209 (77%) of the 271 priests. Two consistent types of disagreement appear in Table 6. The first is evident from inspection of the first row where it can be seen that rater A placed 26 subjects in the Developed category. Rater B placed 11 of these in two lower categories. The second is noted in the third row where rater A placed 35 cases in the Underdeveloped category which rater B had placed in the Developing category. Hence, when rater A described a person as Developed, rater B tended to describe him as somewhat less mature. But when rater A saw a person as Underdeveloped, rater B tended to see him as Developing.

Disagreements which occurred between the two raters over the category into which some priests should be placed were resolved. As can be derived from Table 6, 62 such disagreements occurred. In such situations, case conferences were held. At the case conferences, the authors argued out their differences. No use was made of the test data at any time in making these decisions.

The final result of the ratings and case conferences was the following distribution of priests: Developed, 19; Developing, 50; Underdeveloped,

TABLE 6

INDEPENDENT RATINGS OF SUBJECTS INTO FOUR
DEVELOPMENTAL CATEGORIES

Rater B

		Developed	Developing	Underdeveloped	Maldeveloped
Rater A	Developed	15	4	7	0
	Developing	1	39	5	0
	Underdeveloped	1	34	139	4
	Maldeveloped	0	1	5	16

179; Maldeveloped, 23. It should be emphasized that no claim regarding population proportions is intended here.

Another series of conferences between the authors was held. The authors reviewed the cases which were contained within the categories. On the bases of the psychological reports and the notes which they independently took during the rating procedure, a composite description of each type was generated. Particularly instructive cases[1] were noted. These descriptions were then reevaluated by the consultants and were revised and refined into the following four chapters of the report (Chapters IV, V, VI, and VII).

The psychological test data were analyzed according to the taxonomy of development derived from the psychological reports. These analyses are reported in Chapter IX. Basically, the average scores on a series of variables were computed for the men placed in each of the four categories of development. Tests of significance of differences were then run.

Not all the quantitative data collected were statistically analyzed. Given the temporal limits of the project, it was necessary to delete from formal analysis the quantitative ratings made by the interviewers. These, however, were available to the authors and were helpful in the categorization of subjects into developmental categories. Also deleted from statistical analyses were the following psychological test variables: the ratings of Ideal Self and the Church on the Identity Scale and the priest's own ratings of his real, ideal, social, past and future selves on the Faith Scale.

---

1. Transcription of the tape-recorded interviews, some of which were utilized in the preparation of the illustrative cases, was made possible, in part, by a grant from the Loyola University of Chicago Committee on Research.

A Note on Control

The core methodology used for this investigation was the clinical interview. While considered by some (cf., Bolgar, 1965) as pre-scientific, this method is both fact-finding and heuristic. The latter is true because many of the facts that are uncovered by the interview stimulate precisely controlled studies. Admittedly, this investigation was not an experiment in the traditional sense of implementing a highly specific manipulation of variables and sharply defined control groups. Definite consideration was given to a parallel evaluation of control subjects; however, such procedures were decided to be irrelevant. Strictly speaking, there was no one definitive control group apparent to the investigators. Further, since the resources for the project were fixed, inclusion of a control group, largely for ritualistic reasons, would have reduced the number of priests interviewed by 50 per cent. At the same time, the eventual taxonomy from Maldeveloped to Developed that was used in this study provided data for relative comparisons among rather discrete groups of priests.

CHAPTER IV

THE MALDEVELOPED

Two principles were applied in selecting men for this category: first, a long-term history of difficulty, dating back to the earliest life experience of the individual and associated in some way with the faulty resolution of the initial growth problems of life; secondly, serious psychological problems recognizable as major difficulties which interfered in a marked way in the individual's personal life and work. We will not describe each maldeveloped individual according to a specific psychiatric diagnostic category. Rather we will describe the general characteristics of this group, the ways in which their problems are manifested in their day-to-day living, and also describe some of the questions related to identifying and helping them to a more adequate adjustment.

These men are not the stereotypes often popularly associated with serious psychological difficulty. All these priests function in responsible roles in society, even though more than one has a history of psychiatric hospitalization. They function with difficulty; the stress is usually noticed by those around them but is not often interpreted accurately. These are the sort of men who are thought of as a little eccentric at times, or perhaps as difficult to live with or hard to work with. Some get themselves into serious trouble from time to time. Others never experience public trouble at all. They seem cooperative, quiet and reliable. There is no one satisfactory universal pattern by which one can recognize the maldeveloped. They appear rational because their disorders are emotional rather than intellectual. In technical terms, they suffer from affective disorders rather than logical disorders. This frequently leads people to expect more rational and orderly behavior from them than they are capable of producing. We are speaking now, not of priests who are in fact in psychiatric hospitals, but priests who are interacting with their peers, their people, and their superiors every day.

The number of the maldeveloped in this cross-sectional sample is relatively small. As previously noted, it is felt that another sample of the same size would yield similar results. In other words, it can be presumed that across the whole population of priests the percentage of maldeveloped personalities is small. They are still capable of functioning as priests, although their effectiveness is hampered by their psychological difficulties. Because they have emotional rather than logical disorders, they may seem to be better adjusted than they are. They reinforce this impression through the use of intellectual defenses to keep themselves together. In other words, the problems they experience are within them, and do not show necessarily on the surface. They can be masked, especially in a profession in which a person can maintain an accepted distance from others, by their appearance of controlled rationality. They do not, however, experience their emotional lives in the same manner as normal, healthy individuals. Their emotions are disrupted and in turmoil; they cause them pain and move them to the use of repressive and controlling mechanisms of defense. They adjust, then, through these defenses rather than through the proper integration of their emotional lives.

To put it in simple language, they do not feel about themselves, nor do they react in relationship to others, in the relatively integrated manner which is characteristic of well-developed persons. They cannot handle their feelings directly, and they are frequently made very anxious by them; their defenses, such as rationalization or projection, enable them to live with the disorder without admitting it to themselves. These intellectual defenses are something like wallpaper on cracked plaster, giving an integrity to the surface which would not otherwise be present. It is a deceptive and fragile covering, however, which is very vulnerable to any marked change in conditions. The use of defenses in a systematic way gives rise to certain forms of behavior which we call symptoms. Symptoms are signs of something going on inside the individual; marks, in other words, which are very informative if we are able to read their meaning accurately. The symptoms observed in these individuals are the edges of their defensive adjustments. What shows to the outer world is not the disorder directly but the psychological device which the individual uses in order to keep the disorder under control. That is why it is possible to identify a certain number of intellectual defenses which are characteristically employed by this group of men. Intellectualization is a process, for example, by which a person is able to deal with his problems because he drains all the emotion out of them and is able to speak of them in a purely intellectual way. The intellectualization of experience takes the human fullness out of it. It comes across as detached although intelligent; it comes more from the surface than from the depths of the individual using it. People who use intellectualization can talk about their personal problems in a very detailed way because the defense enables them to do this without really experiencing any of the pain connected with the problem. This is characteristic of the defenses employed by the maldeveloped.

A clear example of the use of intellectual defenses is the early middle-aged professor who has been in psychoanalysis for a number of years. Both his own intellectual work and his mode of psychotherapy utilize his great intelligence to maintain control over his extremely disordered emotional life. He is passive and feminine in his own personal identification, a homosexual in sexual experience, and has had extensive problems with alcoholism. He values himself very little, mostly because of his negative feelings about his own homosexuality, and lives a very lonely and isolated life, his only satisfaction coming from teaching. He manages to keep going mainly on the strength of his intelligence, realizing that his religious identification and his celibacy give him respectability. That is what holds him together.

The symptoms of the maldeveloped are frequently misunderstood or misread; they do not seem as seriously handicapped as they really are. One would think that a rational, logical, and calm approach in dealing with them and their difficulties would work. It is only when a bishop or superior is frustrated in trying to relate to these people in a relatively normal way that he begins to understand the depth and convolutions of the emotional difficulties which the maldeveloped experience.

Take, for example, the young parish priest, oldest of a large number of children in a desperately poor family, who never experienced affection from his father. The intense rage he feels toward his father has never been resolved and it expresses itself in dealings with any male figure. Similar to this man is the slightly older parish priest who never knew his father because he abandoned the family when he was an infant. The priest has had difficulty with all the authority figures in his life; even in his faith life he feels abandoned by God the Father.

The emotional problems of the maldeveloped are associated with poor early family backgrounds. In every case there has been a major disruption of the accepted family pattern. Psychological trauma has been connected with this — some psychological wound inflicted on the person which has never healed, an emotional deficit that has never been made up by later compensating experiences. Maldeveloped priests carry their problems into the seminary and the priesthood with them, showing them in different ways at different stages of life; they are always related to this common infertile ground of emotional deprivation during early child-hood. The sources of this trauma are not the incidents in themselves. In some instances these may be experiences had by other persons which are worked out more smoothly because the individual has not been exposed to the worst aspects of the situation, such as the constant fighting be-tween mother and father. Different factors, such as the early presence of other concerned adults, may make up for the loss of one or the other of the individual's parents. The key element, as far as the maldeveloped is concerned, is the unresolved traumatic event which continues to have ragged and unhealed edges. They suffered greatly at an important forma-tive stage in life. To use Erikson's terms, they experienced a major distortion at the very time in their lives when they should have been developing a basic sense of trust. With the maldeveloped, nothing makes up for what is lacking in their early home life experiences.

The maldeveloped have experienced one or the other of the following distortions of the family picture: separation of parents who have proved incompatible; divorce of the parents for the same reason; desertion by either mother or father; psychological distance from the parents even though they remain married to one another; death of one or the other parent at a crucial stage in the individual's development. Great emo-tional turmoil precedes or accompanies most of these experiences. This is particularly true in those families marked by separation, divorce or desertion; these may have been preceded by years of hostile wrangling on the part of the mother and father.

Characteristic, then, of this group is the deep flaw in the relationship of the husband or wife who are the subject's father and mother. This has long been recognized as extremely significant in the healthy develop-ment of the child's personality. The present research merely illustrates again what previous psychological studies have already pointed out: any marked distortion of the parental relationship and the normal home environment has serious consequences on the psychological development of the children. A further characteristic of this population of mal-developed priests is the presence of strong, over-protective mothers with whom the individuals frequently over-identified because of the lack of a father figure or because the father figure was a weak and passive person. This is a consistent finding, giving further evidence of the emo-tional distortion of the child's early world, and disclosing one of the clear sources of his later emotional difficulties. Because of the presence of dominant, over-bearing mothers and the lack of any real masculine figure in the environment, many of these subjects have experienced persistent difficulties with their own personal male identification. They never knew a true man upon whom they could model their behavior at the most important stage of their growth; the scars of this persist in the later stages of life. We have already pointed out how individuals who have not learned to relate to a father figure in a healthy way have serious disturbances with any of their later relationships with authority. So, too, they may expect from the authority figures they meet later in life a kind of fathering behavior which they never knew in their childhood. This often perplexes the authorities with whom they deal because, although these individuals look relatively normal at times, they cannot help but manifest their inability to deal smoothly with authority figures.

If all this is true, what do these men look like? How do they manifest these internal difficulties if they can seem only mildly disturbed, or, at times, not disturbed at all? We will list and comment on some of the ways in which these people reveal their inner problems through their outer mode of adjustment.

1. They may have severe, psychotic breakdowns which require hospitalization. As was mentioned earlier, the number of these is small in the population of priests who are currently functioning. There are, however, some men who have had serious personal difficulties, who have received psychiatric treatment, and who are now functioning in an acceptable manner in pastoral work. Their adjustment may be tenuous, and they may need medication or the continuing support of therapy, but they are capable of performing priestly functions, derive a certain amount of satisfaction from them, and would like to continue insofar as they can. Severe breakdowns, however, do not come just from overwork or out of the blue. They are the signs of serious problems and they are frequently related, as has been described, to early family difficulties. These men are, of course, the most obvious of the maldeveloped because they have had to get professional treatment for some extended time. It is clear that they will never be able to withstand the pressures of life with the same resiliency that is common among better developed persons. They are, however, capable of a certain amount of priestly activity.

2. They may have persistent conflicts with any and every authority figure in their lives. This is clearly related to the absence of a healthy father figure with whom they could identify during their growing years. The conflicts of later life are rooted frequently in their own emotional distortions rather than in real life situations. This internal difficulty, which may at times be the chief manifestation of a severe problem, makes it very difficult for authorities to interact in an effective manner with these

persons. There is very little that a person in authority can do correctly because he triggers the strong emotional reaction which the person feels because he has been deserted or disappointed by his own father. Rational arguments do not avail; this person cannot help but reveal what he has missed in his emotional background through the manner in which he interacts with the authorities in his life.

3. Sometimes the difficulty is very subtle, hardly noticeable unless you take a close look at the individual. The deep problem is kept beneath the surface of everyday behavior by very strong intellectual defenses. This is very common in the lives of gifted individuals. Although they have great internal problems, they are able to keep them under control through the strength of their own intellects. They are very good at explaining away their deviations, which may be very secret and very well protected, through the use of rationalization. They can make their inconsistent behavior sound consistent. This enables them to live without experiencing the anxiety which they would normally feel if they faced the truth about some behavioral difficulty in their lives. For example, the maldeveloped person might engage in homosexual acts and still be able to maintain a very smooth public presence. He isolates deviant behavior through these intellectual defenses and does not face his own inconsistencies. It takes a close look, however, to properly identify some of these men.

4. The individual may live out a much more bizarre identification. This is rare. There are cases of priests now functioning whose adjustments are clearly disturbed but who seem to get away with it. For example, an individual may make a very eccentric adjustment, living a disordered and unproductive life, but still perform priestly functions in his own unique way.

Perhaps a classic example of this type is the early middle-aged priest whose parents were divorced when he was an infant. At the age of five he proclaimed himself for Christ at a fundamentalist revival meeting in a dramatic and forceful way. He considers this early event the true equivalent of ordination to the priesthood, a reality which was only formalized by his later official ordination. He conceives of his priestly work in a grandiose, overdramatic, and highly personalized way, playing the role of the intense prophet, and masking his delusional focus on himself through his high intelligence. He is a seriously disturbed person who makes a bizarre appearance but who continues to function in the Church.

The wonder with this type is that their symptoms are not more accurately read and interpreted by others. It is as if they were waving flags and asking for someone to recognize the fact that they have serious difficulties with their emotional lives.

5. The individual may withdraw from society and live as a loner who cannot work effectively with others but who structures his life carefully so that this is never really demanded of him. His inability to be close to others is sometimes masked by or excused on account of a presumed style of piety which justifies this kind of withdrawn behavior. Sometimes the loner, who stays at a distance from people because they are liable to hurt him, can serve very well as long as his environment is not disturbed, especially if he can employ compulsive defenses. If the loner is forced into a change in which he must relate more closely to people, there may be a major dislocation in his emotional life, and he may break down in a more obvious way. Extreme withdrawal, however, is a clear sign of some sort of disturbance.

For example, the young priest-teacher who cannot speak of his early life very clearly at all; whose only memory of his parents is one of their arguing with each other; a man who looks back to puberty and his experiences as a compulsive masturbator as a turning point in his life. He says that he felt so much guilt over this that he felt it necessary to retreat from the world in order to shield himself from sexual stimuli. He attempted to join a contemplative order at the time, but when he was told that he would have to wait a year, he joined another religious community (although he has attempted several times to join the contemplative order since). The pattern of flight from his own basic impulses has ruled his life and shaped his choice of the priesthood, in which he is quite poorly adjusted. He is presently seeking more isolated work to be able to withdraw even farther from others. The main way in which he attempts to keep himself psychologically intact is through the use of obsessive-compulsive defenses. He stays away from others, claiming that he has no close friends in his religious community, no one, in fact with whom he can speak about himself at all. Through his obsessive tendencies he tries to exercise control over his every action, keeping them all in place through some conscious effort. So, for example, he even consciously offers up to God beforehand the action of blowing his nose.

This man's life is filled with signs and symptoms of the severity of his underlying disorder. They are apparently not understood by those around him who see him as quiet, withdrawn, and serious. They do not apparently suspect that here is a far more serious problem than eccentricity.

The individual is literally barely holding himself together through a very painful use of neurotic adjustive techniques. As the interviewer notes: "He resolves his problems primarily by reading; he is given to flight as his primary way of dealing with any kind of intense feelings. Even though he has rigidly enforced his obsessive thinking and has greatly controlled his life by his obsessive behavior, he still seems to lack the ego-strength to carry on for very long. . . . The long range prognosis for this man is extremely poor. The likelihood that his obsessive-compulsive defenses may break down and lead to a schizophrenic break is rather high."

In other words, we have a priest with a life-long problem who is trying to keep himself together with fragile, compulsive defenses, and who, through efforts to join a contemplative order or to get more withdrawn work, is telling those around him, as best he can, that he is disturbed. They do not seem sensitive to the severity of the problem and may not be until he has a major breakdown.

6. The individual may be chronically depressed or chronically anxious. These are signs that some processes are going on inside of him with which he has not come to terms. These interfere in a marked way with his functioning, but he is frequently able to keep up some semblance of pastoral work — at least saying Mass, and being available for sick calls. He is not a very happy-looking person, and his anxiety manifests itself in indirect ways, such as physical illnesses; but he is seldom recognized as a person with a serious emotional problem.

Thus, the pastor in his late fifties whose present anxiety has been increased by his assignment to a parish for which he must take sole responsibility. He makes a good and reliable appearance but his inner uncertainties and conflicts make him incapable of functioning independently. He characteristically tries to resolve these depressing problems by eliciting sympathy from others. This is a regressive defense, one that reveals the infantile level (seeking mothering and comfort) at which he presents himself to others. He probably looks just like a "worrier" to other priests who hardly suspect the deep inner difficulties.

7. The individual may adopt a very perfectionistic style of defense, keeping his emotions under strict control by trying to live a life that is in complete accord with some kind of external requirements. He is to be distinguished from the person who tries truly to lead a good life because of the underlying emotional problem to which this perfectionistic behavior is really directed. He does not seek holiness as much as he establishes control over his own strong emotions. Sometimes these get

out, through very small cracks in his defenses, in an unexpected show of anger that is literally just a tip of a large and jagged iceberg.

8. Sometimes there are very obvious problems which observers of the individual attribute to a lack of self-control rather than to an inner emotional problem.

For example, the individual may act outwardly in a homosexual manner or he may become a severe alcoholic who seems unable to maintain any sense of responsibility for himself or his obligations. Ordinarily, when these problems become severe, these priests are hospitalized or given special assignments in which they can get continued psychiatric assistance. Frequently, this kind of breakdown is the priest's ultimate effort to communicate to the world around him. It is a mixture of self-punishment and symbolic psychological language which reveals the seriousness of his difficulty and the amount of help he really needs. Sometimes, however, these problems are misinterpreted and the individual is given supportive encouragement rather than psychological assistance. He will just keep breaking down, or he will find new and perhaps more dramatic ways of expressing his psychological difficulties.

Common to many of these situations is a strong underlying hostility, one of the disordered feelings which is so strong that its presence makes the individual highly anxious. He defends, then, against the existence of this strong feeling through one of the psychological maneuvers which we have described before. The withdrawn young teacher possesses strong feelings of hatred toward his parents. He muffles these, however, by his defensive adjustment. Even his barely audible speaking voice is a sign of his efforts to keep everything quiet within.

Common also to these persons are extremely negative feelings toward themselves, a diminished sense of self-esteem, anger toward themselves, and a great lack of comfort with themselves. They are uneasy in life, and find it difficult to accept, much less love themselves in any way. It is difficult to believe this is true of some of these persons because they can look so acceptable on the surface. They may even have realized a respectable amount of achievement in life. None of this is sufficient proof of their worth to them, because this has been so effectively undermined by their early life experiences.

It is also characteristic of these people that they cannot deal well with the show of emotion in others. Because of their own faulted emotional development, it is almost impossible for them to deal effectively with aggression or the expression of any strong feeling, whether it is enthusiasm or affection, from other people. They may long for one or the other of these things, but it is across a gulf which they cannot bridge. This adds to their pain and contributes in the long run to their isolation.

Frequently, these men are wrapped up either in the past and their own emotional history, or in the future which has not yet come into being. They do not have a good sense of the present, cannot relate realistically to their immediate responsibilities and cannot plan in a truly effective fashion. They live focusing either on the past or on what has not yet come to be.

Some concluding remarks are in order before we review in greater detail other individual examples of the maldeveloped population. It is necessary to repeat the fact that the symptoms of which these people give evidence to can be misunderstood, especially by superiors or other authorities in the Church. These men are still functioning, still trying to demonstrate by means of their symptoms the fact that they are seriously ill. They will continue to act out until some effective response is given to their internal difficulty. It is very hard for them to talk about what their real trouble is, largely because they cannot get out of themselves to look at it directly. That is why they choose to speak in the symbolic language of symptoms. They do not know clearly what they are saying and they may even deny that there is any serious problem. Their whole communication, however, makes it clear that there is a severe inner problem which cannot be ignored.

It is also clear that the maldeveloped priests could have been identified at an early stage of their life through some form of psychological evaluation. These individuals did not develop their problems within the seminary or the priesthood. In every case the problem existed before application to the seminary. It is also clear that the psychological disturbance played a role in the motivation of these individuals for work in the priesthood. The present research clearly indicates the wisdom of careful screening programs for seminary applicants; early evaluation of these persons might have helped them to make better decisions and to receive the benefits of psychological help earlier in their lives.

It is important to note that there has been a philosophy of treating these persons which has defined health as getting people to adjust, not through a fuller or healthier personality, but simply functioning again within the priesthood. This is a very limited definition of health and may contribute to their difficulty if return to priestly functioning is thought to be synonymous with cure. Lastly, it must be observed that some of these men can, in fact, continue to function in the priesthood if there is some effective response to their difficulties. That is to say, some of these men need a quiet and not very demanding parish. They may need continuing psychiatric support and superiors who are willing to tolerate a certain amount of eccentricity. With a wise combination of support and treatment, some of these priests can continue to function on a limited basis in the future.

Part Two: Case Histories

We will now examine, in somewhat greater detail, some case histories which should help provide an understanding of the life problems of maldeveloped persons. One case history[1] will be presented at length, followed by a few briefer ones. They are not all alike in age or background; they are, however, similar in the painful struggles that have marked their lives.

This diocesan priest is in his early fifties. He has been and remains an associate pastor in a large diocese. His ministry has been, according to his own evaluation, mediocre, although he has derived satisfaction and success from preaching and from working with women's church social groups. He does, however, describe his professional life as a failure, an opinion that appears to be seconded by his peers and his superiors. The central fact of his adult life was a period of alcoholism which extended for about fifteen years of his adult life. After appropriate treatment he has made a recovery and has not been drinking for about three years.

He responded to the interviewer in a very warm, sociable, but anxious way. His attitude was one of overcompliance to the examiner but self-demeaning toward himself. He spoke very positively about people in general but he rarely related facts about any particular individual. He appears to be a very energetic, intellectually bright but minimally productive person. He creates the impression of considerable warmth and throughout the interview he stressed a liberal and open point of view on life and on the Church. The examiner's reactions to this man were not completely positive. The priest made it clear, through his style, that no one ever got very close to him in a personal way. His intense needs to be cared for and to be supported made it difficult to establish and to maintain real or affective interpersonal relations. This man is classified as a maldeveloped person. He is, nevertheless, able to perform certain useful functions in the Church.

---

1. Frank J. Kobler, Ph.D., was primarily responsible for the preparation of the four major case histories in the present report.

When asked what he considered to be the most important things that he was doing now as a priest he replied:

> In addition to saying the Mass and administering the sacraments my greatest role is that of preaching . . . giving leadership to the people to enable them to cope with the problems that they face today . . . and then I like to project a personal friendliness to people so that they feel there is some place where they can go, that somebody cares, that they can be heard and that they are going to be treated with a full, honest evaluation of themselves.
>
> . . . There are a lot of elderly people in our parish . . . and they have lost the security blanket of the traditional practices of their religion. And I think that my role is to point out that even though there is a great deal of change going on, the substance remains the same and that it is being revived and enriched.
>
> . . . This is where a priest (like me) can do a great deal in reassuring older people of the stability of their faith.

Here is an older man, a failure in the eyes of many, a chronic alcoholic, a psychosexually immature and emotionally childlike person, a man who is diagnosed as a moderately severe psychoneurotic who is, nevertheless, able to perform a useful service to people and to the Church. He accepts with enthusiasm the changes in the Church, and he uses himself as a bridge for older people to help them to retain the use of their faith in their daily lives. This positive work is, however, strongly tinged by a deep sense of failure at not having made a greater success of his life. The source of his failure and his attempt to heal it over by an appeal to faith comes out clearly in the following exchange:

> A seminarian asked me one day not too long ago, 'Are you a pastor?' And I said, 'no,' and he said, 'How long have you been a priest?' And I told him about 28 years. And he said, 'Well, don't you want to be a pastor?' And I said, 'I haven't really spent that much time being concerned about it.' I've thought about it. But I feel that because of my faith that I am where I am because of a reason. I don't have to know it. As long as I am acting in a priestly way that, therefore, I am pleasing to God. And this is all that is important to me.

This priest has repressed all negative feelings toward his parents and his family. His father came from Ireland and worked his way into a position of considerable local prominence. Apparently his father obtained two advanced degrees without the benefit of much early formal education. The son was the next to the last of several children and he had very little relationship with his parents. His oldest brother married about the time that the future priest was born. His father had thought of becoming a priest but gave up this idea. He describes his parents as "very dynamic people yet very understanding and very warm." His father is described as a "very friendly person" and "very expansive" and "completely unselfish." "There was always a tremendous respect for my father," he noted. With his mother he states that he "communicated beautifully," and that "I was always conscious of her being available, that to her everything was centered in and for the family." The mother and the father agreed never to argue in front of the children so the family saw no expression of anger in the home. His father was away from home frequently during the first four years of the boy's life. Despite his many subsequent problems he cannot describe his family experience except in very positive terms.

He states that he liked all his siblings and peers, yet he shows little if any indication of any close or important relationship to them. All the children, he tells us, competed for the parents' affection. This priest does not name one close friend. Once he became an alcoholic, a friend from another city began paying a great deal of attention to him and aided him in obtaining treatment for his alcoholism. When asked about his friends, he replied:

> My friendships were flexible, you might say. If you were to ask me today which of the priests that were my classmates are still friends of mine, I would say a lot of them. But I couldn't say that any single one is especially a friend. There are just all of them. It's a sort of free lance type of thing.

A central difficulty in this man's life has been his loneliness. He has not been close to others in a healthy give-and-take way. Rather he has demonstrated a need to be placating, to be compliant in the presence of feelings of hostility, of rejection, and of unjust treatment. This is the style of adjustment he uses with his religious associates and superiors:

> The problem with authority figures was a big thing to me. It happened in different circumstances —with different pastors and with the Bishop. I didn't realize I couldn't handle alcohol and as a result I got into a confrontation with the authorities, and so finally with the help of God I was able to realize that I was an alcoholic and that I had to quit drinking. And that's it. And I haven't had

a drink in three years. . . . I was going to show them that I didn't have a drinking problem . . . until finally these blackouts were a corroborating thing for me.

When asked what things he liked about himself and what things he disliked about himself he replied as follows:

I am reasonably healthy . . . and I have at least an average amount of intelligence. I have a capacity for fantasy which I didn't realize until recently is very important in my life. . . . This is fantasy not in the sense of being way out but in the sense of being a dreamer. . . . I don't consider myself an expert in any one particular field, but yet I don't feel terribly threatened in any project. . . . Perhaps that sounds a bit ambiguous or a bit strange to put it that way. For example, I don't know how to paint but I wouldn't be a bad painter if required by circumstances to paint. And if I didn't do too well at it this wouldn't bother me too much.

This is one of the more revealing passages in his interview. It suggests two sources or two conditions for his "failure" in his priesthood and in his personal life. One is the disproportionate emphasis on fantasy as a way of escaping the demands of reality and as a method for extending approbation to himself. The nature of this fantasy, particularly as it related to the developing alcoholism and its remission, the confrontation about drinking with his pastors and other superiors, the underlying repressed resentment and depression: all these would be appropriate areas for understanding and for helping this man.

Another significant factor in his maldevelopment is the presence of ability, health, energy and of some talent and the associated failure to focus or to utilize these resources in some manner that could be accepted by himself, and approved by his colleagues. This priest has achieved little in his life that would give him sufficient status and self-respect. He has attempted to find status in his preaching, but this has not really satisfied his needs. He needs something more than success at preaching; an assignment, a job, a focus for his life. His statement that "I don't consider myself an expert in any one particular field" is his own soft way of speaking of his despair, his loneliness and his sense of worthlessness and rejections. If a diocesan priest cannot become a pastor, and some cannot, then it is very difficult for him unless he has some other job classification and position that has status and approbation in the ministry:

There are a few things that I would like to do that I haven't done. I would like to fly a plane. I mean to be able to fly whenever I wanted to. I have always been adventuresome, if you want to put it that way. . . . I wish I were less sanguine and more choleric in my way of acting. This is negative in me and ties in with my fantasy. . . . Only under pressure will I work or be productive . . . otherwise, I'll daydream around and away from the job. I am disorganized in my work and I procrastinate and waste time by daydreaming and worrying about the job or work.

The difficulty in this man's life does not arise from a single source, such as an inappropriate work assignment; it springs from lacks and maladjustments in his personality. He is disorganized, he uses fantasy in place of, or to avoid productive work, and he has not learned to work with people. He manifests disproportionate amounts of anxiety that lead to his periodic disablement.

The thing that I dislike in myself is the business of not accomplishing all the things that I wanted to. I don't want to accomplish in the sense that to accomplish you have to get yourself involved. I often purposely commit myself to something that I don't have to, so that I can get myself involved. This is because I know that it will force me to do more. (He gets himself overinvolved in tasks so that he can be motivated to produce but then he fails more often than not.) I have a tremendous capacity for impatience. I have a terrible temper, but very few people ever know about this.

This man resents being misunderstood by his colleagues and superiors. He resents what he describes as the false judgments that have been made about him. He resents the misjudgments about the style and the caliber of his work. He resents priests who are organized, effective, successful and productive.

He feels that others do not understand and appreciate him. To his colleagues he is, in his words, " a mystery wrapped in an enigma." He thinks that they are envious of him, particularly of his broad range of interests as well as his wide knowledge which is reflected, he feels, in his effective preaching. He builds his life in great part on his preaching ability and his facility in communicating with and responding to groups. If this has, in fact, an objective basis in reality, it is clearly an area where he should receive support and encouragement. Isolated from some kind of "job classification" to make up for his not being a pastor, this preaching is not enough to strengthen him.

The great crisis in this man's life was his confrontation with the authorities in the Church at the time when his alcoholism became a serious problem. He describes how this was mishandled, what the sources of his resentment are, and how it might have been handled more therapeutically and justly:

> They handled the thing miserably, but thank heavens this has been rectified now. I was sick at the time and I didn't really grasp it. They didn't step in and see to it that I was correctly treated with a hope of recovery. At that time they gave me the great advice and made the great decision that I should go home and stay with my family and that they would get in touch with me. Then for months I heard from no one (in the Chancery). So I thought that if they don't care, I don't give a damn either. So I decided with the help of a friend in New York to get a job. But the hand of the Lord intervened there. This friend was an alcoholic too and he flew in to help me because he felt this was the time to help me. I was disspirited and negative at the time but I felt that here was a friend, and when he asked me, 'Do you mind if I talk to the authorities?' I said, 'Go ahead. I don't care what you tell them.' So he talked to them and he forced them to a certain extent to let me go in for treatment. I went reluctantly because I was tired of fighting alone and I was scared. And shortly the whole thing was clarified for me and I was helped and became well.

Here is a man who had a serious drinking problem for many years. This problem was tolerated, covered over or ignored by the authorities until it reached a crisis stage. Even when it was realized that the man was ill and disabled, the issue was avoided and hidden. He was sent home by his superiors. Finally, in desperation, when this priest went out himself to look for a new job he found a friend who recognized his illness and who was sufficiently energetic, perceptive, and humanitarian to step into the situation and to provide the appropriate treatment. Even this friend had to fight the authorities to secure prompt and proper treatment. From this man's experience it seems clear that superiors and other responsible people could be more sensitive to such problems and could establish appropriate policies and procedures for the treatment of alcoholism in priests. His alcoholism is one of the notable events in this priest's life. Six years ago the Bishop confronted him with his heavy drinking and it was a really traumatic event in his life. The priest had denied the drinking problem until it became so severe that he had blackouts and memory losses.

In a deep personal way this priest is incredibly alone and has been since early childhood. The most important person in his life was a man half a continent away, who came to him, but who responded to his alcoholism more than to the man himself. One of the major difficulties in this priest's life has been with authority figures. He has looked to them for support and they have not extended it. In this relationship with his parishioners he uses his role as a priest, rather than his own personality, to develop relationships. He rarely relates to anyone as a person on a genuinely human level. His personal relationships with women have been as limited as have his relations with men. He relates to women in groups and by preaching to them. He reports that he has never had a date in his life. He has little idea, derived from experience, of what it means to be in a responsible relationship with another person. He perceives the role of women as that of caring for men. Rarely, if ever, has he been able to express or to receive affection.

He perceives himself almost exclusively as a priest and not as a person. It is the role of the priesthood that provides his identity. This central role identity needs constant reinforcement from his parishioners. He derives his strength from being a good preacher, especially to alcoholics. This work reinforces his life-long posture of keeping himself distant from people. Because of this, his work becomes a defense against life rather than a creative expression of it.

This priest uses his faith and his religion as an excuse for his social role. His faith is vague and childlike. The Church provides the structure for his life. He actually employs his priesthood as a defense against accepting the responsibility of adult life.

This priest is, however, functioning adequately, if painfully, at the present time. The priesthood offers him the necessary controls to continue at this level of functioning. One can predict that if he becomes depressed he will return to drinking. If he is assigned to rewarding tasks within his capabilities, such as preaching retreats to alcoholics, he will very probably be able to maintain his present acceptable functioning. He needs much reassurance and support, and he seeks and receives them through constant activity in Church and AA meetings.

His thought processes are regressive and primitive. Some of his statements are totally unintelligible. He has a mixed neurosis involving compulsive behavior, gross denial, and intense intellectualization. Under stress this condition could regress into more severe pathology.

This priest's difficulties may well be related to his upbringing, to the family life which he keeps in a hazy and pleasant fantasy of recollection.

Although he looks fairly normal, and his bouts of alcoholism have seemed a puzzle to his superiors, he is a severely disturbed individual who has acted out his difficulties because he could never face and deal with them directly. He has lived a painful and difficult life and needs response to his own person in order to maintain his present level of adjustment.

Further Case Histories

We will now inspect some briefer reports on other subjects who have been rated as maldeveloped persons. The purpose of this is to allow the reader to develop an understanding of this population in breadth as well as in depth. As in all the other categories, the subjects of the maldeveloped classification do not belong to one age group or one occupational setting. They are linked together, however, by the serious disruption of their home environment.

A clear example is an associate pastor in his early thirties. His parents experienced constant tension in their marriage because of the father's petty criticism of the mother who could do nothing at all to please him. She accepted his fault-finding without much outward expression of her hurt feelings, although she occasionally shared them with this son who would one day be a priest. This built up their resentment of the father at the same time that it accentuated their feeling of powerlessness to deal with him. At one period in the marriage the father drank quite heavily. The marriage, however, endured even though the tension in the relationship of husband and wife has never been resolved.

This is probably related to this priest's sudden and unexplained move to enter the seminary over his father's strong objections. He made the decision impulsively as if he were trying to prove to himself that he could do something worthwhile on his own and as a reaction to the strong controlling influence of the father. Unfortunately, this priest had two assignments in a relatively short time after ordination, meeting in each one a pastor whose authoritarian attitudes presented to him again the image of a controlling father. These experiences embittered him strongly and rekindled the feelings of worthlessness and powerlessness which he experienced in his own family life. He still labors under the burden of this bitterness, avoiding other priests and authorities, and fully decided to keep to himself in order to avoid being dependent on others or having others dependent on him.

This man suffers from a severe obsessive-compulsive neurosis with accompanying strong feelings of anxiety, guilt, and personality inadequacy; these have reduced his efficiency and have left him depressed, fearful, and quite vulnerable to stress. He not only feels unable to cope with his inner sexual drives and dependency needs in any effective manner, but his fear and distrust of others has caused him to pull away from even the possibility of close emotional contacts. He has become progressively isolated and self-preoccupied but this avoidance technique has not really helped him. It has only increased his pain and frustration; now he turns his anger at God for having let him down. His rejection of God, however, has also become unbearable because of the guilt which he feels; he tries to atone for his rejection of God but once again he finds that he cannot live up to his expectations and falls once more into the vicious cycle of helplessness, despair, and guilt.

This priest is overreacting to his unresolved dependency which had its roots in his family situation. His father never permitted him to assume any independence or make any decisions for himself; this gave rise to an underlying resentment in him because he has always been made to feel obligated and guilty, striving hard to please his father but never receiving any emotional support or encouragement in return. His subsequent problems in life and in the priesthood have their roots in this unresolved relationship with his father. He has not, of course, found the independence and security which he had hoped to discover in the priesthood after his somewhat impulsive decision to enter the seminary. He has, in fact, had many severe problems which have involved him in this recurring cycle of frustration and guilt. His recent efforts to express his frustration in relationships with women have only deepened his guilt and made him feel less adequate to the challenge of forming close personal relationships. He is in extreme conflict because he wants sexual satisfaction while at the same time he knows he cannot love another person adequately. The inconsistency of this situation causes him great pain because he realizes that he is not living up to his own expectations nor those of the vocation which he has chosen. He also feels compulsively drawn to express his sexual needs. This constellation of difficulties has sharpened his sense of worthlessness and self-doubt. At the present time he is not sure where he stands, vacillating between over-control and self-indulgent behavior. His underlying rebellion against a cold, indifferent, yet controlling father figure seems to be re-enacted in his relations with unresponsive pastors as well as with God whom he simultaneously loves and rejects. Unless this man receives psychotherapy, there is every likelihood that he will not be able to sustain himself in this unremitting situation of conflict. He will either leave the priesthood or he will remain and become more isolated, lonely, and despairing and his work and relationships will suffer accordingly.

Yet, another example of the serious disturbance which can be traced back to early experience is the middle-aged pastor, born the last child in a medium-sized family. His father was, according to his description, a passive and dependent person while his mother was extremely obsessive and compulsive in her attitudes and behavior. This man grew up very isolated from his peers and spent a great deal of time with his mother. She started him in school a year ahead of time and this complicated his already difficult situation in relating to his age mates. Everyone was older than he and this merely accentuated the difficulties he was already experiencing. He was also inept at sports and had little opportunity to involve himself with the other boys. He compensated for this by throwing himself into his studies and doing quite well. This man can now recall that during these years his mother frequently talked to him about the idea of becoming a priest, emphasizing how attractive this would be and how pleased it would make her. He does not recall consciously making this decision to become a priest on the basis of her influence, but it is quite clear that the mother was the only individual to whom this young man was close and that she left little room for other vocational alternatives.

This priest related throughout the rest of his educational history much in the way he did in grammar school. He even used recreation periods to study from time to time, avoiding sports, and established no close friendships. After his ordination this priest switched from being a zealous student to being a zealous worker. He has overworked, taking on several jobs at a time, ever since the time of his ordination. He seldom takes any time off, even now in his position as a pastor.

This priest describes himself as a loner. Isolation seems to have been a chronic situation in his life ever since he left his mother. As the interviewer notes, "In talking with the man it is evident that there is a significant amount of rage that is kept carefully under control by avoiding interpersonal relationships and by staying close to a very rigid code of behavior. This priest identifies highly with the priesthood and feels that the stereotyped behavior of the priest enables him to control many impulses that would be difficult if he had to react to his impulses spontaneously."

This priest's unresolved dependency has been transferred from the mother to the Bishop; this has resulted in many confused feelings about himself as a priest and about his relationship with the hierarchy. This priest is so dependent and in so much need of acceptance by his bishop that he cannot express any of the deep anger which he feels within himself; he cannot even express constructive criticisms which he might like to offer. The very possibility of expressing these things makes the potential loss of his superior's affection too much of a reality.

This priest has had a life-long problem which he has been able to handle through mechanisms of withdrawal and through obsessive defenses. He is able to administer a parish but he never has and never will involve himself in any personal way with his parishioners. These are jobs which he assigns to assistants while he remains aloof and distant. As long as he is able to maintain this role he should be able to maintain his adjustment. There are certain difficulties connected with this adjustment which must be pointed out.

Presently there are some signs that this individual's anger is getting more difficult to control and that he is unsure as to how to handle this. He never had allowed this anger to get out of control before or even to find the slightest kind of expression. As it builds up inside of him now, it causes him to feel quite fearful about what might happen if any of it escapes. Balancing this against the reality of life around him causes him to have experiences which are quite paranoid in flavor. He suspects, for example, that the bishop is disinterested in him and that many of his parishioners actively dislike him. He can give no evidence for any of this and it seems to derive from his own inner psychological difficulties. He uses the defenses of rationalization and projection to hold himself together. At the present time he does not have the capacity to look deeply into himself with any insight. This is complicated by the fact that he is beginning to wonder about his relationship with his mother and he is having difficulty controlling the emotion which threatens to break through in this area.

This man is caught in a very difficult position. He really cannot function in any other situation than the one in which he finds himself. He needs emotional support but he cannot ask for it and, psychologically speaking, cannot even accept it unless it is given in a very indirect way. If he can continue in a parish where he gets some distinct recognition and where he can be gratified by administrative rather than personal tasks, he will continue to adjust successfully. It is quite possible that this priest, unless he develops greater insight into himself and a greater capacity to control the feelings which now threaten to break through, may turn to alcohol as a means of maintaining his adjustment. The paranoid features of his personality will also become more obvious as he grows older but he is not now motivated for psychotherapy nor is he presently a good candidate for psychotherapy. The best thing that can be done for him at present is to strengthen his defenses and to alert people who work with him to an understanding of the rather tenuous nature of his adjustment so that they do not press him beyond his capacity to respond.

More dramatically disturbed is the man in his late thirties who has served both as a pastor and as a teacher. He is filled with anxiety, feelings of depression, and the pain of many personal conflicts. He desperately expresses his desire for help but feels that he has no close friends to whom he can turn.

This is related to an extremely deprived and traumatic childhood in which he never knew his father and only learned in his teens that he was illegitimate. He tries to protect his rather fragile personality by isolating himself from others and from the pressures of life. This has failed frequently, leading to depressive periods which have become more intense recently. He has considered suicide and psychiatric assistance has been urged upon him. When he feels this deep insecurity, he prefers the idea of running away from his problems. He feels markedly alone, unloved and unlovable.

This person is confused in his own personal identity and this seems related to his upbringing by a mother and grandmother who, according to his account, seem to have been emotionally disturbed themselves. He is, as a result, very ambivalent in his attitude toward his mother and toward women in general. He has little energy to involve himself in the work of the priesthood. He cannot separate his personal problems from his life in the Church. Because of his family history he also has continuing difficulties with male authority figures.

This priest, who was very honest and open in the interview, is seriously disturbed, marginally adjusted, and seems to be getting worse instead of better. He needs immediate professional treatment.

Yet another type is exemplified by the monk who is in his early forties. According to his own account, he had no strong feelings of identification at home where his mother seems to have been a rather neurotic and dominating figure, given much to psychosomatic illness. He got little attention during his formative years because of the serious illnesses of some of his brothers and sisters. Much of his own insecurity and sensitivity were, therefore, repressed at this time and have remained so throughout his life. He recalls an atmosphere of brooding and anxiety, especially generated by the mother. This is all the more poignant as he recalls that a façade of happiness and composure was presented to the community in which the family had a rather prominent position.

Serious defects in this individual's adjustment did not, however, appear until late adolescence. He found himself filled with feelings of estrangement in college, insecure in his capacity to compete with others and totally unable to choose a vocational objective. He said that he was overwhelmed with a desire to work for the welfare of some oppressed groups in society but, having made an abortive effort to do this, he suddenly left school and applied to the monastery.

This person is seriously disturbed and has been so for many years. He is quite poorly related to the world around him, lives in a universe generated by his own distorted thinking, and experiences genuine feelings of grandiosity. This serious disturbance is under good control because of the monastic life and its schedule and the expectations this makes on his behavior. This control is not by any means firm, however, and, although his problems may not be suspected by many, he is truly living in a world of his own which could break down at any moment. At the present time his adjustment is clearly maintained by the conditions of the life which he has chosen.

A final example of a maldeveloped person is the severely disturbed neurotic man in his early forties who was quite anxious during the whole interview experience. He spoke in a loud, excitable voice and frequently became lost in his own thoughts so that he would drift away from the question at hand until he would suddenly come to and say that he had forgotten the question which had been asked. He is, in the words of the interviewer, "an obsessive-compulsive person who is racked with guilt and torment over his inability to control his hostile and erotic impulses. He is a product of a disturbed and unstable family background in which his parents were in open conflict with each other. He was subjected to a rather strict, demanding and critical maternal figure who not only failed to meet his affectional and dependency needs but tended to frustrate his need for independence and identity. In spite of her rejection, he has emotional and erotic ties to her and this makes denial of his need even more hurtful to the extent that he feels rage and resentment towards her. Because of his helplessness he had to repress his rage and try to conform to her rigid expectations and standards for fear of being punished. . . . By the time he entered adolescence he was still emotionally constrained and rigid but he found it difficult making and keeping friends except a few who were, as he was, docile, inhibited and withdrawn. He attempted to find a way out of his unhappy predicament by entering the seminary during his teen-age years but even in this choice he simply substituted one authoritarian, rigid and repressive situation for another."

This man has had persistent problems since the early days of his life, all of which have been related to this basic situation of being dominated so extensively by his mother. He has had many serious problems and has suffered a great deal emotionally as a result of these. He has functioned reasonably well as a priest mostly because his work enabled him to be on his own. He has experienced a recurrence of his infantile conflicts regularly; his anger is now displaced on the Canon Law of the Church which he obsessively finds quite restrictive and too rigid. He seems, in the words of the interviewer, "to be living his original conflict over unloving and oppressive authorities who do not understand or care about his need for a warm and understanding authority figure to fulfill his dependency needs. He is growing more fearful and uncertain of his future because of the changes occurring in the Church." This man is caught in a terrible bind, fearful of any variations in the Church but unable to react except by withdrawing more and more within himself. He has had psychotherapy but it is clear that his situation is worsening and that he may be headed for a more serious breakdown, especially as he heads into later middle age.

It is clear that the maldeveloped have extraordinarily painful times in adjusting to the problems which they have as a result of their upbringing. In some cases, the priesthood offers some source of personal identity and control and the individual manages to make some kind of respectable adjustment within it. The stress is always very great, however, and, in many cases, it is not clear whether the individual gives or gets more in his work as a priest.

CHAPTER V

THE UNDERDEVELOPED

Psychology is hard-pressed to define the normal and the abnormal in a completely satisfactory way. It has traditionally been hesitant to draw a sharp line across human behavior, staking out one side as completely healthy and the other as completely unhealthy. The patterns merge, blend into one another, with positive and negative traits shading off as these qualities become at times almost indistinguishable from each other. All psychological description is, then, an approximation. This is so because man is different from mountains and landscapes whose physical features vary little with the passing years. Man is dynamic, made to grow, constantly shifting. It is, therefore, difficult to plot his true dimensions at any single point in time or space.

The concept of growth allows us to take into account the problem occasioned by our imprecise notions of what is normal and abnormal as well as the dynamic quality of human experience. Growth is a concept that allows us to view man in accord with the developmental tasks of the various stages of his life and to see with what effectiveness he has achieved the kind of growth appropriate for him at any given time. We can take a look at an individual and see whether, in fact, he is growing or not. We can attempt to understand his growth and the factors which affect it either positively or negatively. Interrupted or arrested growth can be investigated to determine the reasons why an individual has not gone beyond a certain point in unfolding his own true personality. The concept of growth allows us, in other words, to stay much closer to the way human beings operate and frees us from having to fit them exactly into rigidly defined categories. Growth allows us to understand, to see forward movement, to appreciate the sideways direction of human beings as they try to adjust to some snag in their development, and to tease out the frustrations that may come at one time or another, bringing growth to a complete halt. This dynamic vision of human development is indispensable for understanding the American priesthood.

The largest segment of the priests under study have not achieved the kind of growth which current psychological theory would expect from a group of men of their chronological age and vocational responsibility. Without speculating in detail, except to relate growth difficulties to earlier life experiences, we may describe a large proportion of American priests as underdeveloped. This classification is quite broad and, while the term has negative connotations, it should not be taken totally in that sense. The classification of underdeveloped covers a wide range of personal adjustments and suggests a failure of growth rather than the presence of illness. It also suggests the presence of capacities which have not been realized rather than the presence of psychological obstacles which can never be overcome.

It should also be noted that the classification underdeveloped can be applied equally well to many American men. In a sense, one might say that it is normal to be underdeveloped in our culture. That does not mean that it is healthy or that it is the optimal mode of adjustment. Rather, it points to something about the relative character of the state we describe as normal. When we look at the men functioning in society in responsible positions, men who may not display underdevelopment on first inspection, we are confronted with the possibility that there is more psychological evidence of unrealized potential than there is of complete personality development in the people we call normal in our culture at this time in history. This matter will be discussed again further on in this report. It suffices now to present this as a background notion, especially in the light of the fact that no profession has allowed itself to be inspected to the same depth that the American priests have been through the psychological interviews of the present study. We do not have directly comparable data. The data that we do have on certain other professions suggest a widespread difficulty of psychological underdevelopment across many professions. This is not to excuse this state nor to idealize it; it is to observe it as a background against which any group of professional men must be understood at this time. There is no reason to believe that the population of priests is radically different from the male population from which they have come. The study offers no conclusive proof that they are worse than the population from which they have come. However, neither does it explain away the fact that the carefully selected men, who have a long period of training through which they are observed very carefully, are psychologically underdeveloped in the very areas which are crucial to their effective functioning as clergymen.

It is important to keep in mind the fact that we do not understand psychological health, or normalcy, except as a relative concept, an ideal, the features of which we can describe, but the realization of which is a constant task of life. The mature person pursues his growth through facing and dealing constructively with the stream of new experiences which await him in every season of life. There are tasks appropriate to the later years of life, after the main work of the individual is accomplished, which cannot be anticipated before this and which presumably can only be prepared for by the successful achievement of all the earlier stages of growth. The person who has moved maturely up to this last phase of life will undoubtedly pass through these last challenges successfully. His life is, after all, a dynamic whole and the roots of his later adjustment are deep in his childhood experiences. The underdeveloped person does not handle successfully the challenges of his current adult state of life because he has not passed successfully through all the previous stages. There are tangled and unresolved issues, the tendrils of which reach back to childhood; they manifest themselves through the distinct character and tone of the psychological life stage which he has not completed. In other words, the behavior and attitudes of the adult reveal clearly to us his true profile of personal development, throwing into relief for us the phase of growth which is incomplete. This turns us away from conceptualizing the underdeveloped priest as a sick person and permits us to view him, in accord with our developmental model, in terms of the uncompleted work of an earlier stage of life. The underdeveloped priests of the United States can be understood if we realize that they have not accomplished the tasks which are appropriate to the developmental period known as adolescence.

Before we can describe the underdeveloped priests, we must survey the tasks of adolescence itself. We are not speaking of the physical changes which ordinarily take place in adolescence. We speak rather of the psychological tasks of adolescence. Some of these are, of course, related to the physical changes which people ordinarily identify as the most visible aspects of adolescent growth. The physical changes parallel the profound personality changes which accompany the transition from childhood to adulthood. The individual looks like a child at the beginning of adolescence and like a man at the end. This is a very complex period of growth, and it is not surprising to find that many factors can interfere with its smooth and free-flowing development. The failure of psychological growth at adolescence can cause the person to use certain adaptive mechanisms which mask but do not really change the fact that he is not a fully developed adult. The task of adolescence has been summarized by Lidz (1968) in the following way:

> Achieving a successful integration depends upon a reasonably successful passage through all prior developmental stages, but also upon the solution of a number of tasks specific to adolescence which leads to a reintegration and reorganization of the personality structure to permit the individual to function as a reasonably self-sufficient adult. One of Erikson's major contributions to psychoanalytic developmental psychology was his emphasis upon the crucial importance of late adolescence. Now, the young person must gain an ego-identity, an identity in his own right and not simply as someone's son or daughter, an identity in the sense of a unique consistency of behavior that permits others to have expectations of how he will behave and react. He will have, in a sense, answered the question 'Who am I?' and therefore others will know who he is. The achievement of ego-identity usually requires the concurrent attainment of the capacity moved toward interdependence with the person of the opposite sex: an intimacy that properly encompasses far more than the capacity to have sexual relations, or even to enjoy orgastic pleasure in the act. It concerns an ability to dare to form a significant relationship without fear of loss of the self [299–300].

In other words, the individual puts himself together during the adolescent years so that he emerges with a reliable and consistent sense of his own personality and his own role as an agent of relationship to himself and to others. The individual must learn to be himself and, just as important to any definition of health, to be able to share his unique self with another person. He must learn the tasks of devotion and fidelity during his adolescent years, not as bywords but as the qualities of personality which flow naturally from a well-developed sense of identity. The individual is preparing himself for the early adult tasks of deep friendship and love, the double seal on the life of the person who is capable of true intimacy. The individual who has not completely settled the questions of adolescence is severely handicapped in the face of further living. Erikson has raised the question of whether an individual can achieve any meaning at all in life until these problems are successfully resolved. A good deal of the behavior which we see in presumably adult people who have not in fact completed their adolescence tells us that their struggle for identity is still going on, that their longing for intimacy is still unfulfilled, that they are, even though they be captains of industry or cabinet members, basically underdeveloped persons. The rest of their lives, in a sense, becomes an effort at solving problems that were not solved at the correct time. Solution at a later date is, of course, very difficult but it is not impossible. What is important to note here is the fact that an underdeveloped person's life will radiate from that very point in the developmental scale at which growth stops.

There are other ways of conceptualizing the tasks of adolescence. It is useful to cite them here because, although the language may be different, there is a convergence of understanding which supports the general picture which has thus far been developed. Peter Blos (1962) in his book *On Adolescence* discusses the ego in adolescence, outlining the challenges to the person as he develops an authentic sense of his individuality. For example, he notes that during adolescence, "Ego interests and functions become stratified into a definite hierarchy. Selective ego components are elevated to a dominant position; others are subordinated to them. This irreversible fixity in the ego's relations to the outer world, to the id and the superego, based on a hierarchical order of ego interest and attitudes, is referred to as character. Character does not acquire its final countenance until the close of adolescence (p. 175)." He relates the successful ordering of the ego interests to a vocational commitment that is a true choice. He continues, "The ultimate aim of adolescence as a whole, namely, to endow the individual with a stable arrangement of ego interests and with sexual differentiation and polarization is the core of the sense of identity. Both these achievements have to be exercised and refined in interaction with the outer world (p. 177)." He emphasizes the same point later on:

> The ego at adolescence has the task of counteracting the disruptive influence of infantile trauma by pathological solutions; this is achieved by the employment of stabilizing mechanisms, and finally by processes of differentiation, stratification, and integration which are the psychological hallmarks of a cohesive personality (p. 190).

Or in discussing the emerging self, Blos goes on to say:

> It needs to be emphasized that the self has a long individual history and does not emerge as a psychic formation at adolescence. What is new at the entrance into adulthood is the quality of the self, its relative stability and the effect it exerts on both reality testing and realistic self-evaluation as the basis for thinking and action. Subjectively, the young adult feels he is a different person after the adolescent turbulence is over. He feels 'himself,' he senses a unity

of inner and outer experiences instead of the fragmented excesses of his adolescence. This all amounts to a subjective self-experience which Erikson has described as 'ego-identity' [pp. 191–192].

To sum up, the person, after adolsecent growth has taken place, possesses an understanding of himself which he now brings into all his later life activities. Difficult as it is at times, adolescence prepares the individual for genuine adult living. A true adult can share himself with other people. The developed young adult knows who he is and senses the direction in life that is right for him. He is secure in his sexual identity and has a clear perception and a sensible respect for his intellectual and physical capacities. He is ready, in other words, for life as a grown-up person. He has the psychological equipment, as it were, to make himself present in life in accord with the truth about his personality, to reveal himself in a trusting and human way and to accept the self-revelation of others with a sense of responsibility to them.

It is clear that many men fall short of this description of early adult development. These are the people we designate as underdeveloped. Their later life will always reflect the fact that their adolescence was never truly closed. The underdeveloped priests have assumed adult responsibilities. They have done this with, to one degree or another, an incomplete idea of themselves, and their abilities, as well as an unfulfilled capacity for close and trusting relationships with other persons. These priests demonstrate, through their modes of adjustment, their efforts to live as adults even though they have not reached psychological adulthood. These modes reveal their problems in the terminology used by the researchers who have presented us with a clinical picture of adolescent growth. The underdeveloped priests have difficulty in relating to themselves in a stable and reliable manner; they lack a true sense of gravity about themselves as human persons. Blocked in dealing with their own identity, they frequently assume the identity conferred upon them by others or through a role which they are asked to live, such as that of being a clergyman. This does not represent an identity that flows from within them as much as one given to them from the outside. They have, in many cases, never made the kind of vocational decision which reflects the reordering and stabilization of the ego that takes place during the adolescent years. For many of these individuals, no conscious vocational choice based on their own interest and abilities ever took place. In fact, for a great many of the underdeveloped the choice of going to the seminary was made by other people and at a very early age. The prospect of becoming a priest was one that was rewarded with respect and affection in the family and the neighborhood. It is difficult to establish any one point of vocational choice based on self-perception. Indeed, their lives have been notably shaped by the expectations of others rather than the discovery of themselves.

Parallel to this unsureness about self-identity is the almost non-existent experience of intimacy during their adult years. It is well to remember that intimacy does not here refer only to sexual intimacy. We speak here rather of the ability to put one's own personality in an open and vulnerable relationship with another human being, to get close to another person in the richest and best sense of that phrase. Intimacy can mean something as simple as developing a true friendship in the adult years of life. Among the underdeveloped, however, the experience of true friendship is rare if not non-existent. They clearly reflect their lack of growth through adolescence in the way they form relationships with other persons. Reflected in their own statements, there is a generalized lack of closeness with anybody in their lives. The people whom they describe as friends are frequently comrades, people with whom they spend time, but hardly individuals who could be considered as within the range of an intimate relationship. They exhibit an uneasiness about closeness which was reinforced by their training for the priesthood. Seminaries formerly de-emphasized human relationships and so contributed to the frustration of their students' adolescent development.

An example of the underdeveloped is the parish priest and teacher who relates through a shallow affability in an effort to please others. He is very undeveloped and, through a series of affairs with women, seems to be seeking the comfort and reassurance he never knew from his stepmother. He feels that sexual experience with women is developmental for him, but, in actuality, he uses women to authenticate his masculinity while he holds them off through the defense of his priesthood as a bar to any real commitment to them. He has very little insight into his behavior and thinks that he is a good fellow.

Along with a lack of closeness with other persons, which many of the priests seem to envision as a privilege not allowed them or a danger to be avoided, they exhibit a lack of understanding of their own emotional life. They handle their feelings through repressive and intellectualized defenses. Indeed, one is struck by the human isolation of these men, the almost unconnected manner in which they lead their lives, even though they find themselves in the midst of people all the time. There is a distance, reinforced by cultural and personal factors, which they find difficult to bridge and which they generally avoid through the use of one or the other of the previously mentioned defenses.

These facts about the underdeveloped priests do not mean that they are failures; neither do they suggest that they are totally inadequate. The research reveals unfulfilled possibilities rather than pathology, lives lived through adjustment rather than through spontaneous experience, lives dominated by the subject's failure to pass through the developmental stage of adolescence completely. The underdeveloped priests have difficulties which are typical of the adolescent or pre-adolescent stage; they reveal patterns of defenses which cover over these lacks in growth but which do not make up for them.

It is important to note the strengths of these men even as we describe their growth problems. They are quite intelligent and most of them will remain in the priesthood. They are capable of achievement, although this frequently flows from their efforts to realize an identity from outside themselves because they lack one that comes from inside. These priests function in an adequate manner if we measure only in terms of the service functions which they are called upon to perform. In general, these men are not serious behavioral problems. They are not, for the most part, noticeably neurotic (this might be different if they moved from their semi-protective environments). They do not as a class misbehave sexually; they do not drink too much; and they do not cause many problems for their superiors or their inferiors. They are much better understood if we think of them as not fully alive, as persons who are psychologically impoverished, as men who could be happier and more vital persons if they had resolved their adolescent problems.

It is possible to speak of these men in terms which were employed by Karen Horney (1950) in her book *Neurosis and Human Growth*. She speaks of individuals who have not realized their true selves in life but who have put their energies into trying to develop an idealized self. In other words, she speaks of a person who, because he has never truly experienced or expressed his own identity, cannot bring forth the riches of his own personality and so adjusts by the strenuous method of trying to be that which he is not, an ideal self outside and separate from the psychological truth of his own personality. Horney suggests that the modes of inadequate adjustment which she describes are seldom found in the pure state. She describes the neurotic process of growth and says that, in real life, this is most often seen in mixed types so that "it would be more nearly correct to speak of directions of development than of types." By extension, it is better to speak of directions of underdevelopment rather than of pure types of underdevelopment. The underdeveloped priest is not stalled in the sense that he does nothing. He chooses, somewhat in the manner in which Horney speaks of it, a way of presenting himself in life that is not in accord with what he is truly like.

The underdeveloped bolsters himself with adjustive devices in the face of life and its difficulties; he attempts to present himself as adequate, and to try to forge some kind of integrity in his life experience. This is a very difficult and trying process for him, even when he is not able to admit it consciously. An underdeveloped person who is protected from the challenges of growth or excused from accepting them simply does not grow. It takes an extraordinary person to develop the insights and the convictions required to overcome an unstimulating environment. An ordinary man finds this almost impossible and, if he is already underdeveloped psychologically, he characteristically settles for the amount of growth which he has achieved. This is the style we see in the underdeveloped priests of the United States. The priesthood offers them an environment of protection in which they are rewarded in many ways, through respect and security for example, even when their personal efforts do not always merit favorable responses. As long as his basic needs are cared for and his lack of development does not urge him to achieve anything more in life, the underdeveloped priest will change very little unless he is confronted with a major dilemma of choice from which he cannot really escape. An example will make this clearer. A child does not learn to speak intelligibly as long as his parents or older brothers and sisters translate his language-like noises for him. He does not learn because he does not have to; he is getting along fine just the way he is, receiving the responses he needs without additional effort on his part. He will not learn unless the older children in the family or the parents stop responding to his baby talk. So for the underdeveloped person; he will not begin to grow unless the significant figures around him stop reinforcing his immature behavior through accepting it without challenge. The underdeveloped priest clings to the techniques of adjustment which substitute for full growth as long as he need not confront what he is really doing.

To sum up: an underdeveloped person who does not experience the demands of growth in his environment will not grow. He continues to function through some major adjustive pattern which takes the place of real growth.

An example of the underdeveloped priest who will not change much is the priest in his late thirties who moves through life without much closeness or conviction about what he does. As described by the interviewer, "He likes people and is liked by them, but his relationships do not run deep. He is a congenial person, uncomfortable with strong emotion and deep commitment. His career sustains him. In it he finds most of his emotional satisfaction. He does not evince a strong or deep faith. His teaching theology is not a sign of his religious convictions but it is a part of his ecclesiastical career. . . . He does not have the courage to take a deeper look at himself, his Church, and the society in which he lives. . . . A great deal of his potential will remain just that — potential — unless other forces become operative to transform him."

These adjustive patterns can look good until they are closely inspected. It is worthwhile to examine a few of them because they are so characteristic of the ways in which underdeveloped priests present themselves in life. These styles of adjustment provide the mechanism through which he maintains himself in an underdeveloped state without perceiving the inconsistency of his position or the true dimensions of his lack of growth.

An individual may use the mechanism of compensation in order to disguise his lack of growth or his personality weaknesses. So a person who finds it difficult to deal closely with people may absorb himself in administrative tasks and even develop a certain amount of skill at these. There is nothing wrong with being good at administration; it is not, however, desirable when it takes the place of some other aspect of neglected personal growth. Through compensation a person may also seek gratification in certain areas of life when he is frustrated in accomplishing as much as he would like in some other area. It is not uncommon to see underdeveloped priests allowing themselves certain freedoms of behavior and experience in order to make up for a lack of interpersonal effectiveness. Much of the underdeveloped priest's difficulties with psycho-sexual identity are expressed clearly through the compensatory mechanisms which he employs in order to balance these problems off. These may include excessive vacations, sports activities such as golfing, expensive hobbies, or expensive tastes in housing and automobiles. It is frequently the case that the individual who makes up in one area of his life what he lacks in another is quite unconscious of the process.

The lack of development possible in men is also well illustrated by the pastor who in late middle age was recently transferred from a large and prestigious parish to a less desirable one. His reaction is one of anger and anxiety and he plans to deal with the new situation through compensating himself for the loss by "winding down" into a semi-retired and apathetic pace of life. He has emphasized good times all his life: eating, talking, drinking, singing, hunting and fishing. His passive-aggressive personality is manifest in his ulcers and in his alcoholic problem. He is totally against change in the Church and blames Communism for the present erosion of things. His own faith is superficial, a perfect match for his very self-centered view of life. He is looking forward to moving to another country to spend his time fishing after he retires.

A man may adjust to a lack of his own development through fantasy. In his own imagination he is the conqueror of new worlds, the person who is at last recognized for his true worth, a man who stands up to the bishop, or who fights for the downtrodden in openly successful fashion. These fantasies need not be grandiose to fulfill the function of substituting for real growth. The underdeveloped priest makes of himself in these kinds of visions what he truly does not make of himself in everyday life. This is a fragile mechanism with which to adjust to life. It is the style, insubstantial at best, of the man with big plans and little follow-through.

An example of a man who hardly works in the priesthood at all is the middle-aged pastor who, as he describes it, "putters around," spending his time with superficial activities and never getting down to any serious work, although he indulges in wishful thinking about it. However, he enjoys the respect he gets as a priest although he dreads much of the work connected with it. His only enthusiasm is for his pets; he spends much time in incidental hobbies; his only worry is whether he will have financial security in retirement.

An underdeveloped person may adjust to life through identification with some person or institution from which he can draw strength and a sense of personal worth. In other words, the underdeveloped priest may adjust to life through the role of the priesthood rather than through his own personality. This occurs in the lives of men who have never learned to identify themselves properly and who must depend heavily, therefore, on the external supports of the role characteristics of the priesthood. This kind of adjustment is badly shaken when changes are introduced into the role or institution with which the identification is made. It is clear that many underdeveloped priests are uneasy about actual and possible changes in institutional policies or regulations, such as celibacy, because so much of their identity comes from the role of the priesthood. Change the role and you disrupt the adjustment in a notable way. Celibacy, a value little realized in their lives, is something that underdeveloped men wish to preserve because it is an extrinsic facet of their identification, something that makes them special in the eyes of the world, something, in other words, that is not a sacrifice but a support for their own persons.

Some persons are so underdeveloped that they scarcely seem to exist; they hardly seem to make an impression on the world around them. They are like invisible men, locked in by their own limited growth to a withdrawn and bland kind of existence. Such is the young member of a religious community whose work consists largely of the impersonal tasks of merchandising Church goods. He has hardly any relationships with others, and very little positive force in his own personality. He likes celibacy because it fits his needs very well, giving dignity to the good-natured listlessness of his life. His plans to be effective in the priesthood are largely fantasy, and he will not move far away from his present isolating and undemanding work.

An individual who is underdeveloped may adjust through introjection in the process of taking on the external values and standards of the environment in which he finds himself without really making them a part of his own personality. This is the kind of mechanism that is employed by many of the men whose faith is largely defined in extrinsic terms. They have accepted and made their own values of the Church for which they are spokesmen but they have never questioned or thought through the issues connected with these things.

A middle-aged pastor typifies the entrenched and underdeveloped priest who has reduced the world and its wisdom to the dimensions of his own personality. He lives by cliché, not by faith, and his notion of ministry is very shallow. He is not a strong person and his only real enthusiasm is for watching sports on television. He is not really close to anyone and lives on the surface of life, worried now only about what will happen to him after he retires. He has, in fact, never developed much as a person, but he believes that he has all the answers to the world's problems.

An individual may adjust to life through projection, that mechanism through which the individual blames those around him for his own problems and is, therefore, free from having to deal with them inside himself. This is the kind of adjustment in the underdeveloped priest who blames the authorities of the Church for his own difficulties and who expects them to solve his difficulties for him. The bishop is frequently the object of the projective adjustment of this person who goes through life feeling that he has always had bad breaks, bad superiors, and very little help to make much of himself.

A person may adjust to a lack of development through reaction formation, a psychological mechanism by which he prevents disturbing desires from being expressed by expressing the opposite attitudes or feelings in exaggerated form. The person who is constantly condemning sexual difficulties may be doing such in order to excuse himself from having to examine his own inner life.

Far more characteristic of the underdeveloped priests is the use of mechanisms of emotional isolation, repression, and regression. Through emotional insulation the individual protects himself from being hurt by withdrawing into a passive stance toward life. He gives us initiative and waits for things to come to him, allowing himself very little freedom of movement on his own. There is a neutralization of the emotional life consequent upon this mechanism of adjustment and a concomitant dulling of the personality of the individual who uses it. Many underdeveloped priests employ this method of adjustment. It is not that they are unfeeling persons; it is that they do not wish to have their feelings hurt by life and that they retreat from any situation which may have this potential. These priests find ready-made justifications for this retreat in some of the ascetic literature which warns heavily against any closeness with other persons. Although responsible intimacy is universally recognized as a sign of maturity, many priests have been instructed to avoid dealing with intimacy completely. This interpretation of the ideal of personal relationships for priests rationalizes perfectly the use of this adjustive defense, reducing the person's capacity to overcome it. The priest who withdraws into a passive stance in life is certainly not rebellious but he is not very constructive either. He settles for a life in which the major decisions are made for him by other people and seems to ask for very little from life. He does not get very much beyond the feeling that he has kept his own emotions safe from damage. The person who adjusts in this fashion may feel that it is necessary for him to do this if he is to achieve salvation.

Closely allied is the mechanism of isolation through which the individual manipulates his life, removing the feelings from the situations or activities to which they should logically be attached. He also may divide his life into a very compact mentalized affair through which he can separate incompatible attitudes without resolving their conflict in any mature fashion. This is a strong and effective defense which defuses the individual's life and thus saves him from having to deal straightforwardly with his own emotional reactions.

An example of a man who has great ability and who, in effect, has been isolated by it, is the middle-aged provincial superior who has, in one way or another, been in authority almost since ordination. He is a very intelligent man who has never related in a truly personal way with others; he never really has had to. He has experienced real anxiety in recent years because of the challenging of authority by younger clergy. He cannot understand it and, because of the rigid controls that he has exercised on himself for a lifetime, he never will. He has been effective in many ways but he is still basically quite underdeveloped.

Another defense which is sometimes employed by the underdeveloped personality is that of regression, through which the individual actually reverts to an earlier developmental level and employs the emotional responses appropriate to that time in his life in order to adjust to the stage at which he actually finds himself. This is frequently the style of adjustment employed by priests who have never satisfactorily resolved their own family relationships. They attempt to recreate within the priesthood, their parish, or their religious order the same kinds of relationships which they had in their homes. So, for example, an individual who was extremely dependent on an autocratic father, may recreate this mode of relationship with all the superiors he may have in his life. He does not really relate to them as an adult but as a little boy responding to his own father. So, too, the individual who regresses may settle for the kind of secure homelike atmosphere where all he needs to be is a good boy in order to be rewarded and to experience enough satisfaction to carry on. He is satisfied with the same kinds of rewards that he knew as a child and is very frightened at the prospect of giving up this pattern which is so gratifying for him. So, too, he may react with the hurt attitudes that are found in young children when they do not receive enough attention, making a scene of sorts to get a response from the superiors or the bishop. This is a very defective mode of relationship because it is not only a rejection of growth but a movement in the opposite direction.

A clear example of a priest whose lack of development was masked by his assignments is the early middle-aged pastor who became quite ill after being shifted to a small parish from a major job in his diocese. The fact that his personal development was seriously lacking was obscured by his intellectual strengths and his generally conforming attitudes toward Church authorities whom he felt he had served very well for many years. Only when his basic inability to adjust to the changes in the Church brought him into conflict with younger priests did it become clear that he was underdeveloped. In middle age he had to face a very painful situation: an invitation to resign that seemed to invalidate his previous years of service. He seemed abandoned by the very authorities he sought, like a good boy, to please for so many years. His depression and physical illness since this time have made him restless and unhappy. His lack of development makes it difficult for him to cope with life at a time when he should presumably be at the height of his powers to contribute.

A further observation might be made about these ordinary priests who, because of their lack of development, turn to an adjustive mechanism as their main mode of dealing with life. They are ordinary men, but they are exempt from many of the things which ordinary men face and deal with in the course of their lives. For example, the underdeveloped priests move in a world in which they need not necessarily be responsible for the life and nourishment of other persons, as they would be if they were heads of families; they need not take on a personal obligation for long-term indebtedness; they frequently have neither the benefits nor the possible liabilities that are normally associated with the work of other professions. These are, however, major personal experiences, the positive effect of which on the development of the ordinary man cannot be underestimated. If a man never has to be individually responsible for the welfare of another person, if he never has to make a mortgage payment from his own funds, if he never experiences the praise nor the blame that is common in the professional world for the work that he does, then he misses potentially developmental experiences which are unavoidable for most other people. He is freed of these things, in theory at least, in order to devote himself more fully to his other work. This shearing away of responsibility may, in fact, have the opposite effect from the one that is intended. It may free individuals from certain obligations but it also prevents them from undergoing the experiences by which they might develop their own persons more fully. This restricted range of human experience, far from freeing these priests for greater growth, contributes toward keeping them in the underdeveloped category.

PART TWO

CASE HISTORIES

We will now examine some case histories of priests who are considered underdeveloped. This lack of maturity is frequently masked by situational and occupational conditions. Most of these men live, in some measure at least, by psychological defenses of which they themselves are not fully aware.

This diocesan priest is in early middle age. He holds an important administrative position in a moderate-sized diocese. He has also been very active in a national organization. This priest has had relatively little direct, sustained parish work.

He presented himself in the interview in a warm, friendly and quite animated way. It was immediately obvious that he had given considerable thought not only to the interview, but also to himself as a man and as a priest as well as to the changing society and Church in which he found himself. He was an extremely thoughtful, articulate, and introspective person. It was clear that he was experiencing great stress in his life as a person and as a priest but that he would probably remain in the priesthood. He comes through as a very dedicated and productive man, and his general psychological adjustment was thought to be essentially normal, although emotionally and socially he was "underdeveloped."

This priest describes his family life in very positive terms as warm and accepting, although disrupted and replete with change and turmoil. Because of illness in his family and because of reduced economic circumstances he had to live for periods of time with relatives.

> So I was really kind of growing up in two families, in both my mother's and my aunt's house with really the intention of going to the seminary, and that, as far as the Irish Catholic family is concerned, was a sufficient reason to automatically consider you a kind of free floater. It was not wrong to be living with your aunt and uncle until your parents had re-established things economically. 'He is going to the seminary anyway you know.' The old lady was sure none of us will have him anyway. 'He belongs to God.' I've often thought of what effect this had on my own life — good or bad — maybe my unusual childhood is related to the problems I have in maturity or to other problems. . . . My childhood was a warm one but offbeat.

When this priest was asked what youthful experiences he viewed influential in shaping his present life, he replied:

> Oh, yes, let's say the rigidity of the home — the need to adhere to the good old rock-ribbed principles of how you treat people . . . the lack of deep personal warmth toward one's children. . . . You know there is a particular Irish type who believed in strength and good discipline, but very little warm human affection in a demonstrative way. . . . And I don't know if I was adequately prepared for life growing up in this fashion. . . . It has been a problem for me in my attempts to take what is a very warm and physical nature and to mature successfully. I think that I would have matured at a much earlier age in my life were I able to integrate this type of desire for warm human relationship. My emotions have always

been controlled, like a volcano type of thing. . . . I knew there was love in my home but it was difficult to express it to other persons in a mature, well controlled fashion. . . . The horror of even discussing anything sexual plus the typical seminary training at that time, I think, did interfere with handling problems of my manhood. At least it did to the extent that it kicked back into a much later age. I was having problems and trying to resolve problems, let's say at the age of 26 or 27, that I should have been handling at 17 and 18.

Both he and his father had a problem with excessive drinking. He sensed his interest in becoming a priest in early childhood; this remained constant in his life, a central source of personal integration, and also set him apart from and above the other members of his family. An early and continuing problem with the control of his sexual impulses, with his identity as a man, and with establishing any productive and close interpersonal relations with women have formed a plaguing constellation of difficulties in his life. Such satisfactions as he had in life are derived from his work and not from other people. Work becomes a mode through which he relates to people and also protects himself from any closeness to them. He is presently attempting to achieve a greater closeness to people and has had some limited success. His relationships with men are comfortable and productive; his relationships with women make him very anxious and cause him to pull out of them. He describes his own difficulties:

Most of my sex information came from the wrong places. . . . I was scared about sex in a way in which you shouldn't be at all. I was afraid even to be seen near a girl which was a terribly unhealthy thing in my life with lousy information and a very guilty feeling about it. I was going to the seminary and got strongly attracted to women. . . . These sex impulses and attraction to women have bothered me for a long time especially recently because of a problem I had getting close to a particular woman. Drinking gets mixed up with this too. . . . And I have a real struggle going on in my life concerning which of the many views about this whole area is the proper one. . . . This is not only a personal difficulty . . . or a lack of maturity on my part . . . a lack of personal integration. But I have become more calm about it and accept it, and I slowly begin to achieve some sort of integration where I am not so terribly frustrated, so worried because this integration in myself is lacking as of yet. . . . Drinking is a problem, not only in the frustration that arises from the limitations on what you can do in and for the Church, but more directly for me in the proper handling of my own sexual tensions. Because I have this desire to be better integrated in the sexual area, and I recognize that I am not, I see the need then to be a lot more careful in my use of alcohol. . . . It is only recently in my life that I fell in love with a person, a woman, and I went through a year and a half struggling with that relationship, to try to understand it, and to determine if it were good or bad. . . . And here I found out things about myself that were hard to admit. What I thought was my warmth and my reaching out to another human being was really to a big extent rooted in selfishness and not a generous sacrificial love. . . . So I am not really sure what love is all about. It was a shock to learn that so much of what I gave was self-centered when I should be giving and teaching unselfish love to other people. . . . And it wasn't only the physiological satisfaction but, more important, it was trying to satisfy someone from an emotional point of view—that you are loved and appreciated and that you're happy, and that there is someone who really thinks you are great. You know that once these things are fulfilled you don't really give a hell of a lot of thought to the other person and her needs. . . . This is what eventually caused both of us to break off the relationship.

Because of his strong dependency needs, he related well to authority in the earlier years of his life. Currently his stance toward authority is much more ambivalent and critical, although basically accepting:

One of my chief problems has been in maturing to the point of really thinking . . . and making true judgments on your own. . . . Because I found out later that you really can't have any strong commitments to faith or to anything else unless you go through that thinking and judging process. Before, I had equated loyalty and love for the Church and the priesthood with the ability simply to receive and to pass on uncritically. The type of authoritarianism which I very deeply espoused kept me from making legitimate independent judgments. I think that there are a lot of independent judgments that I have made in my life that are really not so much independent judgments as they were rationalizations or things decided to make me feel comfortable. To give things an honest look has come into my life at a much later time than it would normally.

. . . To do this was heartening to me. I don't have much of a problem in self-esteem because I feel that I am reasonably talented and I've got some fairly good brains. . . . And that makes it all the more astounding to me that a home environment such as mine and a type of a church system and training could have precluded me from having the intellectual honesty to insist that it is part of human life to make responsible judgments. Not just to take it as a given and to pass it on to others. . . . Sometimes, I laugh at myself when I look back now at the utter stupidity of my sitting there and telling a person something that I really hadn't thought through myself and saying this has got to be it and nothing else.

This priest has some insight into his lack of development. He sees the roots of his limited social and emotional growth in the authoritarian and rigid structures of his family and priestly training. He clearly recognizes his high level of vocational competence as well as his limited heterosexual development. His fortunate and fortuitous work assignment is the great sustaining force of his personal and professional life.

The central spiritual experience in this priest's life is his daily offering of the Mass. Religion is essentially a cognitive and intellectual experience for him. He presents many doubts of a mature sort about his faith, but he is able to accept them and to integrate them into a positive and deep acceptance of God and of the Church. The strong feeling that he can and does participate in changing the Church at critical choice points with significant churchmen is a key factor in his on-going self-acceptance and adjustment. His productive and challenging job, the status and the protection of the priesthood, his deep intellectualized spirituality: these factors keep him in the priesthood. He experiences a threat to his vocation in the periodic drive toward resolving his need for sexual expression and emotional closeness with women as well as in his excessive use of alcohol to expedite close interpersonal relations. In responding to his priesthood as a part of his life this man says:

Basically I have a strong belief in Christ. . . . I regret that I don't know Him or love Him as much as I used to. . . . But I have a very fundamentalist point of view that Jesus Christ is the Son of God, and I have a very fundamental belief in the Church as truly being God's will that it should exist. . . . It may be something mysterious but very real to me and true that within the context of the Church the idea that for whatever reason God decides that some people should be blessed in some way by Him, to try to be of service to others concerning the things of God. This I believe very strongly. I believe that whatever His reasons may have been that in the light of His Divine Providence there exists a God who wishes and wills me to be a priest and do His work. . . . I think a lot about this. . . . That it may be my personality, my life style, my human needs that are satisfied in the priesthood. There is a lot of that there, but also there crops up in all my doubts and problems the fundamental belief in my vocation to the priesthood. . . . I feel my priesthood in two things: one, in the office where I offer the Eucharist and in the immediacy of the people present. . . . It's an act of faith for me that in the Mass what I am doing is tremendously important for these people. . . . The other areas where I feel my priesthood is in the job I have. . . . This job I have felt over the years is not my priesthood ebbing away — but I have come to accept this work as a truly priestly service to people through trying to reconstruct the Church whereby its laws and norms are going to be of pastoral help to people.

In the Church we have to grasp the idea that it is possible to live with a certain amount of turmoil. . . . The polarity between groups is an inevitable consequence of the whole thrust of the new role of the Church and of trying to bring the Church into a new way of relating to the contemporary world in which it finds itself without losing any of what is deeply fundamental and essential to her as far as her nature is concerned. I am concerned in this with our leadership, with the attitude of the Holy Father, with the attitude of the authorities in Rome, with the intransigents who still remain on the leadership level, with the judgment of the young people, who, given the intransigence say, 'Oh, hell, we are just going off and we will see you around. It really isn't worth belonging to anyhow in that type of context.'

I am also concerned with what would happen to me and to the Church if the rules on celibacy were changed. I have thought a lot about it and read a lot and my conclusions are precious few and kind of negative. I don't think that most of the men that I know are leaving because of the atmosphere of sexual permissiveness, to go and get married. . . . I don't believe either, as some do, that the majority of men leave because they are very self-willed people. . . . I think it's more a question of being willing to accept what the Church must do to maintain its teaching and doctrine. I think that a man has to come to grips with that. And I must say that just because so many who leave say they don't believe anymore I don't consider that in them there is a loss of faith. . . . The guys I talk to and still know have in their own lives a deep wonder as to whether or not their being a priest in this particular fashion and in this particular way is doing what is expected or required of them by God and by themselves. I am sure that not everybody puts it in these terms. It is hard to crow when the other guy falls you know. In these men who leave I don't sense any deep loss of faith in Christ and in the general Church of God. They just tell me right out that it is the structure.

He wonders if the "thinking patterns of priests are changing"; if these are surface changes or if they go more deeply; what the rate of change is and if the basic values of priests are being transformed. In his discussions with many people of authority in the Church (part of his job) he became "convinced in a hurry that a study of the priesthood was the necessary and only way really to find out what priests are thinking," and that "some assurance is needed that you are not just getting isolated pockets of opinion." "The questionnaire, the tests and the interviews," he felt, "were the first time in a long time that many priests had a real good chance, outside of with their confessors to delve into their confidential life."

This priest spoke clearly and convincingly of how he acquired his present job. For him this job assignment has been productive and quite important in his life. For other priests such a job assignment has been destructive of both vocation and personality. He was asked how he got into his specialized field:

It was the will of the Bishop. I think that this is a commentary on our system, that a Bishop in a diocese happened to be stopping over one night in a rectory where I was a curate. His chief specialist in my area of expertise was with him. I had a question about an intricate case for which I had a solution. The specialist was pleased and became convinced that I was pretty good. And I guess the two of them talked it over and said apparently that I am not too dumb, maybe we can use him.

I've often thought of this, that we don't have, at least haven't had, a systematic approach to job applications and job specifications, so that we very seldom really know our personnel that well, what their strengths are and what their weak points are. I think that everyone tries to make a good effort to fit the square peg into the square hole, but so much of it is by chance, and I suppose it really was by chance that I got into my work, the Bishop said, 'Look I want you to be in the chancery office for a year and you see if you like it. If you think you can keep your sanity doing this kind of work which a lot of people view as purposeful and useful, then maybe we'll send you on to St. ——.' Well, this is about how it happened. A year later the Bishop said one day, 'Well, do you like it?' I said, 'Yes I guess I do,' and he said, 'Well, we like you so go ahead and study, and then I went to graduate school, and here I am.'

In summary, this underdeveloped priest grew up in a troubled household where he found little ready identity for himself; he is rarely able to express any degree of anger even now. Neither can he deal with the anger of other people for each other. He had a very traumatic separation experience when he was five years old that left him with the feeling that he really wasn't wanted as a person. The real value that he could have would come from becoming a priest. This was consistently reinforced by the aunt and uncle with whom he lived as well as by his parents. His virile image was questioned again just before puberty when many of the neighborhood kids challenged his manhood. He has never resolved this basic identity problem, and has continued to question whether he is really a man throughout all of his life. He dated in high school but never effected any kind of close relationship. He tried as recently as a year ago to achieve a relationship with a woman but was unable to go much further than talking with her in a very protected environment.

This priest has an active emotional life in which he finds himself being very drawn towards other people and especially towards women. However, because of his lack of development, he experiences a disproportionate amount of inhibition which really keeps him from effectively creating close relationships. He remains in the priesthood because his image of himself is more that of a priest rather than that of person. His job in the priesthood also offers him a great deal of satisfaction. His rewards come mostly from the activities that he carries out in the chancery rather than through pastoral activities. The distance of his present work is also functional in that he does not actually have to relate too closely to people in his official work. It has satisfying safeguards that are important for him. He is entering the years of the "success crisis" where he realizes he doesn't have much opportunity or much time to change his life if he cares to do so. At the same time he feels many longings to try new things; as a result he has established some friendships with men about his age who feel free to talk about the difficulty of closing in on middle age. He keeps at a safe distance from really developing even though he can describe his problems well. For example, although he verbalized a lot of openness and says that he would like to consider marriage, it is really unlikely that this man is going to get close enough to another ever to do this. There is a danger with this man: if he becomes aware of how isolated he has made himself, he may well become an alcoholic. There are already indications that he is using alcohol as a solvent for his emotional stiffness.

This man is functioning quite well in his job now and is very highly identified with the priesthood. If he remains in his present position and does not experience any serious threat to himself, he will continue his productive role and will probably build relationships that will be as rewarding as his personality allows. He is, however, basically under-developed and does not possess the resources of personality to move far from his present mode of adjustment. It serves his immaturity well, bolstering his sense of dealing with people, giving him status, and keeping them at a safe distance. His drinking and his abortive exploratory rela-tionships with women indicate the unresolved problems beneath the surface. He is, in fact, a lonely and isolated man living beneath the respectable protection of his job. He may well have serious problems if his present life situation is altered in any way.

Further Case Histories

A closer look at some more underdeveloped personalities enables us to see the wide range of lifestyle and backgrounds in which this adjust-ment is found in the priesthood. As in all the classifications, it does not belong to one age or one kind of work.

There is, for example, the high-ranking Church official who has sub-stituted achievement for being close to people in his life and, while he has succeeded in accomplishing many things, he finds himself puzzled now at the isolation he experiences as a result of the distance he has put between himself and others. This man, in his mid-fifties, has demon-strated a drive for achievement all through his life. It is clear that some species of ambition, some desire to please others and to receive recogni-tion from them, has been a ruling dynamic in his life. He has displayed competitive and mild perfectionistic patterns in religious activities as well as in sports and school work. This priest was one of those persons who was popular in a somewhat distant kind of way, an individual who really did not make or seek close friends. To please authority has become the most important motivation in his life, dating back to his early earnest efforts to be approved by his hard-working father., Even as he describes this and his consistent later efforts to please Church authority, he is not fully conscious of how much this has been operative in his own career in the Church.

At the present time this man relies on a very rigid interpretation of canonical structure as a defense against any kind of changes in the Church. He admits, however, that if his superiors in the Church were to alter their perception of Canon Law, he would readily change his understanding of that and of the Church as well. He does not seem to sense his own quite frank dependency on authority figures at all nor of the lack of intrinsic convictions implicit in this attitude. He has many good qualities and these have, without a doubt, contributed to his success in achieving a position of importance in the Church. He is efficient, industrious, and dedicated to doing a good job. He does not, however, have a very well-differentiated personality and operates only within the realm of pleasing authority. He is clearly underdeveloped and may experience greater problems unless he develops some genuine insight into his mode of adjustment to life.

A priest in his early fifties gives us a picture of an individual who has made his way through life, not by developing his true personality, but by making himself "lovable" in the eyes of others. Through this mode of adjustment, he never needs to enter into any genuine or mature relationship; he keeps conflict at a distance and preserves a good feeling toward himself. This is hardly a way of being truly alive and he has had to fortify this adjustment with alcohol because of his frequent experience of depression and loneliness.

This man has sought attention from others all his life and cannot explain, except in the vaguest terms, why he decided to become a priest. It seems from his statements that it was consistent with his drive for maternal and social approval. The priesthood has enabled him to play a role and establish some identity; it has also conferred upon him a sense of security and a feeling of being admired by others. The priesthood, as a role of ministry, has never been internalized. The character of this man is not very deep and he tends to use regressive defenses in order to avoid adult responsibility. He seems friendly to everyone but has no relationships that mean anything in the long run. He is comfortable with teenagers because they make no great demands on him. It is significant to note that this man began drinking when he was in the seminary and considered himself an alcoholic by the time he was ordained. This priest has had a problem of chronic alcoholism ever since. Alcohol, of course, has been his bridge to a friendly world, a clear substitute for any kind of genuine growth. He is grossly immature, and, despite his age, is still in conflict over his personal identity. He will continue to relate by being "lovable" for the rest of his days, hoping that he can keep away from drinking, but never realizing its true dynamic significance in his life.

A clear example of a young man who has never broken through the crust of narcissism which has encapsulated him in his own personality is the thirtyish immigrant priest who presented himself in a charming but superficial manner during the interview.

He is quite shallow and detached, but quite unaware of how isolated and self-concerned he truly is. For example, he says that he would not marry if he were given the option. This is not, however, a sign of virtue as much as it is additional evidence of his inability to reach out in a meaningful way to another person. He is, in fact, indifferent to everyone but himself. He states that he would not feel the loss of anybody who might die or be taken away from him in his life. This man is very narcissistic and his gratifications come only when people need him. He has mastered the art of smiling and being pleasant so that others will respond to him favorably. Beneath the charm, however, lurks a very adolescent and underdeveloped personality. His identity is quite diffuse and his commitments are, even in his own descriptions of them, very shallow and short-termed. He avoids authority, working his way around it rather than meeting it straightforwardly. He might be described as a man who has slipped through the system nicely by minimizing confrontation while he does pretty much what he feels like doing when he feels like it. There is no room for other people on the center stage of his own concern.

This man is very satisfied with himself. He has practically no insight into the superficial way in which he currently describes himself and his work. He says that he is totally involved in his work but, when questioned, he cannot define exactly what his work is. He says, for example, that he feels that he is working when he watches television. This person, in short, only looks effective; the priesthood serves his underdeveloped personality very well, but does very little in return.

Yet another example of an underdeveloped young man is the good-looking priest in his early thirties who depends heavily on the role of the priesthood for his personal identity. He has little insight into himself, describing his life as happy and free from conflict. It is only when one looks closer that one sees that this is not quite true; this person is far less in actuality than he seems when he stands in his roman collar as the official representative of the Church.

There was no strong identification with his father because of the latter's chronic alcoholic condition during this priest's developing years. The mother dominated and provided for the family. He developed an early interest in sports which enabled him to get considerable acceptance from other boys. This remained on a generally superficial level and did not go beyond the rather narrow dimensions of athletic activity. He describes himself as afraid of girls and says that, despite the façade of athletics, he has never felt assertive as a man. He looked good all the while, however.

This priest is a classic example of the individual who goes through life putting all his energy into avoiding conflict. He maintains what there is of his identity by keeping people at a distance, maintaining a moderate position on everything, and depending on other people for his deep needs of support and approval. He is truly less secure than he imagines and very dependent upon the identity which is conferred on him by the role of the priesthood. This role provides an automatic entrance into relationship with others and, because of its status, is a source of great personal satisfaction for him. He is not, however, a deep person and he functions at an immature level of personal development.

A good example of the kind of serious problems that can come into the life of an underdeveloped man in middle age is the pastor, nearing fifty, who managed to get through on his administrative skills until more recent years. His lack of genuine personal development was always masked, even from himself, and he is now in the middle of a situation which he does not fully understand and to which he cannot respond very effectively.

The most traumatic event of this priest's life occurred when a psychotic woman in his parish began showing him much attention and affection. This priest was caught in the bind of being very flattered by this attention, a type which he had never received before in his life, and feeling very guilty about getting involved with a married woman. They became sexually involved nonetheless, and, after a time, this priest resolved the problem by having himself transferred to another parish. The woman, however, pursued him there, became severely alcoholic, and had to be hospitalized after a psychotic episode. This incident has caused this priest a great deal of guilt but the rewards of the relationship have also left him wanting to get involved in a similar manner again.

Why has all this happened? This priest is a passive and dependent person. He will not really reach out for another relationship like this but neither will he ever be able to look inside himself and put together the pieces of his personality which made him the prey of such a situation. He is, however, going to school on the side in order to prepare himself for another career if he has the opportunity for marriage. He rationalizes his purpose in going to school so that he does not experience conflict about it. He is currently, however, in an agitated depressive state, trying to resolve his guilt over this woman's hospitalization while he also wants to avoid any possible conflict with authority. He is obviously in need of psychotherapy but is not inclined to seek it at the present time. He is caught in the pressures of a man who has reached mid-life without ever reaching maturity. He literally does not understand what is happening to him or how clearly his present conflict expresses his lack of personal development.

One last example gives us a clear understanding of how some underdeveloped men substitute ambition and power for any real development of their personalities. This man, in his early thirties, lacks insight into how important power and status are in his life. Nonetheless, these are the dynamic forces which most influence him and which give him his greatest satisfactions in his work in the Church. He is presently secretary to a high Church official, a position with obvious rewards for a man with his personality characteristics.

In the words of the interviewer, he is "a moderately defensive, normal individual with a fairly well-ingrained authoritarian personality pattern that is characterized by too much control over his feelings and emotions, over-conformity to authority and rules, rigidity in his thinking, impatience and intolerance of the failings of others, a striving for power, status and control with underlying feelings of personal inadequacy which he has repressed." He came from a repressive family atmosphere and has transferred what he learned there to his life in the Church. His desire to please and the rewards that came to him for being a good boy have, in fact, marked his career in the Church just as they did at home. Choosing the priesthood provided him with practically the same structure which he knew in his family. He has not only been able to adapt himself to the highly structured way of life but he has achieved an excellent opportunity to get satisfaction for his dependency needs as well as his needs for power, respect and status. These needs are far more real in the lives of some underdeveloped priests than many people would like to believe. Becoming a priest has enabled this individual to hide behind his spiritual leadership role so that he has not had to involve himself in any really personal or close way with other people. He is really not close to anyone and prefers to deal impersonally and professionally, priding himself on being proper, while he is really being quite impersonal. This priest has developed close ties with other clergymen who share his outlook. There is a tone of self-righteousness running through the lives of persons who are underdeveloped in this manner, one that disposes them to seek power and authority because they look on themselves as the rightful inheritors of these. This priest is very rigid and demanding in his expectations of others and displays frequent impatience and intolerance with those who deviate from what he expects of them.

This priest does not really realize how much the priesthood has done for him in satifying his deep psychological needs. He would probably be unable to admit this because the priesthood has provided such a shelter for him against a more fully developed life. He would be extremely threatened by any prospective change in the law of celibacy because this would unsettle his adjustment. He believes that it is absolutely necessary for the priesthood. The real reason for this rigid belief is because his cool kind of celibacy is so necessary for his psychological adjustment. He is the classic company man who, in the long run, does not do the company much good because so much of what he actually does benefits his own personality rather than anybody else. Despite his seeming surface propriety, this priest is a very underdeveloped person underneath.

CHAPTER VI

THE DEVELOPING

Before we look closely at the group of priests that are described as "developing," we should remind ourselves of some of the main features of personal growth. Man does not move from one stage of life to another by leaps. Neither are any of the stages of his life completely static and immutable positions. The nature of human development is dynamic. Man is not designed or put together by blueprints; there is nothing automatic about the process because it is strongly affected by the life experiences of the individual. Brammer and Shostrom (1960) have summed up the essential truths about personal growth in the following manner:

A. Growth is *progressive* and *cumulative;* that is, it moves by steps and through stages.

B. Growth is *integrative* and *disintegrative;* that is, growth is a building- and fitting-together process as well as a tearing-down process. For example, childhood patterns must be disrupted before adult patterns can become operative.

C. Psychological growth depends upon the twin principles *maturation* and *learning.* Maturation implies a potential for development which unfolds under the proper stimulating conditions when the organism is ready to respond. Restrictive environments and restrictive adaptations of the individual, such as overly intense psychological threat and consequent defensiveness, inhibit psychological growth.

D. Finally, psychological growth is dependent upon contact with people (p. 64).

Forces that interrupt or thwart the kind of emotional learning that is essential to orderly development can prevent an individual person from progressing through the normal stages of growth. Interference with emotional learning is ordinarily related to the important persons in the

107

individual's life; for example, the parents or those who, for one reason or another, take the parents' place in the individual's life. It is likewise important to remember that the environment in which the individual lives can either aid or frustrate him in his personal development. Again, the environment is an amalgam of people, attitudes, rules and cultural customs; in some way or other, the ethos of a particular age may influence for good or for bad the ease with which an individual passes through the developmental stages. Just as it is possible to frustrate human growth, it is also possible to start it going again. Human growth, however, does not leap over unfinished stages. No matter when it is taken up again chronologically, the individual passes through the emotional phases that he missed because of whatever frustrating circumstances he encountered. In other words, the growth process is fluid and sensitive to its psychological surroundings.

In normal and healthy situations, the average person does not go through the growth process without certain problems and crises. When the atmosphere is distorted so that there is interference with learning, the problems can be sharply intensified and the individual can, as a result, find himself stalled instead of moving forward. This arrested growth, however, need not be permanent. The person is plastic; his structural and personal environment can change so that he finds himself once again in the midst of the growth process. It is this kind of experience in priests which we describe in this chapter. This is the story of individuals whose personal growth was suspended or delayed for a time and who, at a later date in life than they expected, find themselves challenged by problems of growth. It is quite possible, in the way that we use words, to describe this population as immature, if we mean this word in the sense that the growth of these individuals is not commensurate with their age. Although this is true, the use of this word may lead us to miss the most important truth about this group: they are moving again, finding new aspects of their own personalities for the first time in their lives. They therefore reflect vitality, a sense of purpose, and a determination to move forward that is sometimes stronger than that of developed priests.

Two questions are important here. What kind of things have interfered with the normal expected growth of the priests under study and, secondly, what tripped off the growth process again in their lives? The fact that there was a lack of full development in these individuals is related to many of the factors that have been discussed in connection with the underdeveloped subjects of this study. In summary, they are ordinarily related to the early childhood experiences, to the way in which the individual learns to deal with himself and others in his early family life. The seeds of many later growth problems are planted at this time and so it is with the present population. For example, many priests were reared in rather rigid and authoritarian home atmospheres in which parental demands on the child's behavior were very great and in which the children did not experience healthy affection from their parents. Frequently, the father was absent, or suffered from some other symptomatic difficulty, such as overdrinking. In these circumstances the future priest tended to identify with the generally more tender mother figure. The prospective priest, however, lived in an environment wider than that of his family, an environment which reinforced the attitudes and ways of looking at the world which was so much a part of the family experience itself. This kind of experience is by no means exclusively that of priests but it is characteristic of the kind of circumstances which can effectively inhibit the emotional development of the individuals who go through it. We are presuming, of course, that in all other ways the individual is normal and healthy, suffering no organic defect or major physical illness. The lack is clearly in the psychological atmosphere and this has a powerful suppressive effect on the emotional development of children. The subjects of this chapter, then, resemble in many ways those described as underdeveloped. The difference lies in the fact that the unfinished business of growth has been taken up again, that instead of being stuck rather firmly with the patterns familiar to the underdeveloped, these persons have struck out to deal once again with the challenges which they did not confront at an earlier time because of the repressive character of their early years.

What can cause an individual to break out of the confines of underdevelopment, even at a rather late stage in his life? What, in other words, are the kinds of psychological occurrences which start the individual's personality unfolding again? The circumstances are varied, they are perceived differently by those undergoing them than by those observing them, and they are difficult to place in one inclusive category. The crust of underdevelopment may be pierced, however, by some unexpected shift in the basic relationships in the individual's life. For example, those with whom he has been closest, his parents possibly, may become aged, or even die. They move gradually out of the orbit of active and satisfying relationships and, when this is accomplished, the individual may discover that he has no close ties with others. The resultant experience of loneliness, with its shock and anxiety, demands an adjustment on the part of the person involved. He may do this in many ways, of course, but not all of them may indicate positive growth. There are regressive possibilities here; these may be the result of a variety of occurrences which interfere with the psychological adjustment of the underdeveloped adult. He may, for example, turn inward, begin drinking, or use some other ultimately destructive defense to ward off the necessity of dealing with the positive aspects of the challenge implicit in the incident which has taken place.

An individual may find himself suddenly shifted from one form of work to another. For example, many missionaries find the adjustment from missionary work to some assignment in the United States extremely difficult. This total transformation of their environment, demanding that they change their focus in work and relationships, can be very jarring. The individual priest who is healthy may find it difficult to make this kind of shift; the person who has not fully developed may find it disruptive. He can no longer go on with the same kind of adjustments with which he balanced out his underdeveloped personality in some other country. He may become very anxious and uneasy upon being assigned to some form of work in the United States, such as fund raising or teaching in a seminary. His anxiety and restlessness may be the only clear signs of the kind of growth crisis which the individual is experiencing. Frequently he resolves it by returning to the missionary setting without really coming to grips with the kind of questions occasioned by the change in his life circumstances. He may also, of course, deal with these challenges in a constructive way. The possibilities of this are very great. For example, a person may find that the reasons that he preferred the work to which he had been assigned formerly are no longer valid in the light of new self-knowledge. The possibility of returning to the former work may now become threatening to him because this work no longer meets his needs. These situations can become very complicated, can elude the observation of even the most sensitive superior, and can, because of the kind of expectations placed on men in the priesthood and religious life, cause a man to pull back from growth in order to avoid the dilemma caused by the change in his life.

An excellent example of development in an older man is the pastor in his late fifties who had to begin growing again as the result of an assignment change. After many years of leading a carefully sheltered intellectual life, he was assigned to parish work. Under the pressure of younger priests and in an assignment that was very difficult for him to accept, he has moved considerably forward, becoming personally involved in the transformation of the parish and making a success both of this enterprise and of his own adaptation. His potential for this kind of adjustment lay dormant for years, as sheltered as he was; because of circumstances he has had to grow and has done so with integrity. While far from a fully rounded individual, he has still made considerable progress and should continue to do so.

The man may have a new educational or personal experience which shifts his view of the world in which he lives and makes him examine his convictions and his pattern of life more closely than he has ever done before.

Many priests and religious have had this kind of self-confrontation forced upon them by the Second Vatican Council and the changes which have permeated the environment of the Catholic Church ever since. The shifting nature of the age itself, self-investigation, the development of a more personal approach to one's self and to one's work, the input of reading, workshops, and other extended educational experiences, both formal and informal: all these can have a powerfully disruptive effect on a formally effective mode of adjustment to a person who is not fully grown.

A person may be moved to examine his own development through the experience of a serious illness or even through some major kind of failure in which he is somehow involved. For example, an individual may be engaged in a form of work which, in this more demanding age, may be eliminated because of inadequate financing or changes in some other policies. The person who has made considerable investment in one form of work may find the sting of failure both unexpected and totally disruptive. It is one of the major forces in precipitating new growth in an individual in all walks of life. Here again, a more non-productive solution may be attempted but this could not be classified as growth.

A person may begin growing again because of a profound religious experience, although these experiences are rare, and are not usually cited by the priest population as a reason for new growth. It is difficult, however, to define simply the nature of a religious experience. Many priests, looking back on the course of their development, feel that the whole process has had an important religious dimension. They feel that the power of the Spirit has been active in them and, while they may not describe an intense or singular religious experience, they feel that their faith has indeed been involved in the circumstances which have caused them to re-examine themselves and their goals in life. In the same way, an individual may have a new personal experience which is surprising in character and quite dramatic in its effects on his adjustment. He may find that his formerly secure sense of himself is now dislodged because of an experience with another person, frequently a woman, which has brought into his life a kind of value and a quality of experience that he never knew before. This is not infrequently the reason for profound changes in the lives of the priests and religious under study. They find they have tasted something which they formerly felt was not available to them and that its effects on them are positive and powerful. The realm of personal experience is probably the most potent as regards the reinitiation of growth in the life history of the individual. This is not surprising because human growth is linked at every stage to the persons who are involved in our lives. For many priests this new experience of persons has a religious dimension to it which only increases its effect, challenging the individual to inspect again the set of values by which he has lived and the nature and depth of his commitment in faith to the religious beliefs which are his. Quite often this kind of confrontation leads the person far more deeply into himself than he has ever been before. He begins to put aside the very controlling defenses with which he has restricted his life experience and he moves into human realms which he can truly say he never knew existed before this kind of experience occurred.

What do these people look like when these changes occur? Here again, it is not possible to write one description to cover all the possibilities. In fact, the individuals themselves may not have a clear idea of what is happening to them. It is only on reflection that they begin to see that something new has come into their life and that, as they have pursued it, they have also restructured their view of the world around them.

An example of a person who is beginning to develop because he has truly sensed the isolation and loneliness that his failure to develop brought into his life is the middle-aged priest now pursuing a graduate degree in social science. From a rigid and authoritarian home, he submitted always to his parents' commands, repressing his own personal development in the process. After years of intense work, a style of adjustment he employed to express his unresolved sexual and aggressive feelings, he found himself with no friends. The pain of this occasioned his insight into his partial responsibility for his own alienation. He has made efforts to move and has, in fact, made some progress, so that now he is, as the interviewer described it, "reveling in his new found openness and unexpected comfort with himself." He has only begun, in middle age, to take up the tasks of personal growth and he is moving slowly but in a positive direction.

The individual may only be aware of the symptom that tells him that something has changed in the world in which he once felt fairly comfortable. He may find himself anxious or restless, negatively reactive now to the formerly unquestioned structures which surround him. He may hurt in some vague way which he cannot describe even to himself because he is not comfortable with his own emotional life and its significance. He may, on the other hand, find himself experiencing an urge to move and develop even when he cannot explain this to himself nor choose with complete certainty the best means to achieve it. This is what occurs with men who move forward. The situation, however, can be different.

Others whose adjustment is dislodged may regroup their defenses and present themselves with a new array of symptoms which are really the signs of their digging in against the possibilities of new growth. They try, in other words, to quiet their anxiety by reinforcing rigid defenses which have been torn open by some occurrence or other. They may also remain in the underdeveloped category through defensive adjustments that are obviously non-productive, such as drinking, exploitative sexual relationships, or more severe withdrawal. We are concerned, however, with those for whom the change in their life occasions a step forward, perhaps a timid and uncertain one, but one that leads them forward nonetheless.

Psychologist Sidney Jourard presents a description of this experience from the inside, noting that, although change is going on all the time, it is experienced only in certain moments of time. Something like this seems to happen to the priests who are the subjects of this study. Although they can only describe what has happened to them in terms of certain concrete experiences in their own world, certain shifts in their own feeling, certain changes in the values in which they believe, what they say is well described by Jourard (1968):

The awareness of change is frequently the experience of *surprise:* the unexpected has just been presented to us. The world, or my own bodily being, is not as I had believed it to be. One of the expectations about being, my concepts and beliefs about the world, has just been disconfirmed. The awareness that things are different is not growth, though it is a necessary condition of growth. A growth *cycle* calls for (a) an acknowledgment that the world has changed, (b) a shattering of the present experience world-structure, and (c) a restructuring, retotalization, of the world-structure which encompasses the new disclosure of changed reality (p. 166).

There are few analogies to guide us as we try to understand the elements that are part of this kind of change experience. One of the few directions in which we can look for the careful observation of the process of positive growth is that which takes place in the experience of counseling or psychotherapy. The essence of this kind of therapeutic experience is not something magical or mysterious; it is rather the personal growth of the individual who seeks some kind of help in order to further his own personal development. It is true that this individual may have serious symptoms or life problems, the conflictual nature of which he experiences painfully and often without insight. The therapist, in other words, tries to create the conditions in which the individual can continue to grow to his fullness; he is not "cured" by some mysterious art of the psychologist or psychiatrist as much as he is enabled to draw upon his own strength to complete what is lacking in his own growth. As Karen Horney (1950) has put it:

> We cannot cure the wrong course which the development of a person has taken. We can only assist him in gradually outgrowing his difficulties so that his development may assume a more constructive course. . . . We want to help the person find himself and with that the possibility of working toward his self-realization. His capacity for good human relations is an essential self-realization, but it also includes his faculty for creative work and that of assuming responsibility for himself (pp. 333–334).

If the experience of counseling provides us with the circumstances in which a person who has had a difficulty with psychological growth tries to overcome it through marshalling his own strength through the relationship with the therapist, then the characteristic phases of growth which occur in this situation tell us something about the systematic challenges which have to be faced by the priest who finds that he is a developing person. Before we discuss in detail the life history and developmental problems of some developing priests, we must review the typical psychological experience that occurs in progressive personal growth.

Carl Rogers (1961) has presented a description of the growth of the person in therapy as a process in which the person moves not from one fixed point in life to another fixed point even though such a process might be conceivable. He sees individuals moving on a continuum along which they shift from one fixed point to a passage of change or, in his

words, "from rigid structure to flow, from stasis to process [p. 131]."
He goes on to propose seven possible stages of the process. These give
us the flavor of continuing growth and its characteristic dynamics as
they are experienced by the developing priests.

In the first stage the individual is in a very fixed position. You might
say that he is stalled, that he has not moved beyond a certain level and
that there is little sign that he will. He holds to this, in other words, and
defends himself against psychological movement. He may remain, for
example, at a very adolescent stage and use intellectualized defenses,
such as rationalization, to justify his adjustment. Rogers (1961) describes the individual in this way:

> There is an unwillingness to communicate self.
> Communication is only about externals.
> Feelings and personal meanings are neither recognized nor owned.
> Personal constructs are extremely rigid.
> Close and communicative relationships are construed as dangerous.
> No problems are recognized or perceived at this stage.
> There is no desire to change.
> There is much blockage of internal communication (p. 132).

At the second stage of the process there is a slight loosening in the
emotions and in the way the individual talks about himself. This seems
to occur, according to Rogers, when he has the experience of being
listened to, of being "received." This loosening of the formerly rigid
self continues throughout the process of development with a consequent
greater freedom of self-expression. There is progressive opening of the
self, and an increased awareness of the person's identity during this
period of growth.

The process for the developing priests follows this same general trend.
The individual has been progressing through life unaware of many
aspects of his own personality, settled in as it were, at a certain undeveloped stage of growth without much awareness of his true situation. In
fact, he may perceive himself as healthy, in no need of change, and as
pretty much in control of his life and work. It is important to appreciate
the fact that individuals who are frustrated in their growth do not consciously or deliberately keep themselves back from full growth. They
are coping with life as best they can with the psychological tools which
are theirs as the result of growth experiences up to that point. For the
priests in this study, the psychological adjustment which precedes some
phase of further development is usually heavily defensive. The priest

may not really be aware of his arrested development, although he occasionally may be made uneasy by the signs of this which he can perceive in his life. For example, he may feel very uneasy in dealing with authority or in dealing with members of the opposite sex. He may feel uncertain about himself, his own convictions, or his future plans, preferring passively to accept what the Church and his superiors prepare for him. He does not let himself understand the possible significance of these adjustments. He tends to preserve a picture of himself which is at variance with what he is really like. He expends his energy, however, in trying to enlarge this unrealistic self-ideal so that he continually moves away from his real self and is, in effect, not really in touch with himself at all. This seems to be quite characteristic of the men who operate without very much insight and at a very early level of psychological development. For them the Church is frequently an extension of their own rigid, religious, and highly structured family life. The only way of adjusting to their own family life was to accept it passively and to move in the directions which won them approval and affection. This approval from others was frequently strongly reinforced by the individual's choice of the seminary. Whatever the defenses may be, they remain in place until some event or chance occurrence dislodges them and makes the individual experience, even in a vague way, affect his own vulnerability.

This problem is well illustrated by the pastor in his mid-thirties who has resolved his relationship with his mother only in recent years. In fact, the resolution of this relationship may lead him eventually to leave the priesthood, so tied up were his mother's wishes with his perseverance in the seminary. She prevailed on him to remain in the seminary on two occasions, including a short period when he dropped out before ordination. Since his ordination, however, this priest has been involved in three affairs with women, all of which he describes as beginning innocently and getting out of hand as he got more intimate with the persons involved. This is not just a question of temptation or weakness, but a sign of this person's unfinished psychological growth. The affairs with the women are clear evidence of his confusion about his own identity and his relationship to his dominating mother. The affairs, however, have brought this man to examine himself seriously, and to begin to probe deeply into his motivations and his adjustment in the priesthood. This causes him considerable anxiety, which he converts into psychosomatic symptoms. Nonetheless, he is moving ahead in an effort to deal more maturely with his conflicts. He recognizes his own lack of development and, although he is confused and in pain, he is developing. It would not be a risky prediction to expect him to leave the priesthood within the next few years.

We see in this case, much as it is noted in the continuum proposed by Rogers, a gradual loosening of the rigid defensive posture which the individual has adopted as a life style. He begins to sense that he does have feelings and that he should listen to them rather than always look away from them. This is frequently an exhilarating kind of experience because, for the very first time, he looks within himself for an understanding of his experience rather than always to the world outside of himself. Characteristically, the individual begins to move out of himself, away from isolation and toward relationship with others. There are further psychological stirrings within him, although he may not be able to accept and make these experiences truly his own as yet. Priests who are developing begin by dealing with involvement, taking a cautious step forward while being prepared to beat a hasty retreat. It is very difficult for them to pull themselves away from the rigid backgrounds which have shaped their lives until this time. They are very careful as they strive to maintain a balance between what is new and desired by them and what is traditional and expected of them. This causes the kind of conflict which they may not be able to ignore any longer and which moves them to a much closer evaluation of their personal growth and development and the values by which they have been leading their lives.

Their initial approach at this stage is frequently highly intellectualized, an effort to learn more about themselves through books and seminars so as to neutralize the troubling human experience which may have come unexpectedly into their lives. They want to learn about sexuality, the formation of personal identity, and the mystery of relationship between men and women. All these things have been unknown territory for them, forbidden by extensive repressive defenses which have blocked off many aspects of their development. They have lived up to this point through looking at life in an intellectual way. Now there is something totally new in finding that they are unified persons whose possibilities for experiencing life are much richer than they had ever dreamed. This is the kind of crucial experience of the self which makes the individual abandon the former carefully secured positions of adjustment and strike off into the unknown territory of himself. The outcome is hard to predict. For the individuals involved, the experience is a very difficult one to understand. They frequently do not have any help in trying to interpret what is happening to them. Traditional answers do not speak to them anymore but they find it difficult to believe that there is another way to live.

Clearly, for a man who has lived according to one form of adjustment for many years, the challenge of finding that there is more to life than he suspected may lead him to reconsider his vocational commitment and his ideas of the faith, the priesthood, and the Church. This is not unusual in the developing person because, once he has set his foot in a positive and forward direction, he really finds it difficult to pull back into a more regressive position. The experience is very disruptive, however, because the individual feels the repercussions of the changes that are going on inside himself even when he cannot understand them very clearly. He is in process, having shifted from a stable and static view of life to one in which he feels a new liberation but in which he may not have a secure center of gravity or a well developed sense of identity. The developing individual makes many mistakes. His behavior gives evidence of his struggles. He moves somewhat tentatively away from the values and supports which formerly guided him. He finds, in other words, that the price of change is high, as high as its rewards, and that once he has begun to change, he cannot step back from it. He must see it through to its conclusion, even if this means a notable change in his life circumstances.

It is important to note here, however, that not every person who is developing will necessarily move away from the active exercise of the priesthood. In fact, it may well be that the individual moves into a new and far more effective position as a clergyman. He is freed from formerly highly restrictive ways of relating with people, is capable now of a kind of closeness which he never knew before, and is able to understand and identify with the experience of his people in a far more human manner. He has been weathered by life, and may choose again the priesthood in the light of this new understanding of himself. This is quite possible, especially when the lack of development in the individual is not the result of serious psychological problems as much as the effect of a repressive and restrictive home and cultural environment.

A clear example of a priest dealing with important personal issues in delayed adolescent growth is the teacher in his late twenties who only recently began to relate to people in a closer manner. His lack of development is related to a very restrictive home life which was dominated by his mother who overcontrolled the children, not permitting much spontaneous expression of feeling. This caused the individual to become very angry but without any freedom to express it outwardly. This anger turned in the only direction it could, toward himself. He was, in his own feelings, always the bad one, and this notably affected his picture of himself. He did not, as the interviewer noted, really have "terribly bad experiences; rather, he hasn't had many experiences" at all. This very restrictive self was sustained through the seminary and has only begun to change in the atmosphere of teaching young people. He is very adolescent in his dealings with high school girls, but this is exactly the sign of his beginning, at almost 30 years of age, to work through this developmental phase of life. It is clear that this new experience, making him more sensitive to people, can increase notably his effectiveness as a priest.

The questions which developing priests frequently raise reflect this kind of developmental experience. They would like to stay in the priesthood but they have found a new side to themselves and what they perceive as the structures of the priesthood do not seem to them to allow its expression. All they have known in the priesthood, as they have seen it, has been the restriction of their personal lives. The developing person sincerely questions celibacy not because he is necessarily going to marry and not because he is anxious to undermine the authority of the Church. He finds this a valid area of inquiry because he has a new appreciation of the values of love and human relationships in life.

There is no point, in any case, in trying to keep people from having the kinds of experiences which open them up to more of life. Developing priests sense little understanding of their experience on the part of higher authorities, however, and they frequently find themselves somewhat in the dark and somewhat alienated from the traditional Church which does not really seem able to make room for them. Neither should it be thought that these men should be spared the anxiety which is the natural concomitant of this growth experience. Anxiety does not necessarily mean impairment. As Horney (1950) has said: "It may mean that the patient has come closer to facing his conflicts or his self-hate than he could stand at the given time. . . . An emerging anxiety also may have an eminently positive meaning, for it may indicate that the patient now feels strong enough to take the risk of facing his problems more squarely [p. 340]."

The self-knowledge which is a product of this kind of growth is not that brand of intellectual knowing which the individual may have been comfortable with earlier in his life. Knowledge kept on the totally intellectual plane is not threatening. Indeed, intellectualized knowledge may keep one's emotions under control by keeping them at a distance. This is no longer possible for the developing person who feels progressively more deeply about life and himself as he moves along the pathway to greater self-realization. As Horney (1950) notes: "Only when experiencing the full impact in its irrationality of a hitherto unconscious or semi-conscious feeling or drive do we gradually come to know the intensity and the compulsiveness of unconscious forces operating within ourselves [p. 343]." In other words, unless the person feels deeply at this time, he will never sense the forces that have made him the way he is, nor will he understand the strength of the defenses which he has employed to maintain himself in a rigid and fixed undeveloped position.

It is important to note that much of the behavior of those who are developing is quite adolescent in character. It could not be otherwise because, in actuality, this is the life stage which many of these men are passing through only at a later time in their lives. You cannot cure adolescence because it is not a disease; you cannot outlaw it, because it is not a crime. Observers of priests may detect this behavior in them when they are developers and they may wish that it were otherwise. It may truly be embarrassing but it cannot be suppressed. That was the problem in the first place. There are adolescent men in every profession, of course, and there is no sensible way to help them except to assist them in continuing their growth. The danger would be to misinterpret this behavior as moral weakness or as failure to deal with temptation. These priests have growing pains, and they can only be helped by those who are able to understand this.

It is also important to note that many young men in the priesthood are developing by the very fact that they are in their early manhood and that they have not had sufficient life experiences to develop at any time before this. Their development begins again, as it were, immediately after the seminary and is occasioned by the fact that they have, at long last, come to work and live closely with other persons. The suspension of this kind of first-hand closeness with a great variety of people seems to be a strong factor in preventing the normal growth of individual priests during their seminary years. The repressive defenses which they learn to use, and which are reinforced by the seminary itself, are very powerful. They begin to crack, however, in the less well ordered but more healthy circumstances of ordinary living. This new awareness has disturbed many priests who have not realized, or who have been somewhat uneasy about admitting the fact that they had to do their growing after their training was over. More typically, however, the priest is able to maintain his restricted level of development for several years. It is only after a multitude of life experiences, disillusionments, and difficulties that he may begin to look anew at himself and wonder about his values and the direction his life is taking. This is particularly true at a time of great change in the Church, such as the years that have followed Vatican II. The shattering of secure surroundings, the multiplication of new ventures, the sudden environment of uncertainty, the new emphasis on the values of personalism: all these continue to contribute to the initiation of developmental growth in the lives of many priests.

It is also significant, as the psychological testing (Chapter IX) that accompanied the depth interview reinforces, that developing priests are clearly coming to grips with life in a very active way. The tests reflect the dynamic process of re-engaged development, revealing these men as individuals who are, in psychological terms, actualizing themselves. They are not falling apart, although they are reorganizing themselves; they are, in fact, trying to achieve a higher order integration of themselves.

We will now examine some case studies which exemplify this "developing" process in the lives of priests. It is interesting to note that individuals can begin to grow again at very different ages and in very different circumstances.

This young diocesan priest works in a large metropolitan diocese. He has been ordained for about a year and a half and is assigned as a curate in a local parish.

This man, although still far from 30 years of age, projected a warm personality which reflected his enthusiasm about his newly acquired self-confidence. Shorter than average and side-burned, he was warm, exuberant, and optimistic. This young man sees himself as progressive, open, and, in his own language, "with it." He feels that recently he has been growing personally and that his life is on the right track. He thinks that the priesthood is the right place for himself although he does express some uncertainty about his future in relation to celibacy and in relation to his ability to get along in the life of the rectory.

Both his father and his mother were born in a large Eastern city. His father was an attorney and a graduate of a distinguished law school. A central fact in this young priest's life is that his father was an alcoholic. This has had a clear effect in shaping his personality and his life style. He describes it:

Father was a very mild person, a very kind and generous man. . . . He had a very severe drinking problem and was an alcoholic. . . . This had a devastating effect on the family. . . . There was constant bickering between my mother and my father. . . . While I was growing up I never appreciated my father. Only when I became older did I begin to appreicate him as a person. . . . I resented him very much for how he embarrassed us. . . . Now when I look back on it I wonder why he put up with some of the things he did. He took a lot from me, from my mother, and from my sister. It was my mother who gave him the greatest problem. . . . She projects her ideas and her way of doing things on others. . . . She is very strong in her concept of the way things should be done. She is very strong, but doesn't think of herself that way. She is a very warm, friendly, and outgoing person, but she has very definite ideas about the way things are and the way things should be done. . . . She dominates and controls by trying to make you feel guilty if you didn't do what she wanted you to do. . . . And she still tries to control me. . . . If I go home she always has a list of things for me to do. . . . My sister finally rebelled against home and especially against my mother and she left. I think that I am like my father in many ways and this is something that when I was growing up always made me very fearful. . . . I never had a very high opinion of Dad and I was determined that I would never turn out to be an alcoholic. . . . I regarded my father as weak . . . although I admired his gentleness and kindness to other people. . . . Yet, to my way of thinking, he was definitely taken advantage of. . . . Now in my own life I may have the same tendencies to be taken advantage of, but I haven't had the experience he had of being married which I think could have been devastating. He wasn't strong enough (with mother and us) where he should have been. . . . I often had the position or role (in the family) that should have been my father's, and I always resented that and wondered why he never did anything or said anything. . . . Mother consulted me and asked me about things in place of father.

This was an unhappy home, one that was psychologically destructive as well as disruptive for the individual in his efforts to secure his identity and to achieve a measure of independence and self-sufficiency. Interestingly enough, going to the seminary brought about the first big change in this man's life. It liberated him from the tense home situation in which he felt continually "tense and nervous." He enjoyed the seminary as years of release and relief for him. In the seminary, "I was a lot more inclined to fool around and to get into trouble now and then for breaking the rules." There was no mother to dominate and to arouse guilt in him;

nor was his father present to make him feel ashamed. He thought highly of his seminary training and he particularly enjoyed philosophy.

Problems are bred in families like his. The role confusion generated by a dominating and coercive mother and a despised, passive father was recreated in his first job assignment in an urban rectory. His first experience in a rectory tells the story:

> In the rectory in which I lived I fought with the idea of rectories, . . . I loved my work but I hated the rectory life and I lived for 15 months in a very typical rectory situation. . . . It ended up with the rector trying to get rid of me and my refusal to go. The personnel board of the diocese had to conduct a hearing and investigation and it ended up with my being allowed to stay but it was still a bad situation. . . . The rector thought that I was too radical. He was the type of person that considered the rectory his home and he was the father. . . . He presented me with three type-written pages of rules and regulations which I refused to go along with. . . . For example, if anyone invited me out to their home I was to refuse unless they also asked him and the other curates. . . . I didn't think that he was serious, but he was very serious about it. . . . He came and removed the doors from our studies so that there would be no secrets between us — that was his reason for that. . . . I told him that he should put the door back on or I was moving, and he didn't, so I moved. . . . But he is very hypersensitive and by doing that, he felt that I was rejecting him. . . . I did try to explain to him that I could not work like that, but it did no good. . . . You know I wasn't looking for trouble but at the same time he wasn't going to push me around. . . . I certainly never looked for a fight. . . . It got to the point where it didn't make any difference whether you talked to him or not; he heard what he wanted to hear. . . . So if he told me to do something or if he told me not to do something, and if I didn't like it I did just what I wanted to do. . . . If he found out, then the words would fly. . . . He backed me into a corner. . . . You couldn't reason with him. . . . I tried to. . . . I hated living in the rectory where I was. I don't see any necessity for living in rectories, and I think that it would be much better if we would try to come up with another solution. . . . That has been my greatest difficulty in the last 15 months, living in a rectory. . . . My professional life has been happy, but my private life has not. Then I started a few adult discussion groups. . . . He thought that these people were trying to by-pass his authority

and take over the parish. He was very strong in that. . . . He thought that the whole parish was a family of which he was the father. . . . So he tried to get rid of me. . . . But I wanted to stay because I liked the people and because I felt I had done nothing that warranted my leaving. . . . I fought it out because to leave would have been a disservice to myself and to all the other curates in the diocese.

The young priest went to the diocesan personnel board. The board heard both sides of the story and he was assigned to another parish. Before he went to the new parish he interviewed the pastor, determined that he could operate more freely and decided to accept the appointment.

The new pastor is ill and has an elderly mother to care for and so was pleased to obtain a young curate to do the work. This young priest can now have his adult discussion groups and engage in other pastoral activities of his choice. "Well, I wanted the freedom to be able to do my work, and to be able to do it as I thought it should be done," he says of his decision to move into this new work.

This young man does not intend to live in the rectory lifestyle of his first assignment. He is sure that there was something wrong there and that there must be an alternative created to this kind of closed-in living. He says:

> The rectory cuts you away from people. You are living a life completely separate and distinct from the type of life that the people are living, and I think it is all very unnecessary. You know I don't think that it is helping me personally either. I mean I could be happier living some other way and probably do a better job of my work because of that. I would like to conclude that in several years everything will be changed and I intend to work with God in the meantime.

This priest wants to have the option of getting married; he wants to live in an environment of his own choice outside of the rectory, and he wants to organize his professional work along lines that he thinks appropriate and productive. He is prepared to confront the authorities to achieve his ends; he has, to some extent, already confronted them and worked out what may be an acceptable program. He relies on his faith in God, his own considerable energies and talents, his strong drive for a radicalized independence, and his hope for the changes in society and in the Church that he feels are working in his direction. His radicalism is not totally wild-eyed. It contains a certain prudence and moderation which center around his unwillingness to hurt others unless they block unreasonably the goals that he is beginning to set for himself. He has an easy conscience both for himself and for the faithful. His thinking on several issues may represent the kind of variation in practice from official Church positions that is common in many priests these days. He does not intend to leave the priesthood:

> I regard the priest as just another member of the community, a profession in its own right, and his personal side is his. Therefore, I am against any type of clericalism. I don't see that a priest should be called Father. I don't see that we should dress in a Roman collar, and I don't think that we should live apart from the way people are living. . . . I don't think that the system that calls for respect for a priest because he is a priest has helped any.

Here he is being the independent radical that his father was never able to be.

At his youthful age he may appear to be somewhat presumptuous when he says:

> Well, I feel that adult education is one of the primary necessities in the Church right now. I don't think it does much good to put all your efforts into religious education, because it's the parents of the kids that are the ones who are most confused. . . . The parents need an awful lot of attention; they can't make any decisions by themselves.

It is interesting that this priest is classified in the category of "developing." He really did not begin to become an effective person until he left his troubled home to enter the seminary. It was the seminary life that freed him to grow, to assert his independence, to release his guilt, to escape the maternal dominance, and to deal with his rivalrous hatred toward his father. He has been able to loosen up, to allow a new and more self-confident self to be put on trial as it were, without losing the respect of others. He is beginning to confront life and its difficulties openly and directly. Prior to entering the seminary his life was marked by withdrawal, hidden resentment, guilt, and anxiety. Now his new manifestations of growth are not particularly easy for his colleagues and superiors to accept. He is seeking closer relationships with people by his methods of working in the parish, by encouraging parishioners to invite him to their homes, and by initiating adult education groups. In doing this, and in succeeding at it, he will certainly be exercising successful

personal independence. In seeking to emancipate himself from the neurotic role thrust upon him by his mother, he tends to over-react; this
overreaction is a blend of warm, energetic and productive missionary
zeal without too much thought and feeling for how he may be under-
mining the more traditional religious and cultural viewpoints. He remains
fearful of getting into situations where he will be manipulated and taken
advantage of as his father was by his mother. This young priest prizes
his ability to control himself in the interests of prudence and moderation
in any circumstances; this is clearly a major positive resource of his
personality. With his new-found growth and independence he is not
going to submit unthinkingly to any rigid set of rules from any authoritarian person. This was rejected when he "left" his mother, that is,
when he finally was able to separate himself from her psychologically.

This man no longer looks on traditional forms of prayers with the
same reverence he once accorded to them. He has a simple belief in
God:

> I really do believe that there is a personal God that loves me as a
> person, and who has the same love for all men, and that He loved
> His Church, and He left the Church with the responsibility of
> preaching His Gospel and establishing and showing His love for
> man. I do believe that this is something that can be done, and I do
> believe that Christianity is something that can work.

He thinks that the community nature of the Church is a vitally important reality. His greatest difficulty in the interview came in his discussion
of the Eucharist, the current theological discussions of which he hopes
will clarify things. It is God's love for him as a person, as he is, that he
feels is the essence of his faith. He views the priesthood as a profession,
somewhat analogous to the law, and he resents having it set apart in
any way. The main function of duty of the priest is to create unity and
communion among the people that he leads.

The most significant event in this man's life and in his priesthood was
the death of his father. Can it be said that the father's death lessened
his commitment to the priesthood? Perhaps this is true with regard to
the traditional authoritarian priesthood that involved the maternal domination and idealization of the son as against the father. But it would be
less true with respect to the new self that he has realized through his
father's death and through the awakening seminary and the post-seminary
rectory experience on which he is trying to build his life.

His future in the priesthood may be less certain than his future in life.

If he continues to grow as he has begun and as he hopes to, he will marry and move into non-institutional, non-clerical work. His personal growth is very important to him now; this search for his full self is at the center of his concerns now. As a developing person he represents a real challenge to the institutional Church but hardly a greater challenge than some other priests that it has successfully nurtured within its confines.

Further Case Histories

The developing person is someone whose growth, although repressed or interrupted for a long period of time, begins again at a later stage in life. He typically encounters the problems that are characteristic at an early stage in life at a time when he should long since have dealt with these. It is not surprising, in the developing category, to find middle-aged men who are still working through adolescent difficulties.

A good example is the man in his early forties who has begun to deal with the elements of his own growth but who has not really been able to integrate his new experience as yet. He is a socially and mentally intelligent man who, in general, is satisfied with his priesthood and his current work, if not with the structures of the Church as they are now. He has what might be described as a type of split personality. On the other hand, he is liberal in his ideas in a moderate kind of way; he can face and understand what is occurring in the Church and even look at his own life and judge that much of his home and seminary education was quite repressive and that this had a sharp influence on his own lack of full development. He knows that something should be done to counteract these possibly negative influences in the lives of others. At the same time, however, he is not free from a deeply ingrained puritanical and authoritarian emotional pattern of life which still influences him. He cannot, in other words, always do what he is intellectually convinced that he should do because he still experiences guilt when he departs from the rigid path on which he learned to walk.

At the present time the principal area of conflict in his life centers around his professional relations with others, especially women. Given the liberalization of ideas within the Church, he gradually has become more and more deeply involved with a variety of women on various levels of his priestly work. He is doing good work in many of these contacts. He has not yet, however, worked out viable ways of handling the affectional and sexual urges that arise in the context of this work. This experience of his own sexuality is something new for him. Because of his repressed background, he is awkward in dealing with it. He handles the guilt that arises from his contacts with women in a variety of ways; confession, discussing his problems with his friends, but also by punishing himself in various ways — for example, he forces himself to recite the breviary even though he considers this a truly meaningless task.

This man also feels uneasy about the amount of time that he gives to interpersonal contacts. He believes in the Church and is a man of prayer, even though in the latter area he is having a difficult time working out his feelings about its formal structure. This priest is moderate in his outlook and is willing to work within the context of the present Church structures for constructive changes. His problem comes from the developmental challenge of trying to learn, at the beginning of middle age, how to relate to women in a mature manner. There are many priests in this category with similar problems. He is by no means an isolated example. Clearly he demonstrates the difficulties which good men experience because of delayed growth.

Yet, another example is a man in his late twenties who has come to re-examine his manner of living and, as a consequence, has opened himself to much pain in trying to grow. Until recent years he related as a little boy to all father or authority figures. He has always needed approval very much and, in fact, has orchestrated his life to obtain these responses from others. Again, he is an example of a man who has just begun to realize how much he identified with the feminine role because of the influence of a dominating mother and the ineffectiveness of his somewhat retiring father.

He has come to understand how he has carried the "little boy" role over into adult life; this insight has made him distinctly uncomfortable. As he notes, he asks himself currently, "Is this all there is?" He is actively inspecting his life and the values and tactics he has employed to get through it so far. Much of this introspection was precipitated by the unexpected death of his brother last year. This young priest's frustration now is his difficulty in coming to grips with renewed growth. His life is now in a state of flux. He always considered himself a small-town boy who looked with a certain amount of distance and awe at the big city type of people. Now he feels more pressed to compete, to move in on what he calls "the big leagues" in order to make the Church more responsive to people. He also realizes that doing this will make him experience more anxiety about his personal adjustment and about the meaning of his Christian faith.

This priest feels a great void in his life because of the lack of a family, that is, other persons with whom he can truly be intimate. He is not concerned merely with sexuality but rather with the overall meaning of healthy adult personal relationships. This man is clearly at a trying but significant point of development in his life. He has the necessary resources to continue his growth, but he also needs help and encouragement to achieve the kind of maturity which he is seeking. He would not have these problems if he were not growing; he would still be the "little boy" getting others to like him.

An example of an older man who has begun to develop again is the priest in his mid-fifties, an immigrant to the United States, who has recently emerged from his very intellectualized world and begun to grow as a person once more. This was occasioned by his going back to school after thirty years in the priesthood. A renewed educational experience opened a new world to him; it also motivated him to look into his style of relationship with other persons and at the manner in which he related as a Christian to current social problems. As a result, this priest is really attempting to make use of every talent he has in order to develop himself into a more effective person and priest. He has not only had many new and interesting intellectual experiences, but he has experienced the trials of emotional growth as well. He has grown closer to other persons and, in the words of the interviewer, "This man, in the later years of his life, has reached a high level of maturity and a general openness and a greater concern for mankind."

Probably the most developmental aspect of this priest's experience has been his newfound capacity to relate closely and responsibly with women. This whole side of his personality has only developed within the last few years. He does not fear this kind of experience but has entered it with a sense of generosity and desire to grow. In fact, this priest is functioning more maturely than ever; all indications point to his confirmed development even though he is in his late middle years.

Yet another and very different example is the contemplative monk who, although he is not quite at mid-life, has had very varied experiences. He left the life of the parish priesthood because, as he described it, he could not face dealing with groups of people as he was required to do as a preacher and an administrator. He knows that his fears drove him into the monastery, fears that were reinforced by his difficulty with academic studies throughout his life. He has had a generally negative idea of himself for most of his adult life and, because he has been rather passive and dependent, he has not been able to respond to his own inner emotional difficulties with much force. This priest always looked to authority for sustenance and always did whatever was necessary to get response and support from them.

This priest has, however, learned a lot recently. He knows that he has been over-dependent and that he has not had a healthy concept of authority. He has begun to realize clearly that he is much too fearful in his relationships with other persons and that he cannot just let this go. He knows that he must do something about it. He has faced his fear of interpersonal involvement and he is willing to take the means necessary to improve his interpersonal life. This priest has discovered, somewhat to his surprise, that he has more resources in his personality than he had suspected. This man, in fact, began to explore his own interpersonal life while at the same time he has been able to preserve his faith and his vocation in the monastery. He has received assistance from a monk-confrere who has had training in psychology and has also begun to participate in encounter groups conducted by a woman; all this has been very helpful to him. He is strongly motivated to grow and perceives the development of his own human potential as an intrinsically religious action. This is not an easy challenge for a man of his years and previous experience but he seems to be meeting it in a healthy manner. He will change a good deal more before he is finished growing, but he is determind to meet the challenges of life more maturely than he has in the past.

Another example of the developing person is the middle-aged seminary rector who has begun to confront his own previous tendencies to be passive and receptive in his relationships with other persons. He knows that his previous passive and docile attitudes enabled him to function smoothly within the structure of the Church because he always accepted people and situations without much conflict. Now he understands that his passive attitude has actually prevented him from being more effective; he knows that he has been remiss in his failure to take more initiative both in judgment and action in responding to the situations in which he has been involved. This priest now recognizes, and this is painful for him, that his passivity was motivated by his strong need to please, to be obedient, and to avoid conflict and unpleasantness. He now matches this insight against his own possibilities for growth; he has actively begun to explore himself in order to develop his own mature assertiveness.

This man has also begun to deal with his long-repressed need for affection and closer involvement with other people. He has resolved this to some extent through his pastoral and counseling work with other people. He knows, however, that his relationships with others were almost always through his role as a priest and never through himself as a person. He shielded himself, as he sees it, from the responsibilities that a man should have if he is truly to be in relationship with others, especially with women. He is dealing with these problems at the present time but it does not seem that he will leave the Church or the priesthood in order to marry. He would, however, favor marriage for priests because of the developmental possibilities of marriage and the fact that he does not believe that it would interfere nearly as much with priestly functions as some claim. This man enjoys being a priest and is effective at it. He has begun to understand some of the emotional reactions within himself which have contributed to his attitudes towards his work and other people over the years. He is working at growing and, while this is painful, he seems to be proceeding in a mature manner.

Developing priests are found in every section of the country, in every kind of work, and at every age level. Their problems have a certain similarity and they can recognize their common struggle to develop as persons. They need some recognition of the fact that their development has been delayed and that renewed growth offers very difficult challenges for them, especially when they meet it in mid-life or beyond. One thing is clear: once a man begins to grow as a person, this becomes the most important business for him in his life because it represents the real search for his own personality.

CHAPTER VII

THE DEVELOPED

Good health, whether it is physical or psychological, has always been easier to recognize than to describe. It is not easy to put into words what amounts to the basic personal experience of living. To understand health, one must take a close look at healthy people and then try to approximate what they are like in descriptive terms. This has been traditionally difficult because healthy people do not fall conveniently into neat categories precisely because they are healthy. One of the signs of health is the way in which people manifest their separate and unique personalities. This is not to champion eccentricity, but wholesome individuality. Healthy people enjoy and exercise the freedom to be different from each other in a constructive manner.

We cannot, however, speak of health as a state of absolute perfection. The developed priests in the present study are found at the healthy end of the continuum of development, the men who demonstrate achieved growth rather than problem or conflict-free behavior. Developed persons have passed through the stages of growth in an appropriately human manner. They may have had to struggle and suffer in order to resolve difficulties along the way, but they have persisted in forward movement and have attained a level of personal integration which can be described as mature. Developed individuals are not finished personalities; they are persons who are still growing, still meeting the challenges of their adult life, experiencing conflicts which they must handle constructively, always confronting the newly evolving problems that never come to an end for any human being.

An interesting example of a man who has achieved genuine development is the early middle-aged pastor whose motivation for entering the seminary was his doubt rather than his conviction about the faith. From this difficult beginning he has moved through many other challenges to a healthy and effective independence.

No steps in the developmental stages are skipped for these healthy

133

people. They do not pass through them without effort nor do they emerge from them without scars. Healthy people look as if they have lived; they do not have an exemption from its wrinkling stresses. That is the way the developed men in the priesthood look. They are not like some mythical children of nature preserved innocently free from the ravages of life. Developed priests have faced and worked through many problems, enlarging themselves and their possibilities in the process. They emerge as imperfect but as well put together, or as psychologists say, well-integrated. They have had, of course, good resources and, in general, favorable conditions for their passage to maturity. These priests do, however, show that they have taken life seriously. Clearly they have been deeply engaged in the process of living.

A major religious superior provides us with a good example of healthy and dynamic adjustment in the priesthood. As described by the interviewer, "he is a very perceptive man who early in his life tended to recognize both his above-average potential and his need for and love of organizing. His mildly compulsive defensive system has served this man quite well. It has allowed him to be quite productive, administratively and professionally successful, and it has also helped him to deal with sexual feelings. . . . I feel that he has a realistic perspective on the limits of his defenses." He is clearly a man who is not a perfect personality but one who deals more than adequately with the problems of life. He is, in a word, healthy.

It is also important to note that there are not many highly developed personalities in any population. Indeed, full growth seems to be restricted to relatively few persons in any culture. There are few comparative data but, for example, in the research done on mental health workers in the United States, Sims and Henry (personal communication) suggest in their study of mental health specialists that the number of fully developed does not exceed five per cent. There is not necessarily something wrong with a profession merely because it does not have a large number of fully developed men. There may be some difficulty for a profession if it presumes that more of its members are mature than they in fact are. It is not to place an excessive premium on personal maturity to observe that a small percentage of persons genuinely attain it. This is not to say that everyone else is sick, for this term can only lead us to misinterpret the fact that most persons are still dealing with growth problems. Most people, in other words, have not worked through completely the stages of personal development. They may be engaged in the task, or stuck for one reason or another at some plateau, but it would be incorrect to apply the word *sick* to all of them. It is also important to realize the difficulties that are involved in defining health, adjustment, or integration. Just as it is hard to make news with good news because of our fascination with that which is bad, so we can describe what goes wrong with man better than what is right about him.

Certain fundamental decisions were made at the outset of this research, however, in selecting the norms which would be employed in discussing the nature of healthy growth and in making clinical judgments about the level of development which the subjects had reached. The first decision was not to accept the definition of health which implied adjustment only within a certain social system, in this case, the priesthood itself. That is to say, one can conceive of a person being adjusted within the priesthood, performing its functions in an adequate if not an exceptional manner, and yet having major, unresolved personal growth problems. In a sense, we can describe this man as adjusted because, with some minimal satisfactions, he is carrying out his role in life. This, however, falls short of giving a definition of adjustment which would stand up outside of a particular social or work structure. The latter, whether a profession, school, or a family, may protect and support a wide variety of fragile adjustments. Health is not just getting along within a certain system. It has a more transcendant aspect; it must hold up outside these limits where it lacks the protection which these structures offer. Maturity endures in any human situation. Judgments about health in this study are based on this latter understanding of it.

Health is not the absence of symptoms nor the absence of conflict. It signifies rather that a person is in good contact with himself and that he lives in a reasonably constructive fashion, that he identifies and deals with his problems in an effective and positive manner. Health is not perfection but a living process of continuing growth. It cannot be conceptualized as a static or permanently achieved condition which, like a trophy, or a uniform number, we can retire. Nor do we possess health as we might a bank account, a house, or a painting. It is more like a good reputation, dynamic in nature, and dependent upon a continued response to life's challenges. It does not exist outside of the persons who manifest it. It is important to note, however, that adjustment does not mean being a famous or outstanding person. Being healthy is not equated with public productivity, although it is not necessarily absent from this either. Many creative people are well developed. Many well developed are not creative in the popular sense. Health is reflected in a kind of productivity or creativity which is interpersonal in nature. Well-adjusted persons are productive through being good husbands and good fathers, through the expression of their health in the significant relationships of their lives. This is particularly relevant for this population of priests, who have fundamental opportunities for this kind of productivity through their pastoral relationships with other persons.

A priest of quite average talents who has used them well because of his personal development is a seminary teacher in his late thirties who came from a sound, if mildly overprotective family. As the interviewer noted, "His feelings of comfort and adequacy in his own family provided him with experiences of warmth and a capacity for intimacy which have generalized to most relationships." This basic experience enables him to deal constructively with his own problems and with the challenges of his work. Although not perfect, he is obviously quite healthy and quite effective and happy as a priest.

Students of human behavior have provided a number of synthetic lists through which they try to describe the characteristics of full development, dynamic growth, or good adjustment. All these terms are roughly equivalent. One of the most useful of these lists was provided by Levine (1942).

His criteria are either found in most other subsequent lists or they can be related quite easily to them. He does not propose psychological adjustment as an easily attained condition. In fact, it is more a goal that people continually seek throughout their lives. His list, and the lists of most other observers, reflect what Freud wrote (1937): "A normal ego is, like normality in general, an ideal fiction." Levine offers the following as the signs of emotional maturity:

A. An ability to be guided by reality rather than by fears.
B. The use of long term values (This would, for this population, point to religious convictions, and an intrinsic kind of religious faith which integrates and supports life's directions and decisions).
C. A grown-up conscience (Here again the internalized aspect emphasizing adult self-control in the light of a good relationship to reality and its demands is important).
D. Independence.
E. Capacity to love someone else but with an enlightened self-interest.
F. A reasonable dependence.
G. A reasonable aggressiveness.
H. Healthy defense mechanisms.

I. Good sexual adjustment with acceptance of one's own gender.

J. Good work adjustment.

No man, then, appears on the scene without problems or without a need to face and deal with his own challenges of growth. Health is a relative kind of perfection. Good health emerges, in other words, as a person integrates or places in proper relationship these various important factors in human living. A well-developed person, for example, is not someone who has totally eliminated aggressiveness from his personality. He knows when and how to be aggressive in the pursuit of reasonable goals and healthy self-fulfillment. Many persons make the mistake of trying to eliminate one or the other of the characteristics, such as aggressiveness or dependence, which actually play important parts in the overall functioning of well-developed persons.

It is also important to note, as Engel (1962) has, that at times the well-developed person will experience in his life certain dimensions which would normally be described as unhealthy functions. Engel offers grief as an example, noting that this disordered reaction is not generally considered beneficial to the total adjustment of a person; yet he points out that the experience of grief also has healthy reparative and adaptive effects on an individual. Grief, an example of a temporary departure in some way from normal behavior, may be essential for healthy functioning.

It is important to note that almost all psychological theorists on man relate the development of the personality through the process of growth to his earliest childhood experiences. It is clear that this is true of American priests. This is not to demand absolutely perfect conditions in the home life and upbringing of the individuals under consideration. This too is a relative experience in which the positive factors that make for growth outweigh the inevitable imperfections that are found in any human situation. It is, nonetheless, clear that many major difficulties, the impediments to growth, have their roots in traumatic early life experiences. This is described in the section on the maldeveloped in some greater detail. However, just as what can go wrong with the individual may be traced back to the harsh emotional deprivation of childhood, so too what is right with the individual can be seen to have arisen from factors that go into a healthy early environment. Essential to this in any home is the relationship between the husband and wife who are also father and mother. If this is a healthy relationship, then the home life will be an environment conductive to the growth of well-adjusted individuals. There is no substitute for this because the emotional learning at this time in life is so potent in shaping the individual's later responses to himself and to others. In other words, the individual's fundamental attitude toward himself, and toward his own possibilities for growth are formed at a very early age. When this is done right, then very little in life can thwart the individual's development towards maturity. When there is something wrong, it is very difficult to make up for what has been missing in the emotional climate of the child's family life.

Saul (1960) emphasizes the importance of continuing growth, the person's ongoing interaction with life and its possible changes, problems, and new challenges. A person is not on automatic pilot. He may be headed in the right direction by the favorable conditions of his early home life and his developmental years, but the mature person must still interact with his environment. This interaction is the way a person expresses his health. As Saul expresses it:

> Mental and emotional health is the adequate achievement of emotional maturity, which means the growth from helplessness and need for love to the capacity to love, to be a good responsible spouse, parent, and citizen; and this depends upon good human relations in the earliest years, for the patterns of these feelings and relationships continue on through adult life [p. 343].

We note, then, the continuity of life. It is not a random series of events but a process whose appearance at one stage is related always to what it looked like at an earlier stage. Nothing happens without reason and without cause as far as psychological adjustment goes. An understanding of the process of human growth enables us to trace back a person's present behavior to the significant situations of his earlier life. The truth of this psychological observation is underscored by the present study.

Part Two: Case History

This developed priest is in his mid-thirties and teaches "religious theology" to high school students on a full-time basis.

He is rugged in physical appearance and yet soft spoken and sensitive. During the interview he was at ease and set up a very personal relationship with the interviewer who responded very positively to this priest. The priest is the next to the last child in a large family; his parents were immigrants from Europe. The relationships within the family were warm and productive, although the relationship with the father was less personal and intense than with the matriarchal mother who strongly influenced the life of the family. The priest describes himself as the mother's favorite child, and he notes that he was careful to repay her psychologically for his favored position in the family once he was ordained.

This man recalls sieges of illness in his early life as notable events which affected his position in the family, school, the seminary, and in his job assignments. Counteracting the dependence and experience of favoritism reinforced by his various illnesses are his strengths: creative intelligence, physical aggression, and financial responsibility. He has, in fact, demonstrated distinct leadership capacities in a variety of roles in his life. This priest has a strong personality and controlling his aggression was not easy. The choice of the priesthood was to a certain degree a function of his efforts to control these impulses. After entering the seminary his aggression became more wholesomely sublimated. He describes it this way:

> I was a very sickly individual as a child. . . . I would say that my mother favored me more than anyone else because I was more sickly than any of the others. . . . She also saw that I was much more responsible around the house. . . . There were many things that I would do that she didn't have to tell me to do. . . . I can't stand anything that's messy. . . . I know of many times that I would tell my brothers and sisters why didn't they pick up after themselves. . . . And many times I felt sorry for mother because she did have a lot of work. . . . My mother was a proud and jealous woman, proud of me in the priesthood. . . . I spent every Sunday after Mass with my mother. . . . She would never accept an invitation to go elsewhere then because 'Father is coming.'. . . . Her kitchen was my favorite place in the house. I'd come in and there was one particular place I used to take. After a while my brother would come along; he is single. Mother would cook dinner, and so he would park himself in that chair. Come one o'clock he would have to move because Father was coming and if he didn't move he was going to have hell on his hands. She would never let it pass. . . . The finest china and silverware was for Father alone. . . . She always called me Father and she insisted that all of my brothers and sisters, nieces and nephews call me Father. She insisted on this and they complied. . . . There were many similar things to this. . . . You know I always saw her every Sunday that I possibly could. It was dedicated to her.

This priest made his decision to join a religious community as a way, as he saw it, to retain the personal independence which he prizes highly.

He decided to enter a community that had no vows. "If it didn't work out, I could walk out," he says. He underwent a variety of individualized and seemingly custom-tailored experiences in the seminary, was sent to Europe to complete his professional education and then he returned to this country for his assignment. From the beginning he was determined to function independently and to do pretty much as he pleased, providing he maintained the fundamental requirements of his job:

> When I came back from Europe my superior tried to limit my hours. At 8 o'clock I was told to be in and to go to bed. . . . I told him to forget this jazz; my work with people required that I be out. . . . I had it out with the superior again and they let me have my own way. . . . I tried to make it clear to them that as long as I was doing my job, saying Mass in the morning, going to school and teaching, etc., that they shouldn't complain. . . . This is what I told the Fathers. . . . I said if a man is over 21 he should know his responsibilities, and if he doesn't, it's his problem. Finally, more or less, they accepted these ideas of mine and they began to do things in their lives the way I do in mine. . . . It used to be that one had to do everything together and you lost your identity. You were lost. I feel that my identity is much more pronounced if I am with people, but also still on my own independently. . . . So, now they do what I do. . . . Now I think we have a good relationship.

Here is a man who, by the force of his will and character, by his own energy and determination, has not only made his own life more functional but has also introduced through his expressed convictions and example some salutary changes in the lives of his colleagues.

This priest also has some very strong and individualistic ideas about how his work should be conducted. He has become a full-time teacher of religion in the local high school. He refused to teach anything other than religion, justifying his position by noting that this is what he was prepared to do and this was where the times demanded that he be. He was also determined to improve on how he himself had been taught religion:

> In grade and high school I was taught religion dogmatically. . . . Everything was forced on me and there was no way out of it. . . . And this was repelling to a kid at that time. . . . It was also disgraceful teaching. . . . There was too much parroting and the students really did not understand the religion. What I wanted to do,

and did, was to challenge the students. I made shocking statements to get them to think, and to question their religion; to ask themselves why they believe it. . . . I must say that my methods are successful. . . . I consider myself to be a truth seeker, and I believe that there is truth in everything, although we may have to call it out. And I will use any source for truth. I try to expose the students to many different views and let them decide for themselves what they should have. . . . I don't believe that the Catholic Church has a monopoly on truth. Once the Church understands the modern conception of man and his needs, she will no longer be paternalistic but will really be a spiritual guide toward the maturity of the individual. To me the priesthood is not a form of prestige or a form of authority, but it is really a way to give service. . . . And I found out for myself that every human being is in the service of everybody and that's what I want to push right through. And this is what I want to have the students see and appreciate. To do this they have to clarify their sense of religion. . . . Religion to me is not just dogma or defining God. Defining God places limits on him as far as I am concerned. I want the students to see religion as more loving. And I must say that a lot of students have come along with me.

This priest is also concerned with his relationships with his peers and friends. These are important to him and they nurture much of his life. He feels strongly that some of the externals and the accidentals of the priesthood are obstacles to effective human relationships and to the development of healthy independence. As an example, he mentions the wearing of his priestly habit:

I am proud of being a priest, yet I don't think that you have to wear a habit to be effective. . . . What is the good of going around in a habit and not being what I am supposed to be? Many times when I have worn my habit people would just move away from me. . . . When I wore my collar people would stand back and wouldn't really open up. . . . At a party I tell my friends, 'Don't introduce me as a priest.' It is not that I am ashamed or afraid of it. . . . but simply that the collar is a detriment to a good and open relationship. . . . This isn't always true. It depends on the circumstances and a priest has to judge for himself. . . . Teaching and the priesthood give me a sense of fulfillment. . . . It is how I can provide others with some sense of life, some sense of value. . . . In teaching I am forming the future. . . . I enjoy helping to make a better life for people. But they must be given the challenges of doing religion on their own. . . . You can't form religion.

Asked about the life of his faith and what he does to sustain and nourish religion in his own life, he replied:

I don't use the rosary and I don't use a breviary. What I do is I read and then I meditate. That's how I prepare for my classes. This has enriched my spirituality.

This priest is strongly for optional celibacy but he would definitely not get married himself if he were given the option. He does not feel that he could be happy in marriage because he would not be as free to carry on his ministry as he is now. He knows that he could never be home at a prescribed hour if told to do so by anyone. Sexuality is not a threatening area for him. He feels that he has normal sex drives and needs and that he could easily have sex relations if he wanted them. But he curbs himself and moves away when such opportunities arise, as they sometimes do in every man's life. He would do nothing to disgrace the priesthood nor bring dishonor on his own individuality. This is not because he thinks that sex experiences are necessarily immoral:

I don't think that pre-marital sex is always sinful. And I don't think that masturbation is sinful at all. . . . I teach a marriage course where sexuality is involved, and my aim is to remove the guilt feelings from the individual. . . . I don't accept the theory of mortal and venial sin. I teach that *sin is sin,* period. I define it as one's lack of response to life. . . . I cannot find an answer yet to all the problems about sex. But I am seeking the answers from moralists and theologians.

He feels that he has seen too much of life and read too widely to feel that much guilt or sinfulness can be integrally associated with sexual behavior.

He discusses his attitudes and his feelings about the place of sex in life and the importance of teaching appropriately about it:

Well, you see I believe that sex is very important in the life of man. . . . I can't be a person without being sexually inclined. I understand the sex conflicts that adolescents and young adults are having because I am experiencing the same things. . . . People are afraid to talk about it and to come out and to say that I am a sexual being.

. . . When I teach about sex I am very realistic in what I say and some people object to this. . . . We discuss the contemporary movies and theater which are largely concerned with sex and violence. I have to tell the truth about life and the sex in it if I am to be believed by them and if I am to get across to the young people the message of Christ.

This young priest is very sociable and personable in his dealings with others. He is now and has always been a leader in the groups in which he finds himself. He deals with others in an open, straightforward and even an intimate way. This does not leave him without faults. He is capable of being a bit patronizing, garrulous, and manipulative. However, these are not major problems. He wants above all to bring life and values to others. A reflective and perceptive person, he is not caught up in any narcissistic self-examination. His opinion of himself is positive and he is rarely troubled by doubts, self-criticism, or feelings of inferiority and inadequacy.

In his work assignments he has demanded and exhibited a high degree of autonomy and independence. He has demonstrated competence, at least in his own mind, as a teacher, counselor, assistant pastor, acting pastor, and as a disciplinarian. He does not complain, seems to accept things pretty much as they are, works in the present, and measures his satisfaction in terms of his service to others. It is anticipated that he will continue to grow usefully and productively in the priesthood.

This priest feels that the Church should be open to all sources of knowledge. His attitude and his behavior are liberal and forward-looking. The Church, he believes, should emphasize spirituality in a vivid, relevant, and expansive way. This man is proud of being a priest and his priesthood is well integrated with his personality. He has thought through the relevant aspects of his life and his profession, and he is content to stand upon and to attempt to share his deep convictions.

This priest is a fully functioning and self-actualized person. In his relations with others he is responsibly intimate, sensitive, and neither passive nor gullible. He manages his time well and makes a real attempt to integrate knowledge and to communicate his wisdom to others in order to stimulate them to do the same. His strong identity allows him to have mature relationships with others. He has a history of appropriate psychosexual adjustments with men and women which allows him to have an open stance toward the meaning and place of sex in life. His primary orientation is spiritual; he actively seeks, through meditation and the search for knowledge, to make his faith real and to communicate this reality to others. He is somewhat unconventional but not in a rebellious or destructive way. The measure of all that he does is its value for his spiritual growth and for the growth of others.

In the various positions of authority that he has held he appears to have demonstrated the qualities of responsibility and sensitivity befitting these positions. The interviewer could not but be aware of some tendency to dramatize himself and his role in life and to manipulate himself and others in the achievement of his goals; these are, however, the inevitable signs of the imperfections that are part of even the most developed men.

Further Case Histories

It is important to recall that developed persons are neither perfect nor free of stress. Developed people deal with their problems in a constructive manner, but this does not eliminate problems from their lives. They do not have flawless life histories nor are they completely perfect in the way they carry out their tasks at the present time. They do, however, represent what human beings look like when they are fully grown.

An example is the priest in early middle-age who presents himself as quite open and spontaneous. The interviewer notes that his ideas reflect intelligence and careful thought and that he is able to express them forcefully and effectively.

His father died when this priest was only an infant, the youngest in the family. This is a good example of how healthy coping with a difficult family situation can make up for a traumatic event in an individual's background. The mother of the family was able to raise the family by herself and to help the children develop traits of independence and responsibility. This individual experienced a combination of freedom and control which permitted him to test his capacities without over-reaching himself; as a result he developed a sense of competence and confidence in his abilities. He was successful and relaxed in school and had a wide circle of friends. He decided to enter the seminary because of the impression made upon him by a priest who took a special interest in him. It is clear that this vocational decision may at least partly be interpreted as motivated by identification with a healthy father surrogate.

Interestingly enough, this priest hated what he described as the regimentation, superficiality, and pedantry of seminary life. He stayed in the seminary, and other developed persons report the same reaction, only because he was able to keep the goal of getting out clearly in mind. During this period his independence and assertiveness caused a certain tension between him and the seminary faculty. He has maintained his independent and assertive style since ordination, although it has been moderated by his general maturity and reasonably good judgment. He is very capable and intelligent and thinks through carefully his work in the priesthood.

This developed person finds the priesthood exciting and challenging. He thrives on the difficult tasks which constantly come to him, and as he responds to these successfully he experiences a deep sense of satisfaction. He is able to recognize areas of dissatisfaction in his life, such as interference in his work by authority, his own experience of loneliness, and the problem of celibacy. He accepts these as necessary evils which are outweighed by the positive satisfactions he knows in the priesthood. This man's psychosexual adjustment is good. He had normal social experiences during adolescence and has integrated his sexual impulses in a successful way into his personality. His sexuality is not a source of guilt or conflict. He is close to many people, actively developing and maintaining relationships which have an appropriate degree of intimacy. He is not, however, unduly dependent on such relationships, nor is he impeded in his activities by the demands of such relationships. This priest represents an unusually well adjusted, effective person who thoroughly enjoys his work, who is realistically self-acceptant, and who is clearly well developed, even though his life has not been free of stress or conflict.

A very different kind of developed man is the middle-aged priest who presently lives the life of a hermit. Despite this, he is alert, friendly, spontaneous and quite able to speak about himself undefensively. This man was able to describe his own problems without denying them; he knows that in certain areas he must meet his own needs and that this does not interfere with his service of God. He is similarly tolerant of his sexual and aggressive impulses, although he does not yield to these or permit them any expression in his life. He recognizes them as aspects of his humanity and neither apologizes for them nor excuses them. In fact, altogether, this priest is able to accept himself in a healthy manner and with very little distortion or need for defensive maneuvers.

On an interpersonal level the subject relates to others in a warm and open manner. He enjoys companionship but has tried to center his life on a very deep and internalized faith, in which his conviction about the importance of prayer is a central value. He believes that his prayer is vitally important for other persons and that his choice of solitude is helpful for carrying out what he perceives as his vocation in life. The interviewer describes him as "a healthy, insightful, self-acceptant individual who has found a life congenial to his needs and that is simultaneously productive . . . within the life he has chosen this priest has adjusted quite well and is a mature, self-actualizing person."

CHAPTER VIII

SOME SPECIAL CONSIDERATIONS

Some special observations must be made about certain older priests within the population. These are men who have adjusted to the conditions of life in the priesthood with integrity and occupational effectiveness, even though these are areas of their personalities which are not fully developed. There is a rounded quality to their lives, an unself-conscious sense of achievement as they look back at their work, a sense about them that everything is now in place, that they have finished the course and kept the faith. These men are remarkable because they seem to have achieved what many other men never do — a genuine peace within themselves. At the same time it is clear that, in certain significant portions of their experience, they have not grown very much at all. This may explain the appealing and impressive qualities which make them attractive as persons. They have a much prized child-like quality because they are, in their relationships with other persons, more child-like than adult; indeed, they have had practically no experience of intimacy and they have not integrated their sexuality in a mature way. They are, psychologically speaking, like admirable children who have been exempt from ever having to deal with some of the difficult growth issues of life. They have preserved a certain innocence through which they have kept at a distance from other persons, never truly drawing close to anyone, yet serving them with an unspoiled and relatively uncomplicated dedication. Their celibacy is that of persons who have successfully looked away from their sexuality, using sublimation through which their energies have gone into their work and their conscientious efforts to live by the conditions to which they agreed when they entered the seminary. They have, in effect, done their best to live within the limits of personal experience which they accepted without question as the conditions of life in the priesthood. And these priests have persevered according to their commitment, partly underdeveloped, but singlemindedly and because they exercised their priesthood during a relatively controlled period of Church life, in an atmosphere that reinforced and protected them.

This is not to criticize these men; they are indeed admirable and they have, within the limits they wholeheartedly accepted, been effective priests. Despite retirement, they remain, as a rule, interested in life, in the changing Church, and in continuing to serve it in some way. Their number is relatively small, but they probably represent the solid, un-questioning core of men, obediently attuned to authority, who have given the Church a sense of stability over the years. They are men the authori-ties could count on to do a faithful job; they still are. Their achievement in living according to their convictions is extraordinary. Their like may not come this way again. It is instructive to note some of their present atti-tudes when from retirement, they survey the Church which has changed so much during their lives. Perhaps surprisingly they are neither impa-tient nor alienated from the changing Church. They support the changes, anxious only that they work toward the religious service of people. On many issues, unlike many younger men, they are quite open, seemingly unthreatened by the possibility of modifying regulations which they have followed without hesitation or question. They are not, for example, dis-mayed by the prospect of a change in the law of celibacy, although they do not feel that this will solve the Church's problems either. They are, as a group, still loyal to authority. They would, even from retirement, respond to its wishes immediately even now. Nonetheless, they are open to a future very different from the past through which they have lived and worked. They just do not feel that what they have done with sincerity can be undone by any prospective changes now. They possess a larger view of life than this; they are quite willing to see what they have done transformed for the greater good of others.

Perhaps a key to this group of men is what the interviewers described as their realistic and unpretentious capacity to accept themselves as they are and not to have misgivings because of unfulfilled illusions about themselves. These men have a good feeling for their own limitations and have not tried to live as though these did not exist. Their concerns in old age do not center on themselves and their own security. They have pos-sessed enough of themselves to feel a healthy sense of accomplishment; they are ready for death but still quite alive. They are, in summary, remarkable subtypes, graced by nature and God, who have, within notable limits, lived out their lives with a sense of purpose and fulfillment — and no regrets.

We shall review some examples of these well-rounded but not fully developed older priests. There is, for example, the 75-year-old recently retired pastor whose main interest in life continues to be the service of people. As the interviewer notes, "He has no illusions about his abilities or what he has done, except to say that he has no regrets over becoming a priest and the years he has devoted to doing his work." He has always accepted authority easily and feels optimistic about the future of the Church. He has never gotten very close to other people, always maintaining priest-laymen relationships with others. The interviewer says that "one gets the impression that his work has served as a sublimating force in his life in that he has been able to channel all or most of his needs for dependency, affection and security through his priestly role." He would like to help younger priests now that he has been relieved of his administrative duties. It is interesting to note that this priest, even in advanced age, retells in detail the manner in which he entered the seminary. It reflects his lifelong alertness to authority and his readiness to defer his own wishes in order to be of service to others. He did not decide to enter the seminary; his father decided for him and he never questioned this. He does not to this very day.

Another example is the man in his mid-sixties who recalls the importance of religious values to his widowed mother as strongly influential in his choice of the seminary. He found himself at home in the seminary where the pious atmosphere of his home life was extended and reinforced. He has continued to generate this environment throughout his life, never getting very close to anybody but maintaining good relationships with everybody. He is a man who has always emphasized deliberation and control in living his life. As the interviewer notes, "He is capable of closeness, but controls it; he tends to be rigid, but forces himself to remain open; he is severely conservative but balances this with liberalism in many ways." This priest, within the limits of his deliberate style, will continue to function in the priesthood, although the incorporation of new ideas will continue to test his capacities for integrating new experiences successfully.

Yet another example is the priest, not quite sixty, the oldest of a large immigrant family. He has preserved the virtues of hard work and dedication which he learned during his upbringing on the farm. The seminary and the priesthood conferred great status on him, and he has been happy with his choice ever since he left home for the seminary. He has always submerged himself in the image of the priesthood, restricting his own personal development because of his concern for the dignity of the vocation. This has left him shy and somewhat lonely at times, as though a reservoir of potential warmth within him has been left largely untapped throughout his life. He has, however, performed dutifully and has experienced many satisfactions because of his fidelity to his work. He feels that he had many gratifying vicarious relationships through his service of others. He has taken himself for what he is and has accepted the difficulties and frustrations of his life without bitterness. He is optimistic about himself and the future of the Church.

Problems of the Retired

It would be a mistake to think that every older or retired priest had achieved a similar balanced view of his work and his life. In fact, it is necessary to point out briefly the vulnerability to severe psychological problems which has come to many suddenly retired priests. Retirement is a relatively new concept in the experience of the Catholic priesthood. Formerly, both theory and practice urged a man who was not physically incapacitated to continue his work until he died. This made the individual's perception of his life, his work, and his priesthood coextensive layers of experience. To put it another way, the role of the priesthood, since it extended right up to the end of life, conferred a strong sense of identity on those who shared it. The person who had a strong personality of his own and an integrated sense of his priestly ministry found this reinforcing but not essential to his own understanding of himself. The individual without a strong sense of personal identity or vocation found the identity given to him through the role of the priesthood to be essential for his own understanding of himself and his relationship to others. The latter, in other words, received their identity from the outside, and needed this extrinsic validation to maintain their idea of themselves. They thought of themselves as priests but not as persons.

This latter group has suffered retirement shock as they have suddenly found themselves without the titles and functions which gave them a sense of themselves. This is a very alienating experience for some of these men because their poorly developed personalities do not bear very well the weight of having to deal with life without the protection and support formerly accorded them through the role characteristics of the priesthood. They are indeed like strangers in a new land, swept by feelings of estrangement and uncertainty as they search for the personal moorings which they never set down in life.

A moving example of this is the retired big-city pastor in his late seventies who continued to live in the rectory where he had been pastor. The adjustment had been very painful for him and, although he was willing to cooperate in the study, he asked that the interviewer come to see him at the rectory which he did not like to leave. He was somewhat uneasy but cooperative during the interview, reflecting clearly how much he had depended on the role of being a priest for his personal support. This became painfully clear at the time of the interview when the old priest was asked to describe his idea of himself. This was quite disconcerting to him. As a matter of fact, he felt that he could not even discuss the subject, interrupted the interview, and went out to get the priest who succeeded him as pastor. He brought him into the room and asked him to speak about his identity for him since he did not feel he could do it for himself.

This illustrated the experience that many older men have felt in the age of retirement; it is compounded of personal confusion, loneliness, and a sense of not fitting in or being very useful to anyone anymore. These men need more than a sense of financial security in retirement; personal psychological security is just as essential. This is a problem whose outlines only appeared as the study progressed. It is an increasing one, however, and one that is serious and painful enough to require further psychological investigation and some systematic response on the part of Church authorities.

CHAPTER IX

PSYCHOLOGICAL TEST RESULTS

Purposes of the Chapter. The present chapter contains analyses of the psychological test data. Chapters IV, V, VI, VII, and IX are based primarily upon the interview data. Are there relationships among the psychological characteristics measured by the tests and the categories of development which were gleaned from the interview data? If there are relationships, are they consistent? What can test data add to our understanding of the categories of development? These are among the questions to be answered in the present chapter.

Background material on the rationale for mathematical analyses will be interposed through the present chapter. It is given with the hope of assisting the statistically unsophisticated while not offending the knowledgeable.

Plan of the Analyses. Results of the following four tests will be reported: Personal Orientation Inventory (POI), Identity Scale (IS), Loyola Sentence Completion Blank for Clergymen (LSCBC), and Faith Scale (FS). Average scores (means) and measures of variability (standard deviations) will be reported for the scales from the four tests. These means will then be presented graphically where appropriate. Visual inspection of the graphs assists one in getting an impression of how the four developmental groups performed on the tests relative to one another.

However, visual inspection alone does not reveal whether the observed differences among the group means indeed reflect actual differences or merely random fluctuations around the same true value. Only a statistical analysis can make such a discrimination. The primary statistical technique used in this chapter is analysis of variance. If the outcome of this statistical manipulation (referred to as *F*) exceeds a critical value, then the differences among the averages which one observes reflect real differences among the groups. However, one can never be totally sure that the differences are real; hence, the assertion that they are real is stated in terms of probability. The assertion is expressed as a fraction of 1.00

in the footnotes of the tables. For example, "$p < .05$" means that the chances are less than five in a hundred that the observed overall differences among the groups are the result of random fluctuation or sheer chance. Another way of saying this is that the differences are "significant" beyond the .05 level.

Once a significant F is found, further analyses are then possible. The purpose of these analyses is the determination of which of the differences between pairs of means is significant. On the bases of the clinical data (i.e., the psychological reports and case histories), the prediction was made that on the tests the Developed group should score psychologically "healthier" than the other three groups; the Developing, healthier than the Underdeveloped and Maldeveloped groups; the Underdeveloped, healthier than the Maldeveloped group. Since these *a priori* hypotheses were available, the *t* technique for determining the significance of contrasts was employed (McNemar, 1962). As in the case of *F*, if an observed *t* exceeds a critical value, then the difference between the two means is significant.

Given the psychological test data only, what would be the "best" grouping into four categories of the priests who completed the tests? To what degree would such an objective grouping on the basis of test data replicate the "clinical" grouping of these priests on the basis of the psychological reports? One technique which can answer these questions is discriminatory analysis (Nunnally, 1967). This technique was applied to the test scores of the interviewed priests.

A Note on Sample Sizes. Only the scores of the 218 subjects who completed the POI, LSCBC, and IS were included in tables which report means, standard deviations, and *F*'s; likewise, these were the scores used in the discriminatory analysis. That is, 53 subjects were excluded because they failed to complete one or more tests by the time of data processing. In the case of the FS, scores from all subjects who completed it in such a way that it could be scored by both judges (that is, were not assigned to a "cannot say" category) were used, regardless of which other tests they completed. There were 194 such subjects.

Tests Considered. As noted in Chapter III, it was not possible to analyze the wealth of data available in their entirety for this report. It may be recalled that the psychologists included ratings in their reports. Further, checklists and rating scales for evaluating the psychological reports were developed and applied to the cases. Regretfully, the analyses of these data cannot be reported at this time. Likewise, certain aspects of the psychological tests await further analyses. Among these data are the ratings of Church and Ideal Self on the IS and priests' ratings on the FS, as described in Chapter III.

Personal Orientation Inventory. Means, standard deviations, and F's of the 12 POI variables for each of the four developmental groups are presented in Table 7. A detailed description of these variables, as of all the other variables considered in this chapter, is found in Chapter III. The means are plotted on a profile sheet in Figure 2. The adult norms reported in the POI manual (Shostrom, 1963) were used in the construction of Figure 2.

Inspection of Table 7 and Figure 2 suggests that the Developing group of priests is generally more self-actualized than the other groups. Differences across the four groups reached significance on one major scale (Inner-Directed) and three minor subscales (Existentiality, Spontaneity, and Synergy). Table 8 shows the results of all possible contrasts between the members of pairs of means of the four developmental groups on the four POI scales which reached significance in the analyses of variance.

Ten contrasts in Table 8 reached significance. The Developing group is consistently healthier than the Underdeveloped and Maldeveloped groups. The Developed and Developing groups did not differ on any variables, likewise, for the Underdeveloped group when contrasted with the Maldeveloped group. The "Existentiality" variable yielded four out of a possible six significant outcomes. Note that in no case was there a reversal. That is, none of the contrasts suggested that a group lower on the developmental scale scored significantly healthier than a group higher on the developmental scale on any of the four variables. This absence of significant reversals on scales of the POI is also characteristic of the scales of the other tests considered in similar tables later in this chapter. This absence of reversals is consistent with the theory underlying the system of classifying respondents into groups which are ordered on a continuum of development.

A Source of Possible Bias. It may be recalled from Chapter III that a significant difference was found between the priests who completed the POI and were willing to be interviewed and those who completed the POI and refused to be interviewed on the "Inner-Directed" scale of the POI (Table 5). This variable also significantly differed across the four categories of development (Table 7). The Developing group was more inner-directed than the Underdeveloped and Maldeveloped groups (Table 8). Hence, it could be concluded that as a group the priests on whom this report is based represent the healthier end of the spectrum of personal adjustment.

TABLE 7

DESCRIPTIVE STATISTICS AND RESULTS OF ANALYSIS OF VARIANCE OF
12 POI VARIABLES ACROSS DEVELOPMENTAL GROUPS

Scale		Developmental Categories				F
		Developed N = 11	Developing N = 39	Underdeveloped N = 149	Maldeveloped N = 19	df = 3/214
Time-Competent	M	17.36	17.79	17.23	15.58	2.59
	SD	3.41	2.83	2.60	4.34	
Inner-Directed	M	84.82	87.74	80.91	77.95	4.25**
	SD	14.35	11.47	11.55	15.68	
Self-Actualizing Value	M	19.55	20.10	19.10	18.11	2.59
	SD	3.64	2.51	2.58	3.49	
Existentiality	M	21.45	21.23	18.48	18.79	5.60**
	SD	4.50	3.65	4.17	5.28	
Feeling Reactivity	M	13.64	14.69	13.35	13.53	1.94
	SD	2.29	3.45	3.02	3.36	
Spontaneity	M	11.18	12.28	11.04	10.11	2.74*
	SD	3.74	3.19	2.81	3.18	

TABLE 7—Continued

Scale		Developmental Categories				F
		Developed N = 11	Developing N = 39	Underdeveloped N = 149	Maldeveloped N = 19	df = 3/214
Self-Regard	M	11.91	12.41	11.79	10.68	2.44
	SD	2.91	2.34	2.15	2.79	
Self-Acceptance	M	17.27	17.69	16.36	15.11	2.51
	SD	4.13	3.61	3.55	4.41	
Nature of Man, Constructive	M	12.82	12.92	12.37	11.89	1.53
	SD	1.78	1.58	2.01	2.00	
Synergy	M	7.00	7.33	6.74	6.58	2.81*
	SD	1.73	1.01	1.23	1.22	
Acceptance of Aggression	M	14.64	15.26	14.55	14.05	0.61
	SD	4.08	3.54	3.46	3.47	
Capacity for Intimate Contact	M	17.27	18.33	16.48	16.74	2.46
	SD	4.43	3.74	3.78	4.19	

* p < .05.
** p < .01.

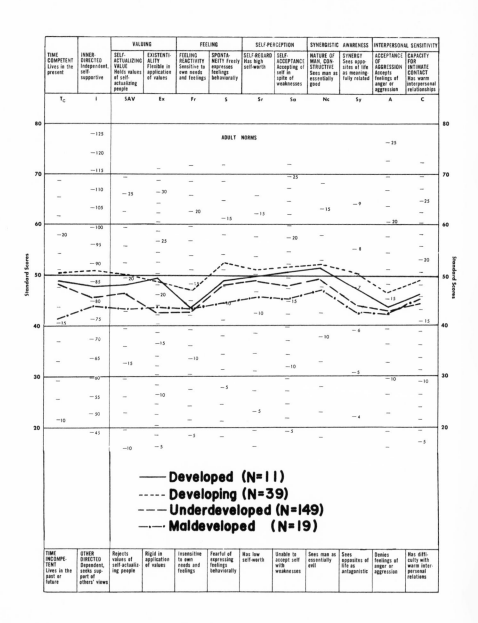

Fig. 2.—POI scores of developmental groups.

TABLE 8

OUTCOME OF ALL POSSIBLE CONTRASTS AMONG FOUR DEVELOPMENTAL LEVELS ON FOUR POI VARIABLES

Variable	Contrast[a]					
	Developed/ Developing	Developed/ Underdeveloped	Developed/ Maldeveloped	Developing/ Underdeveloped	Developing/ Maldeveloped	Underdeveloped/ Maldeveloped
Inner-directed	ns	ns	ns	$p < .01$	$p < .01$	ns
Existentiality	ns	$p < .05$	$p < .05$	$p < .01$	$p < .05$	ns
Spontaneity	ns	ns	ns	$p < .05$	$p < .01$	ns
Synergy	ns	ns	ns	$p < .01$	$p < .05$	ns

[a] All significant contrasts are in the predicted direction.

Identity Scale. Table 9 presents the summary statistics and results of the analyses variance for the 10 subscales of the IS. The means of the subscales are plotted in Figure 3.

Inspection of Table 9 and Figure 3 suggests the Developed group is consistently healthier than the three other groups on these measures which were derived from Erik Erikson's schema. The Maldeveloped group scored consistently below the other groups. Table 10 shows the results of all possible contrasts between the members of pairs of means of the four developmental groups on the six subscales of the IS which reached significance in the analyses of variance.

Table 10 tends to confirm the impressionistic interpretation of Figure 3. That is, the Maldeveloped group clearly shows up as consistently less healthy than the three other groups. The Developing group is not distinguishable from the Developed or Underdeveloped groups or any of the variables. The "Ego-Self" subscale significantly distinguished between the groups in four out of six cases.

Loyola Sentence Completion Blank for Clergymen. Table 11 presents the descriptive statistics and tests of significance for the six subscales of the LSCBC.

Note that all the subscales reached significance in the analyses of variance. A high score on the LSCBC indicates *poor* adjustment. The means are plotted in Figure 4.

Inspection of Table 11 and Figure 4 suggests a pattern of relative positions similar to that found in the plot of the IS (Figure 3): the Maldeveloped group tends to show the poorest adjustment and the Developed group shows the best adjustment. Table 12 shows the results of all possible contrasts between groups on these variables.

Again the Maldeveloped group is consistently less healthy than the three other groups. In addition, the Developing group scored better than the Underdeveloped group on the "Self," "Interpersonal Relationships," and "Psychosexual Maturity" scales.

Faith Scale. The priests' descriptions of mature and immature faith were rated by two judges on an intrinsic-extrinsic faith dimension. The score of a protocol is the sum of the two judgments on this nine point scale. The higher the score, the more extrinsic the faith. The highest score possible was 18; the lowest, two. The mean score for the Developed group was 7.60 ($N = 10$, $SD = 1.96$); Developing, 6.98 ($N = 41$, $SD = 2.87$); Underdeveloped, 8.84 ($N = 128$, $SD = 3.40$); Maldeveloped 11.00 ($N = 15$, $SD = 4.00$). The analysis of variance of this variable across the four groups is presented in Table 13.

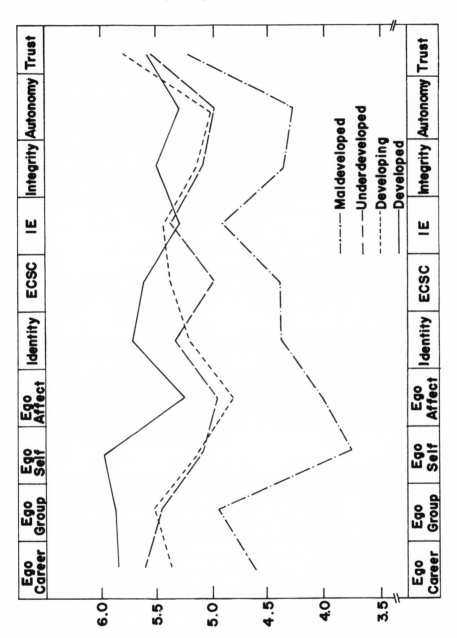

Fig. 3.—IS scores of developmental groups.

TABLE 9

DESCRIPTIVE STATISTICS AND RESULTS OF ANALYSES OF VARIANCE OF TEN IS VARIABLES ACROSS DEVELOPMENTAL GROUPS

Scale		Developmental Groups				F df = 3/214
		Developed N = 11	Developing N = 39	Underdeveloped N = 149	Maldeveloped N = 19	
Ego-Career	M	5.80	5.37	5.61	4.59	4.70**
	SD	1.02	1.15	1.06	1.82	
Ego-Group	M	5.85	5.53	5.44	4.91	1.52
	SD	0.94	1.10	1.32	1.35	
Ego-Self	M	5.95	5.14	5.11	3.79	5.45**
	SD	0.93	1.50	1.54	2.12	
Ego-Affect	M	5.27	4.81	4.96	4.00	4.30**
	SD	0.96	0.80	1.15	1.80	
Identity	M	5.70	5.23	5.34	4.38	5.57**
	SD	0.68	0.86	1.01	1.57	
Expressivity and Comfort within a Social Context	M	5.59	5.37	4.98	4.39	2.95*
	SD	1.42	0.95	1.41	1.44	

TABLE 9—Continued

Scale		Developmental Groups				F
		Developed N = 11	Developing N = 39	Underdeveloped N = 149	Maldeveloped N = 19	df = 3/214
Individual Expressivity	M	5.29	5.44	5.39	4.92	1.74
	SD	0.91	0.73	0.93	0.87	
Integrity	M	5.49	5.15	5.09	4.36	3.07*
	SD	0.86	0.85	1.15	1.58	
Autonomy	M	5.31	5.00	4.94	4.76	1.17
	SD	0.48	0.86	0.82	0.60	
Trust	M	5.58	5.80	5.53	5.22	2.00
	SD	1.02	0.67	0.88	1.06	

* p < .05.
** p < .01.

TABLE 10

OUTCOME OF ALL POSSIBLE CONTRASTS AMONG FOUR DEVELOPMENTAL
LEVELS ON SIX IDENTITY SCALE VARIABLES

Variable	Contrast[a]					
	Developed/ Developing	Developed/ Underdeveloped	Developed/ Maldeveloped	Developing/ Underdeveloped	Developing/ Maldeveloped	Underdeveloped/ Maldeveloped
Ego-Career	ns	ns	$p < .01$	ns	$p < .01$	$p < .01$
Ego-Self	ns	$p < .05$	$p < .01$	ns	$p < .01$	$p < .01$
Ego-Affect	ns	ns	$p < .01$	ns	$p < .01$	$p < .01$
Identity	ns	ns	$p < .01$	ns	$p < .01$	$p < .01$
Expressivity and comfort within a social context	ns	ns	$p < .05$	ns	$p < .01$	$p < .05$
Integrity	ns	ns	$p < .01$	ns	$p < .01$	$p < .01$

[a] All significant contrasts are in the predicted direction.

TABLE 11

DESCRIPTIVE STATISTICS AND RESULTS OF ANALYSES OF VARIANCE OF SIX LSCBC VARIABLES ACROSS DEVELOPMENTAL GROUPS

Scale		Developmental Groups				F
		Developed N = 11	Developing N = 39	Underdeveloped N = 149	Maldeveloped N = 19	df = 3/214
Self	M	45.73	46.00	47.25	49.89	4.94**
	SD	4.17	3.22	3.89	4.33	
Interpersonal Relations	M	43.82	41.77	43.84	48.16	8.33**
	SD	3.97	4.37	4.36	6.54	
Phychosexual Maturity	M	46.00	43.59	46.55	49.53	9.06**
	SD	4.24	3.71	4.27	5.21	
Church, Faith, Religion	M	40.73	42.01	42.00	45.42	3.55*
	SD	4.10	4.08	4.56	6.01	
Priesthood	M	43.91	45.28	44.91	48.74	4.58*
	SD	4.53	4.52	5.04	5.79	
Job Satisfaction	M	42.18	44.77	43.89	48.00	4.46**
	SD	3.84	4.14	5.11	6.76	

* p < .05.
** p < .01.

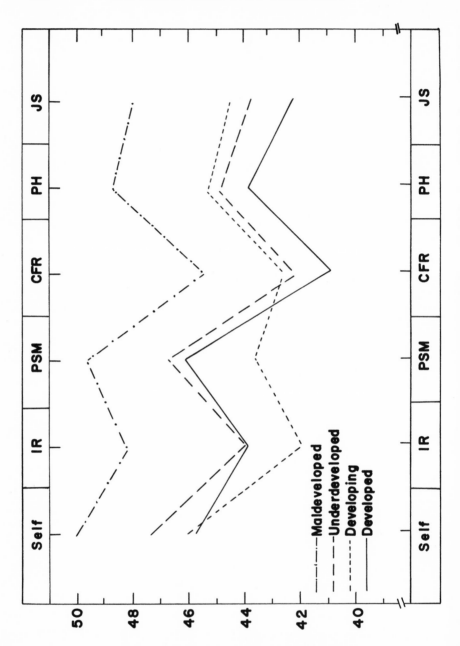

Fig. 4.—LSCBC scores of developmental groups.

TABLE 12

OUTCOME OF ALL POSSIBLE CONTRASTS AMONG FOUR DEVELOPMENTAL LEVELS ON SIX LSCB VARIABLES

Variable	Contrast [a]					
	Developed/ Developing	Developed/ Underdeveloped	Developed/ Maldeveloped	Developing/ Underdeveloped	Developing/ Maldeveloped	Underdeveloped/ Maldeveloped
Self	ns	ns	$p < .01$	$p < .05$	$p < .01$	$p < .01$
Interpersonal Relations	ns	ns	$p < .01$	$p < .01$	$p < .01$	$p < .01$
Psychosexual Maturity	ns	ns	$p < .05$	$p < .01$	$p < .01$	$p < .01$
Church, Faith, Religion	ns	ns	$p < .01$	ns	$p < .05$	$p < .01$
Priesthood	ns	ns	$p < .01$	ns	$p < .01$	$p < .01$
Job Satisfaction	ns	ns	$p < .01$	ns	$p < .05$	$p < .01$

[a] All significant contrasts are in predicted direction.

Since the result of the analysis of variance was significant, contrasts were undertaken according to the method described above. The Developed group was no different from the Developing and Underdeveloped groups but was more "intrinsic" than the Maldeveloped group (p < .01). The Developing group was more intrinsic than the Underdeveloped and Maldeveloped groups (p < .01). And the Underdeveloped group was more intrinsic than the Maldeveloped group (p < .01). Hence, the patterning of significant contrasts is consistent with the predictions from the theory that the development of intrinsic faith is associated with psychological development.

Discriminatory Analysis. How well would a quantitative grouping of the respondents into four categories on the basis of their test scores fit the clinical grouping into four categories of development on the basis of clinical reports describing them? To answer this question a stepwise discriminatory analysis, a complex statistical manipulation, was performed (Program 07M of the Biomed Series) on the scales of the POI, IS, and LSCBC. Only the scores of the 218 priests who were interviewed and who completed all of these tests were considered. The stepwise discriminatory analysis reached a peak in the number of subjects classified at the tenth step. That is, consistent gain in efficiency of classification did not occur beyond the inclusion of ten variables. The correspondence between the classification on the basis of clinical data and the classification on the basis of the test data at step ten of the discriminatory analysis is presented in Table 14.

The *Chi square* value of Table 14 is 44.21 (p < .01). Hence, there is a significant association between the two strategies of classification. The agreement is, of course, far from perfect. The diagonal of Table 14 contains the number of agreements between the two strategies for each

TABLE 13

ONE WAY ANALYSIS OF VARIANCE OF MATURITY OF FAITH
ACROSS DEVELOPMENTAL GROUPS

	Sum of Squares	Degrees of Freedom	Mean Square	F Ratio
Between Groups	211.73	3	70.58	6.53**
Within Groups	2054.25	190	10.81	
Total	2265.98	193		

** p < .01.

TABLE 14

NUMBER OF CASES CLASSIFIED INTO DEVELOPMENTAL GROUPS

Clinical Ratings	Discriminatory Analysis			
	Developed	Developing	Underdeveloped	Maldeveloped
Developed	8	1	1	1
Developing	5	28	2	4
Underdeveloped	24	35	66	24
Maldeveloped	3	2	3	11

of the four categories. The sum of the diagonal is 113 or 52% of the total number of cases. The largest proportionate differences between the two methods of grouping the priests occurred in the Underdeveloped group. Table 14 suggests that their test scores are substantially more heterogeneous than the psychological reports describing them.

It is interesting to note that of the 28 variables entered into the discriminatory analysis, the Psychosexual Maturity subscale of the LSCBC was by far the best discriminator among the groups. This finding adds to the validity of the developmental level scale used to group the subjects clinically. In other words, this finding adds credence to the assertion that the men were in fact grouped according to the level of their psychosexual development.

In Table 15 the 28 variables are ordered according to their importance in distinguishing among the four developmental groups as determined by the stepwise discriminatory analysis.

It should be noted that in the present analysis each variable contributes to the categorization in a unique way. That is, that part of a variable's contribution to the discrimination which overlaps with a variable which is a better overall discriminator is not considered.

Conclusions. The patterning of scores obtained by the priests in the four developmental categories and the statistical analyses of these scores suggest the following conclusions:

A. *The groups psychologically differ from one another.* Average scores on 28 variables taken from the psychological tests were computed. Statistical analyses indicated that 16 of these variables significantly differed across the developmental categories.

B. *These differences are quite consistent.* The Developed and Developing groups consistently appear to be healthier than the Underdeveloped

TABLE 15

RELATIVE IMPORTANCE OF 28 VARIABLES ACCORDING TO DISCRIMINATORY ANALYSIS

Rank	Variable	Test	Rank	Variable	Test	Rank	Variable	Test
1	Psychosexual Maturity	LSCBC	11	Time-Competence	POI	21	Self-Regard	POI
2	Identity	IS	12	Self-Acceptance	POI	22	Inner-Directed	POI
3	Existentiality	POI	13	Acceptance of Aggression	POI	23	Expressivity and Comfort	IS
4	Trust	IS	14	Church, Faith, Religion	LSCBC		within a Social Context	
5	Autonomy	IS	15	Synergy	POI	24	Self-Actualizing	POI
6	Ego-Group	IS	16	Nature of Man, Constructive	POI	25	Ego-Affect	IS
7	Interpersonal Relations	LSCBC	17	Feeling Reactivity	POI	26	Ego-Career	IS
8	Job Satisfaction	LSCBC	18	Integrity	IS	27	Individual Expressivity	IS
9	Ego-Self	IS	19	Spontaneity	POI	28	Self	LSCBC
10	Capacity for Intimate		20	Priesthood	LSCBC			
	Contact	POI						

and Maldeveloped groups. The Developed group looks the healthiest on the LSCBC and IS. However, the Developing group looks consistently better on the POI. The Maldeveloped group appears to have the poorest adjustment in all realms tapped. The Underdeveloped group scores typically in the middle area, neither disturbed, nor particularly healthy.

C. *The test data indicate that the groups are ordered on a developmental continuum in which psychosexual maturity plays an important role.* The variable which discriminated best across the four categories was Psychosexual Maturity. The next best discriminators tended to be variables derived from Erikson's theory of psychological development.

D. *The priest's conception of mature faith is associated with his own personal development.* The data indicate that priests who are personally more mature value "intrinsic" religion more than the men who are less mature. These latter men value "extrinsic" religion. This finding is of potentially major significance for decisions regarding the facilitation of personal growth among the clergy.

E. *There is indication that the sample of priests on whom the present report is based represents, in general, the healthier end of the spectrum of personal development.* There is evidence to suggest that the very fact that a man is willing to be interviewed in depth is an indication of good adjustment. Hence, there is the possibility that the present report is overly benign. That is, the incidence of lack of full development among the clergy may be even more pervasive than indicated in this report.

CHAPTER X

RECOMMENDATIONS

The recommendations of this chapter are related to basic psychological questions which must be proposed to those who are responsible for the continued development of the priesthood: what are your goals or expectations for American priests? This question leads immediately to two others which seem to express the psychological implications of the findings of the present research:

1. Do you put first priority on assisting American priests to achieve greater personal maturity and, therefore, greater effectiveness as priests?
2. Do you rather put priority on American priests' adjusting themselves to the expectations of the institutional priesthood even at the price of not developing themselves?

There is a conflict implied by these two points of view, although it is obviously one that is not impossible to resolve. Those responsible for the exercise of the priesthood should, however, understand the terms of the conflict with which they must deal before they can move to resolve it. There is a problem, even though it may be a problem shared by many other persons and institutions in our culture. The problem arises precisely because a sizable group of American priests are not as developed psychologically as they could be. There is also evidence that a number of them are aware of this and are anxious to grow more as persons and as priests. This basic dynamism is healthy and explains many of the efforts for greater responsibility and self-determination within the Church. On the other hand, those responsible for the priesthood have long-term expectations of how the men who are priests should be recruited, educated and how they should live. These might be described as the institutional expectations of the priesthood, the conditions which, if observed readily, will minimize the stress in administering the activity of priests so that it fits into the pattern of organizational needs. This problem is

173

common to all institutions: how to manage personnel so that what contributes most effectively to personal growth also contributes to the work of the organization. The definition and resolution of these mutual expectations regarding the priesthood and the work of preaching the Gospels is at the very heart of understanding the problem uncovered by this investigation.

One need not take sides to outline this difficulty, but one would fail as a psychological consultant if one does not try to make the dimensions of the problem as clear as possible. If the men who are priests become increasingly aware of the problems which they experience because of their lack of personal development, then they will gradually begin to seek what they consider to be the appropriate remedy for their problem. This movement will be toward those values and conditions of life which provide greater freedom personally and occupationally. They will reject solutions which emphasize conformity to organizational expectations without adequate consideration of what they value in their own personal growth. On the other hand, those responsible for the overall functioning of an organization may not conceptualize the problem in quite the same way; they are preoccupied with institutional concerns and, in the light of this focus, may emphasize conformity to the expectations of the organization as a fundamental consideration for the adjustment of the personnel. This, indeed, seems the case with the American priesthood, where the conflict between the desire for personal growth on the part of priests and the seeming institutional restrictions and expectations for their acceptance of traditional patterns meet headlong. This is not an irremediable problem but it is one that can grow more sharp-edged and complicated the longer its resolution is delayed.

This can be put in another way. The main problem of American priests is not sickness which needs specific psychological treatment. It is, along with that of most other Americans, a problem of incomplete growth, for which there is only the remedy of an expanded and realistic experience of life itself. Whenever individuals have a personal problem of growth, they do not solve it by making themselves conform to expectations outside themselves. Authentic growth is necessarily expressive of the individual himself; it frees him from conforming as a mode of adjustment and commits him to being more responsible for himself. This process of releasing greater growth in persons does not necessarily set them against other people or the organization in which they work. In fact, it usually allows them to contribute with greater cooperation and creativity as well as a greater sense of self-satisfaction. Research on management has confirmed many times over the wisdom of encouraging growth rather than repressing it as the key to an effective organization. Those who are responsible for the organization of the Church must review their expectations on their priest-personnel and ask whether they want greater maturity in them or whether the demands of the institution make it necessary to insist on re-emphasizing conformity to the traditional role of the priesthood.

It is important to keep this general question in mind, even though one might ask: Is it not possible to have both of these values preserved, that is, greater personal development in priests and yet a continuity in the role expectations of the priesthood at the same time? Perhaps this question can only be answered effectively after all the research evidence on the priesthood is completely absorbed by those who read it. It is obvious that no solution can totally ignore the needs of either the individuals or the institution; but no solution will say that changes are unnecessary in either the lives of individuals or on the part of the institution. Psychologically speaking, changes have occurred and will continue to occur. One needs thorough understanding to make decisions that insure the positive course of the continuing process of change. A clear picture of the conflict at the root of possible responses to the problems of the priesthood is necessary before final decisions can be made. No recommendation that ignores the need to reconcile individual growth with institutional aims can be psychologically successful. To sum up these observations: you cannot strengthen the personalities of an institution's personnel without modifying the expectations for conforming behavior on their part; you cannot emphasize institutional goals and demand conformity to them on the part of personnel without limiting their personal development.

The basic problem with American priests would seem to be the need to provide them with the opportunities and the encouragement to continue their personal growth in a successful manner. One must remember the fact that American priests are, psychologically speaking, ordinary men; greater realism about this will allow sensible positive recommendations for the kinds of experiences they require to move forward in their personal growth. To recommend the creation of more opportunities for self-development is not in any sense to pander to some kind of weakness. It is rather to capitalize on their strength, their residual capacity to achieve greater maturity. One must work with what is there, not with what he wishes were there or presumes is there as far as psychological make-up is concerned. Indeed, some of the policies that have been implemented to prepare men for the priesthood have been based on a misunderstanding of psychological reality; these policies, such as removal of seminarians from ordinary developmental educational and social experiences, have contributed to arresting rather than freeing the growth of men who are priests. If one is committed to the continued personal development of priests, one must have a real sense of the nature of the basic difficulty. It is not a sickness that needs a specific medical or psychological treatment; it is a need for increased personal development, and that can only be treated by a more adequate experience of mature living.

It would be relatively simple to write recommendations for American priests if we could conclude that they suffered some psychological illness. A very small proportion of them would be described by this notion of sickness; psychological treatment on a vast scale is obviously not the response of choice for this population. It is true that there are priests who are classified, as a certain number of persons in any profession would be, as maldeveloped. The following seem to be appropriate suggestions regarding these priests:

1) The maldeveloped will always function within the limitations imposed by their severe psychological problems. They should not be expected to overcome them as though these problems were simply bad habits or evidences of weak wills. Greater sensitivity and awareness of symptoms is needed, because frequently symptoms are the only language in which these maldeveloped men convey their message of inner discomfort. A more prompt response to them as individuals would enable a proper diagnosis and course of treatment to be planned at a time when it would be far more beneficial to them. Those who have suffered serious psychological problems need continued support and understanding, and, perhaps in certain circumstances, a greater positive toleration of their eccentricity if they are to continue some measure of psychological functioning in the priesthood.

2) The benefits of an adequate psychological screening program are underscored by the evidence of this research. In every maldeveloped case there was early clear information about these priests' psychological difficulties which would have enabled authorities to make much better decisions both for them and for the Church itself. The signs have been there a long time and skilled psychiatrists and psychologists would have been aware of them at an early period in these priests' lives.

3) With regard to the rehabilitation of the maldeveloped some fresh thinking should be done about the ideal mode of readjustment. Frequently, in the past, the notion of being recovered has been synonymous

with the idea of returning to the work of the priesthood. This may be a dangerously narrow and restrictive ideal to propose for these men. It seems clear that it may be healthier for many of them to be able to move out of the priesthood with minimal difficulty rather than to strive only to readjust to it. A more open attitude to their future possibilities would create a better atmosphere for the success of their efforts to re-integrate themselves.

4) The last point in dealing with the severely emotionally troubled priests is to recall that what is appropriate for them may not be at all appropriate for all other priests. In other words, while psychological screening will help to identify those with serious emotional liabilities and enable one to decide on an appropriate treatment for them, it will not do quite the same thing for the men whose problem is growth rather than sickness.

It is neither realistic nor practical to recommend some form of psychological therapy for the underdeveloped priests of America. While they might profit from it to a certain degree, it would not touch the basic problems nor do much to relieve the situational difficulties which promote and sustain this lack of development. As has been mentioned several times before, these men need a more active incorporation into life itself. They need, first of all, to be stirred to deal with their growth problems and then assisted in every way to do this constructively. Many of them do not really recognize that they are not fully grown; they are so firmly defended by their adjustive styles that they may be insensitive to their basic lack of maturity. The underdeveloped priests are men of good will; this is no indictment of that. Not all of them, however, recognize that they could be more fully grown, that their work could be more fruitful and satisfying, and that they could, in a real sense, experience life in a richer and more productive way. So many of them are fearful of others, cut off from personal relationships, and only tentatively dealing with the adolescent issues of their own identity, that they draw back from the challenges of a deeper form of living. The only long-range way to improve the priesthood as a function of service is, of course, to make it possible for priests to improve themselves. The problems with which they have to deal are not intellectual as much as they are emotional. They must learn a little better how to live in the full dimensions of their personalities. This is an affective rather than a totally rational problem. They are ordinary men who have tried their best to cooperate with a system of training and a discipline of life which have failed to introduce them fully to the real problems of their personal development. Indeed, one might observe that the restrictive and over-idealistic seminary training reinforced aspects of their personalities which really did not need further strengthening (self-control, a sense of duty, docility) while it ignored the areas in which they needed genuine development (personal identity, ability to relate closely and responsibly with others, self-confidence).

The therapy for underdeveloped persons, and these priests are at many different levels within this category, is not a greater insistence on conformity. Psychologically speaking, these men need a greater practical freedom within which to assume their true adult responsibilities in life. Underdeveloped priests need more active options, beginning at an earlier age and extending throughout their careers. They need, in order to overcome passivity and a tendency to go along with life, more challenges to exercise freedom in regard to their own lives and the work which they do. The emphasis, as it was in earlier comments on celibacy, is on the quality of freedom itself rather than on any specific object of it. Unless responsible freedom becomes more clearly the environment within which men may serve as priests, one cannot expect the problems of underdevelopment to be dealt with constructively.

What, however, are some of the specific areas in which greater practical freedom could be introduced into the lives of priests? Freedom and a sense of trust and concern for its mature use should be introduced in those aspects of life which are the most important for personal development. It does little good to increase the freedom of individuals in areas of their lives which are not of great significance. In fact, those responsible for the development of the priesthood might ask, not how much freedom can we afford to give to priests, but rather what is the minimal control of their lives necessary to maintain in order to insure a cohesive and responsible priestly ministry? In other words, what are the immutables, the essential things which cannot change? When these are clear, then it is easier to see the dimensions of priestly life where freedom could be sensibly increased.

It may, for example, be essential to maintain a very clear and healthy relationship between a bishop and his priests if the work of the Church is to go forward. This may be one of the immutables, without which the identity of the priesthood would fragment badly. Is this achieved by control or by increased cooperation, or a healthy compromise of these elements? There must be some essential agreement on the nature of Gospel teaching and Gospel service to the world, but these ends may be achieved by augmented educational and other programs rather than by anything else. In any case, as the qualities which must be preserved are more clearly defined, it will be easy to specify more clearly the areas in which greater freedom could be granted without damage either to the nature of the priesthood or the integrity of the institution.

What, then, are some of the areas of life in which responsible freedom is important for the growth of persons? One might begin with the education of priests, in which programs emphasizing greater freedom have already been introduced to some extent. Priests need to be trained in a more individual manner than was the case when seminary training was characterized by conformity. Seminarians must be helped to understand themselves and to develop fully the special talents which they may have been given for the benefit of the larger community which they will serve as priests. An individualized approach to the training of priests allows greater freedom but it also insists on greater personal accountability. This is the mixture that makes for maturity.

It is the same in the exercise of the priesthood itself. Greater freedom can be allowed in many areas of the personal lives of priests — in celibacy, living quarters, self-support, and opportunities for further education — but only if at the same time there is an increased demand on their professional performance as priests. Up until now the emphasis has been on the rather close supervision of the priest's personal life without much mature supervision of his professional life. Greater accountability for the manner in which a priest discharges his obligations of service can only increase maturity; greater freedom in his personal life can only enlarge his opportunities to use it in a self-developing and responsible manner.

It should be noted, of course, that while there are some risks in enlarging the genuine freedom in the lives of these men, there is not much danger that they will abuse it. In fact, for some of the more lethargic, the problem will continue to be that of getting them to take active and creative advantage of it. These men are not, however, impulsive persons; they are, if anything, just the opposite, more overcontrolled than undercontrolled. There is not much danger that they would use enlarged freedom for purposes that would subvert the institution which they serve. While there will be necessary adjustments to be made to make this freedom truly available to them, a greater consequent maturity will enable these men to serve more cooperatively and more effectively in the priesthood. A much greater fear arises if one asks what will happen if the freedom of American priests is not expanded in a practical manner?

Part of the answer to that comes from an inspection of the priests who are designated as developing. These men are, as a matter of fact, attempting to enlarge their range of personal choices in order to achieve greater personal growth. For many this is an extremely difficult process, although the experience of increased growth makes up for the pain of having to stretch oneself to attain it. Clearly, some of the developing priests are discovering new strengths within themselves which enable them to function more effectively in their work of ministry. They frequently find that they may no longer need to depend on the institution for as much support as they once did. Their strength comes now from within, where a deepened faith and set of convictions provides a more stable bedrock for their work. Others discover that the course of development leads them out of the priesthood, where they feel they never really belongd or which they now feel in conflict with because of new attitudes toward themselves and the Church. It is clear that, if greater responsible freedom is not encouraged for priests, more and more of them will find themselves, one way or another, on the path of personal development anyway. This may lead some to greater dedication; it may lead others to new decisions about their lives. In other words, those men who are closest to a realization that they still have personal growth to achieve will continue to move into this challenge because of its profound personal importance to them. This pattern will continue even if it is unrecognized, unsupervised, and, on the part of the Church authorities, unresponded to.

The developed members of the priest population are people who can also be trusted with more freedom. The fact that they have developed as well as they can reflects the favorable life experiences which they have had. Their maturity enables them, in whatever work they do, to accept new freedoms with confidence and a sense of responsibility. Indeed, the revitalization of the priesthood may depend on reinforcing the men who are most capable of integrating the goals of personal growth and institutional integrity in their lives. One of the great strengths of developed priests is their lack of psychological defensiveness. The developed should be identified for their leadership potential for the future of the Church. More needs to be learned about the developed priests of the country with a view to helping them to continue to grow and also to understand the kind of man who can minister responsibly to others.

This brings us back to the question with which this chapter began. Do those responsible for the priesthood want to encourage individual development, or does this seem too alien to the objective of maintaining institutional integrity? This is a complex question which needs careful reflection. Is the priesthood a profession that can contain and express the personalities of psychologically growing persons? Or is it, in view of institutional needs, a profession in which the man who can shape himself to its demands is the person who is desirable? Only an answer to this question can determine how much growth through responsible freedom one wishes to introduce into the lives of American priests.

The final recommendation of this report is to extend and continue research on the priesthood and other aspects of Church life. It is clear that a more profound understanding of the underlying psychological truths of the present condition of the Church can only be beneficial to it. In the course of the present research, the investigators identified many areas which need more in-depth analysis. To mention a few:

1. A study in-depth of retired priests whose problems are only now beginning to appear. The difficulties of retirement are many and there seem to be special ones regarding personal identity where increased knowledge would be especially helpful.

2. In-depth interviews with a number of resigned priests would enable the Church to have a much better understanding of this serious problem.

3. An in-depth study of seminarians would be instructive, especially in the light of the responsibility they will bear for the Church in the future.

4. A continued program of research on pastoral questions coupled with continued dialogue between researchers and Church officials.

APPENDIX A

PSYCHOLOGICAL RESEARCH ON THE AMERICAN PRIESTHOOD:

A REVIEW OF THE LITERATURE

JOHN J. ROONEY,
La Salle College

There can be no question of the high degree of current public interest in the Catholic Church and in its priests. In television programs and motion pictures, newspapers and popular magazines, changes taking place in the Church and questions raised about the role of the contemporary priest are increasingly featured.

Particularly since Vatican II, Church officials have come to accept change as a normal state of affairs with a concomitant need to obtain accurate information about the status quo and to assess the impact of various changes on its members — particularly those called to positions of leadership.

Increasingly, psychologists and other social and behavioral scientists are being encouraged to help provide such information. Priests and other religious personnel are interested in a better understanding of themselves and their place in the Church, and are generally willing (and in some cases eager) to participate in meaningful studies of the priesthood.

Observations on the priests and religious living these vocations, such as D'Arcy and Kennedy (1965), Dendero (1965), and Kennedy (1967, 1968, 1969), have been received with enthusiasm.

The growth of interest in such research within the Church is reflected in the bibliography compiled by D'Arcy (1968a) which covered a search of the literature up to the end of February, 1967. After tabulating the entries in the bibliography chronologically, he comments:

The earliest reference is 1927. This entire field of study can be said to have emerged not more than 40 years ago. It took twenty years for it to pick up momentum, which it did immediately after the Second World War, reaching its greatest rate of acceleration in the 1950's. It is still continuing a steady growth. It is one indication of the increasing application of scientific methodology to matters in the religious domain.

This remarkable rate of growth, which has continued to this day, has been accompanied by improvements in communications among those conducting research on religious personnel. At one time it was common for studies to be conducted by investigators who were relatively unaware of what others had done. Instead of building on previous discoveries, studies often duplicated one another.

Such isolated research studies are less prevalent today since publication of annotated bibliographies by Meissner (1961), Menges and Dittes (1965), and Menges (1967), the bibliography by D'Arcy (1968a), and several reviews of research on various aspects of this area (D'Arcy, 1962; Dunn, 1965; Rooney, 1968; T. N. McCarthy, 1970).

The professional barriers dividing sociologist and psychologist, accustomed to approaching research from a different perspective and using different constructs, tools and terminology, have been reduced to the benefit of each.

Investigators tend to be less parochial and more aware of the results of studies conducted with denominations other than their own. More and more the research on religious personnel is appearing in the standard professional journals and is being included in *Psychological Abstracts* and *Sociological Abstracts*. The lack of ready accessibility of much of the research published as masters theses and doctoral dissertations remains a problem, but in most respects communication in this area has improved to the extent that new studies can build upon a foundation laid down by previous workers.

At the same time as the concern for more valid and pertinent information about the religious vocation has developed within the Church, the study of occupations or careers has attracted heightened attention from psychologists and sociologists. Theoretical and methodological advances which they have made have provided firmer underpinnings for the empirical data that is being amassed; at the same time these advances have led from an emphasis on "matching men and jobs" to the more complex study of career development which Super (1969) describes as involving a "differential-developmental-social-phenomenological" approach.

Rather than concentrating on a single vocational decision based on similarity of an individual's aptitudes, interests, values, and personality traits to members of a given occupation, there is an increasing recognition that career development involves a series of choices made throughout the individual's life. These choices are made in an attempt to develop an identity as a person and as a member of a particular occupation; they are modified as the individual's self-concept and his image of the occupation change. As Super (1969) describes it:

> Central to a theory of vocational development are the processes of the formation, translation into occupational terms, and implementation of self-concepts. If the theory is to cover the whole life span, a series of self-concept modification and adjustment processes must be formulated. The deciding individual, construing himself and his environment in his own way, is a major determinant of his own career, even though he operates in a context of external determinants. The formation process includes exploration of the self and of the environment, the differentiation of the self from others, identification with others who can serve as models, and the playing of these selected roles with more or less conscious evaluation of the results (reality testing). The translation of self-concepts into occupational terms may take place through identification with an adult role model (a global translation, in which one says 'I am like him' or 'I want to be like him'), experience in a role in which one has been cast (discovery of vocational aspects of the self-concept, as when being drafted and assigned to training leads to the discovery of unsuspected interests and outlets), or learning that some of one's attributes should make one fit well into a certain occupation. The implementation process involves action, as in obtaining the specialized education or training needed for the preferred occupation, or finding employment in it. Modification takes place after entry and with experience as realities cause further adjustments, preservation of the self-concept is typical of the maintenance stage as the established person seeks to hold his own in a changing technology, and further adjustment is called for as capacities and role expectations are drastically modified by aging (Super, 1969).

Conceptual models such as the above have only recently been applied to clergymen. As they have, researchers have begun to direct their attention to such questions as the role of the priest, the situations under which he works, the image he projects, the choice points and stress points he encounters, the nature of the system in which he functions and the changes he experiences as he progresses through the various stages of his career. These questions are stimulating some exciting and significant research. Yet there are more traditional questions which have not been answered satisfactorily. In 1966 the present writer classified needed research on the psychological characteristics of religions on the basis of three questions: 1) What factors are involved in the decision to enter religious life? 2) What characteristics contribute to persistence in religious life? 3) What qualities are related to success or effectiveness in religious life? (Rooney, 1968)

Research has made progress toward answering these questions, but major gaps remain. Conclusions drawn often require assumptions which have yet to be tested or verified. The question of effectiveness has been a particularly troublesome one. Attempts to clarify it have led to a greater consideration of the role of the priest and the situation in which he functions in addition to the more traditional search for an answer in terms of personality traits.

While the above three questions seemed to provide a suitable format for classifying psychological research on religious in 1966, the changing emphasis of studies in the intervening years have made this inadequate for delineating this area of research today.

Other schemata for classifying research on clergymen have been proposed including those of Menges and Dittes (1965), Demereth (1968), and D'Arcy (1968a).

Menges and Dittes employed the categories listed below:

A. Unique characteristics of clergymen and religious.
   A1. Personality. Including motivational, ability and intelligence, and interest variables.
   A2. Background. Biographical and demographic data, environmental influences, conscious considerations in making vocational decisions, etc.
   A3. Recruiting, screening, training, guidance procedures.
   A4. Miscellaneous. Most commonly assessed attitudes.
B. Effectiveness.
   B1. Definitions.
   B2. Personality.

B3. Background.

B4. Procedures.

C. Differences among clergymen.

D. Consequences of being a clergyman.

E. Counseling and therapy with clergymen and religious.

F. Physical and mental health and illness among clergy and religious.

G. Wives of clergymen.

H. Surveys of research and research methodology.

I. Surveys of psychological testing of seminarians, clergy and religious. Demereth developed the following classification:

I. Ministerial careers (the ministry as an occupation).
   A. Mapping stress points.
   B. Recruitment (origins, motives, recruiters, procedure).
   C. Seminary training (including its relationship to parish realities).
   D. Causes of role satisfaction/dissatisfaction.
   E. Age variations — the generation gap in the ministry.
   F. Dropouts.
   G. Comparative studies across denominations, across professions (including case studies).
   H. Significance of professional associations developing among clergy.
   I. Career development studies.

II. Ministry/laity relations (the Church as an institution).
   A. Authority changes and their consequences (democratization, professionalism, grounds for legitimacy).
   B. Factors in competing role conceptions (e.g., prophet vs. priest, agency vs. communion, etc.).
   C. Heterogeneity among parishioners.
   D. The isolation of ministers in their public roles (public vs. private life).
   E. Parish as "theater of the profound" (performances stages for others' benefit; the management of impressions).
      1. Consequences for conflict — especially when not candidly handled.
      2. To what degree does preaching, teaching, etc., influence a congregation's views?

III. Role of religion in wider society. (Empirical and theoretical issues.)
   A. Historical change and institutional capability.
      1. Increasingly differentiated society.

    2. Autonomy without relevance.
    3. The function of doctrine as limiting the possibilities of change.
  B. Should the clergy's goals be primarily societal or primarily Church-related?
    1. Proper role of clergy in relation to subcultural groups.
    2. The gap between action-oriented and withdrawal strategies.
    3. Associational vs. communal bonds.
D'Arcy used the following outline:
  1) Statistical studies of candidates, dropouts and deployment.
  2) Environmental factors in the background of religious vocation.
  3) Studies of religious vocation in the light of vocational development theory.
  4) Psychological characteristics as measured by personality, interest, aptitude and achievement tests.
  5) Studies of illness both physical and mental and of length of life.
  6) Attitudes of and toward religious personnel.
  7) Role studies.
  8) Sociological studies of the structure of religious communities.
  9) Bibliographies.

The present paper has drawn from all three of these classifications but no one of them was entirely suitable for the scope and purpose of this survey. The categories of Menges and Dittes were more comprehensive than required for the present review; yet, interestingly enough, the term "career" does not appear in them. Demereth's outline developed from a conference in which researchers in sociology and psychology met with Church officials from a variety of denominations; it too proved too broad for present purposes.

While D'Arcy's classification is somewhat more limited than the other two, his bibliography included statistical, clinical and theoretical studies conducted by sociologists, anthropologists, medical doctors, educators and psychologists in which the subjects were Catholic religious personnel. The present review concentrates mainly on empirical psychological research in which priests and seminarians served as subjects.

Consequently, for the purpose of this review, the following outline was developed:

  1) Early studies of priests and seminarians.
  2) Mental and physical health of members of this profession.
  3) Research using personality inventories with clerical groups.
  4) Interests and values of priests and seminarians.

5) The role of motivation on persistence and effectiveness in religious life.
6) Effects of seminary training.
7) Role of the priest and the nature of his work environment.
8) Stages of career development in the priesthood.

Early Psychological Studies

Psychological studies of seminarians and priests were undertaken by Sward (1931), who found religious life attracting more than its share of introverted individuals with feelings of inferiority; by Moore (1936), who studied the rate of mental illness among priests and concluded that prepsychotic individuals are frequently attracted to the priesthood; and by T. J. McCarthy (1942), who found seminarians to be less well adjusted on the Bell and Bernreuter personality inventories than norm groups of students in the same grade. Actually, Moore's data showed the total incidence of mental illness to be lower among priests than in the general population; his interpretation that disorders such as schizophrenia, alcoholism and paranoia are more common in priests than men in general was based on the percentage of hospitalized priests exhibiting a given disorder rather than on a comparison of the incidence of each diagnostic category in priests and men in general. Nevertheless, his studies highlighted (even if they exaggerated) the problem of emotional adjustment of seminarians and priests, thus, stimulating additional research and encouraging the development of programs for the psychological evaluation of applicants to religious life. The research that followed from this can be divided into two main types. One of these concentrated on measuring (chiefly through the use of personality and interest inventories) the characteristics of priests, seminarians and applicants to the seminary. The other continued Moore's concern with the extent of illness, particularly emotional illness, among clerical groups.

Some of this first group of studies are concerned with changes occurring during training, some with differences between dropouts and those who persevere, and others with attempts to distinguish those who are more or less effective according to some criterion — most commonly ratings by self, peers or supervisors. The second main type of research following from Moore will be reviewed first before proceeding to the far more numerous investigations of personality.

Mental and Physical Health of Priests

Results of research on the incidence of emotional illness among priests and seminarians have been sought as evidence for the degree of stress which members of this profession undergo as well as for an indication of the type of person attracted to this life. VanderVeldt and McAllister (1962), in their discussion of cases of alcoholism among priests, concluded that the presence of a dominant mother is common among priests and contributes to the development of alcoholism. They also compared symptoms of priests and lay Catholics being discharged from a psychiatric institute (McAllister & VanderVeldt, 1965), and concluded that alcoholism was more prevalent among priests. As with Moore's studies, however, the fact that a disorder is common among hospitalized priests tells us little about its incidence among priests in general. This would be a more valuable kind of information to have.

Studies providing evidence that the incidence of such disorders as alcoholism, schizophrenia, paranoia, depressive reactions or obsessive-compulsive neurosis is either greater or less among priests than in appropriate comparison groups have potential value in contributing to the understanding of personality dynamics which may be common among priests and in pointing up sources of stress to which they may be subject. Difficulties in the design of the relatively few studies done to date make conclusions here highly speculative at present.

Allied to this type of research are studies in which incidence of physical illness or longevity rate is presumed to reflect the degree of stress present in the occupation. Caffrey (1966) found the incidence of atherosclerotic coronary attacks to be significantly higher in a community of priests involved in teaching and administration compared with a group of monastic priests and brothers. The study, however, did not completely control differences in diet and other variables.

Studies of the life span in priests show mortality rates to be consistently lower than for men in general, although perhaps not as low as for teachers or Protestant clergy (Madigan, 1962; King & Bailer, 1969). Since mortality rates are generally less favorable for single than for married men, this might seem to provide a ready explanation for the difference in the figures for Catholic and Protestant clergymen; comparisons of single and married clergy, including married priests in the Eastern Catholic rite, have not, however, provided consistent support for such an interpretation.

Research Using Personality Inventories

The other major type of research stimulated by Moore's findings was the attempt to ascertain whether the priesthood was attracting more than its share of candidates who were poorly adjusted or who had unique and measurable characteristics of personality, interests, values and motives.

Many studies of priests and seminarians have dealt with characteristics present in such groups, but typically the design has not permitted a clear interpretation of whether the results were indicative of the type of applicant attracted to this life, the effect of attrition as some are screened or drop out during training, the impact of the experience in the seminary and the priesthood or to some combination of these factors.

Descriptive Studies With the MMPI

By far, the most widely used instrument for studying personality characteristics of seminarians and priests has been the Minnesota Multiphasic Personality Inventory (MMPI). Studies have typically found religious samples scoring higher on several scales indicative of maladjustment. Thus, T. N. McCarthy, after a review of the research of T. J. McCarthy (1942) with the Bell and Bernreuter, and that of Bier (1948) and Murray (1957) with the MMPI, concluded that:

> Studies of personality traits of priests and seminarians showed a consistent pattern in which the person entering religious life tends to score higher on neurotic scales than do other Catholics of the same age and the same educational and social background, the religious samples tending to be more submissive, introspective, dependent and self-conscious than a comparable sample drawn from the laity (McCarthy, 1960).

Dunn (1965) reviewed several studies of seminarians, priests and other religious conducted since the above three and drew the following similar conclusions:

> The consistency of MMPI profiles obtained from religious samples is most striking. All groups scored high on Pt and Sc. Male religious usually score high on Mf. This pattern suggests that religious tend to be more perfectionistic, worrisome, introversive, socially inept and in more extreme cases, perhaps isolated and withdrawn.

He also stated that ". . . religious and religious applicants show signs of defensive behavior typical of persons with neurotic tendencies." There are a few studies which run counter to these conclusions in that they found MMPI scores on samples of priests or seminarians to compare favorably with the norm group (Fehr, 1968; Gorman, 1961; McDonagh, 1961). There have also been criticisms of the above conclusions as requiring assumptions which may be unwarranted (Dittes, 1967; Rooney, 1967). A summary of the difficulties involved in making interpretations from studies using the MMPI will help place the results in perspective and assist in future research designs.

Limitations of the MMPI

Since Bier (1948) demonstrated that college students and professional students all differed from the general population in the same direction as seminarians — although his seminarians deviated more than the other groups — it is evident that studies which compare the religious sample with a norm group comparable in age, educational level and other background variables will yield different results than if the comparison is made with general population norms. The fact that these latter norms are not actually representative of men in general is an additional complication, but one which need not detract from their value provided they are used simply as a common reference point for comparing studies and not as a standard of desirable performance.

A second difficulty is the requirement that the subjects in the sample to be studied take the test under the same conditions as the norm group used for comparison. In some cases applicants or seminarians taking the test have assumed that the results would be used in deciding whether or not they would be admitted to the seminary or continued in it; such a condition might readily produce greater defensiveness or anxiety than in a norm group where those tested have been told that the results would have no effect on them personally. Other conditions on which the sample and norm group may differ include whether or not the participants are asked to identify themselves, directions given and the general attitude of the subjects toward participating in the testing.

A third problem in interpreting results of research on Catholic clergy stems from the fact that researchers have not all used the same form of the test; instead a modification of the standard form of the MMPI, developed by Bier for use with religious, has been employed in a number of studies. Results from the two forms may not be completely comparable. Skrincosky (1953), for example, found significantly higher scores on Pd, Mf, Sc, D, and Ma, on the modified form than on the standard form with a group of minor seminarians.

A fourth difficulty in interpreting results stems from the use of the K scale which was designed to detect and correct for a tendency to be defensive, to practice an unconscious type of self-deception, or to engage in role playing in responding to items on the MMPI (Welsh & Dahlstrom, 1956; Dahlstrom & Welsh, 1960). This score, or a fraction of it, is routinely added to several of the clinical scales with the intention of correcting such test-taking attitudes. The meaning of the K score is, however, a controversial question with some of the evidence suggesting that high K scores are characteristic of well-adjusted individuals, rather than indicating an unhealthy type of defensiveness (Dahlstrom & Welsh, 1960; Kania, 1967; Rooney, 1967). Since religious samples ordinarily score high on the K scale, this confounds the interpretation of scales Pt and Sc, to which the full K score is added, and scales Hs, Pd, and Ma, to which a fraction of the K score is added. Aside from the Mf scale, these are the scales which research studies on religious have found to be elevated most frequently — particularly the two to which the full K score has been added.

It would seem preferable for studies to compare uncorrected clinical scores of sample and norm groups as well as scores corrected with K.

A fifth problem is one that becomes critical once it has been demonstrated that religious groups really do score significantly higher on one or more of the scales of the MMPI: How are we to interpret the meaning of the deviant scores? Needed are studies which demonstrate how those who score high on particular scales differ from those who score low in other meaningful ways. Kania (1967) has attempted this for the K scale by relating it to a variety of other personality inventories. He concluded that high scores on it reflect a healthy type of defensiveness, low scores a poor self-concept. Similar studies on other scales are needed relating them to additional indices of personality, such as background variables, clinical interviews, ratings, projective devices and observations of behavior.

Since MMPI scales are not unidimensional, item analysis and factor analysis are also valuable aids to interpretation. Studies of the Mf scale, for example, have shown that it can be factored into five sub-scales: personal and emotional sensitivity, sexual identification, altruism, feminine occupational identification and denial of masculine occupations (Dahlstrom & Welsh, 1960). It is more helpful to know which of these sub-test scores are elevated than to know simply that the Mf score is high.

A final consideration is that interpretations based on average scores may mask differences. Profile analysis, which is based on patterns of high and low scores, is generally considered a superior procedure to working with individual scales; such studies require a large pool of cases in order to obtain a reasonable sample of subjects with various patterns of scores.

Until investigators have overcome limitations of the type indicated above, conclusions about personality traits of priests and seminarians based on results with the MMPI must be tentative and speculative; such interpretations can, of course, be cross-checked against other available evidence to test their plausibility.

Projective devices and depth interviewing have considerable potential for tapping the complex intrapsychic realm of the human personality. These methods require considerable sophistication on the part of re-searchers and a heavy investment in time, but they are essential to broaden the relatively limited focus provided by the MMPI and other personality inventories.

Experimental methods have been used but rarely in studying person-ality characteristics of priests and seminarians because of the difficulty in controlling the variables involved. One variable which has been studied by these methods is the attitude of the subject in an experiment and the manner in which this attitude is affected by the experimenter being a priest or a layman. Even for such an apparently simple variable, the results are complicated by such factors as the sex of the subject and the authenticity of the role of the experimenter (Walker and Firetto, 1965; Walker, Davis and Firetto, 1968).

Several other personality inventories, such as the Guilford-Zimmerman Temperament Survey, Cattell 16 Personality Factor Questionnaire and Edwards Personal Preference Schedule, have potential value in sup-plementing — and perhaps clarifying — the results reported with the MMPI; particularly since they are designed to detect individual differ-ences among a normal population — as contrasted with the MMPI which bases its comparison on various clinical groups. These tests are used in a number of programs assessing candidates for the religious life (Coville, 1962), but insufficient information has been reported on them to permit more than a tentative interpretation at present.

Characteristics Revealed By Other Personality Inventories

Relatively little research has been published on the personality of priests and seminarians as revealed by inventories other than the MMPI.

The Handbook for the Sixteen Personality Factor Questionnaire (16PF) cited data on 1,707 priests which showed them to deviate only moderately from the general population norms. The most notable char-acteristic indicated was a higher score on factor I (indicating a protected emotional sensitivity in childhood and a lower than average degree of self-reliance) and a lower score on factor F (showing a serious and sober disposition rather than a happy-go-lucky one). On secondary source traits the priests showed up as somewhat more introverted, anxious and dependent than the norm group (Cattell, Eber, & Tatsouka, 1970). This handbook gives data on a sample of 145 Catholic seminarians. They also were found to be emotionally sensitive, but compared with the norm group, they were more extraverted, self-assured and unpretentious. Whether the differences reported between seminarians and priests are the result of sampling, training, situational variables or other factors is not known. A footnote in the handbook indicates that the data for religious professionals were provided by Rev. Cletus B. Caffrey, Professor S. W. Stafford and Dr. M. T. Draffen (all from Catholic University) and Rev. Donald Clery (Peru), but additional information such as date and circumstances of testing or details of the samples are not given.

The Guilford-Zimmerman Temperament Survey was used by Sutter (1961) in testing 1,693 major seminarians from diocesan theological schools. Compared with a norm group of college students, the seminarians were revealed to be more submissive, introverted, sensitive, feminine and deliberate in the pace of their activities. At the same time, they were found to be more emotionally stable, serious-minded, tolerant, reflective and cooperative.

Lonsway (1967) used the Omnibus Personality Inventory and a specially constructed one to test 585 first year theology students, nearly equally divided between diocesan and religious, from 29 seminaries. Although statistically significant differences were found in a number of other variables, the author concluded that the major differences between his sample and the norm group of college students were that the seminarians showed a greater need for independence, a more trusting attitude in interpersonal relations, and a greater degree of satisfaction with their personal lives. Both diocesan and religious seminarians showed tolerance of uncertainty, interest in social activities, readiness to communicate with people, deep concern for the feelings and welfare of the people they meet and an emphasis on reflection and logic. Comparing the two groups of seminarians the religious were discovered to be more anxious and worried, more social and less practical in orientation, more concerned about interference with the rights of others, more liberal in religious views, more appreciative of the fine arts and less masculine in attitudes than the diocesan seminarians.

The use of undergraduate student norms as a basis for comparison with theology students is a practical expedient based on the lack of readily available norms for graduate and professional students on many tests. It does, however, introduce a limitation which must be kept in mind when interpreting the above results.

Personality and Perseverance in the Seminary

Turning next to studies comparing those who persevere in seminary training with those who drop out, we find results that are not completely consistent. Most research of this type has been done with the MMPI. Hispanicus (1962) and Sweeney (1964) both found Sc, Pt, and Pd to be significantly higher for those who withdraw, although Hispanicus' sample was quite small; Murray & Connolly (1966) reported Ma and Sc to be elevated significantly for dropouts; Weisgerber (1969) found high Pd scores to be the best predictor of withdrawal, with very low K scores also an effective predictor, and other patterns (e.g., Mf and Ma as highest peaks) worth further investigation. Vaughan (1963) failed to differentiate between the two groups, but found the profiles of dropouts to center around Hy-Pd and Pd-Ma peaks.

Barry (1960) developed a scale which successfully discriminated the two groups; he also found the non-persisters significantly higher on all scales except Ma and Hy. Other studies using this scale have not provided confirmation of it as a measure of perseverance (Coelho, 1963; Murray & Connolly, 1966; Weisgerber, 1969), but Carroll (1970) found it to be related to faculty ratings.

It is worth noting that for several of the MMPI scales on which seminarians deviate from the norm group, these studies suggest that those who leave the seminary deviate even more.

The higher Pd score among those who leave is also of interest, perhaps reflecting excessive independence or lack of appropriate control.

Those who persevere generally show up as a better adjusted group on the MMPI than those who drop out or are eliminated. There are, however, a number of inconsistencies in the results. Some of these arise from difficulties in sampling and research design. Additionally, the calibre of person who persists may vary considerably with the demands of the training program, the spirit of the peer group, the quality of faculty and staff and other such situational factors.

Lee (1968) used the 16PF as well as the Kuder and a number of attitudinal response items to compare 60 students who persisted in the seminary with 60 who voluntarily left. The 120 students were part of a group tested prior to graduating from high school who were followed up during college in the diocesan seminary. Although he found the majority of those who withdrew not to differ in personality from the majority of those who remained, the use of analysis of variance, regression analysis and cluster analysis revealed some differences. Persisters were significantly more submissive; dropouts were higher in self esteem. Seminarians who exhibited conformity of attitudes and behavior in social situations and those who were more feminine in interests and personality were likely to remain; those who displayed creativity on the tests were likely to leave.

Personality and Effectiveness

Attempts to relate scores on personality inventories to success in the seminary or the priesthood have most commonly used academic grades and ratings as criterion measures. Wauck (1956) and Webb, Goodling & Shepherd (1958) found MMPI scores not to differentiate between groups divided on the basis of faculty ratings and field work ratings respectively. Weisgerber (1969) concluded, on the basis of faculty ratings of seminarians, that high Pd scores reflect an independence which often produces difficulty in observing religious discipline. Ingram (1963) found a negative correlation between Pd scores and academic performance among divinity school students. Hispanicus (1962) reported a significant negative correlation between Pa scores and faculty ratings, with Pd and Pt also negative and close to significance, and Mf close to significance in a positive direction. Cardwell (1967) found grades of Protestant seminary students to be significantly correlated with Mf and originality and nearly so with Sc and K and Social Responsibility; near significant correlations were found between Mf and intelligence. Thompson (1956), using students from a Lutheran seminary, noted that those with deviant MMPI profiles did not achieve as well as predicted; Webb et al. (1958) and Ashbrook (1962) also confirmed this. Carroll (1970) reported that seminarians differing on ratings by faculty did not differ significantly on the MMPI previously taken as applicants, but did differ significantly on concurrent testing on scales D, Pd, Sc, Ma, Si and Barry's Re scale. Wright (1957), using concurrent testing on Army chaplains rated by a panel of supervising chaplains, found the low rating group to score significantly higher on L, F, Hs, D, Pd, Mf, Pa, Sc and to score significantly lower on Si.

The Pd score was higher in several of the less effective groups, as it was also in the case of those withdrawing from the seminary. Aside from this there was little in the way of a consistent pattern to the results. Quite possibly, the kinds of characteristics which differentiate the effective from the ineffective priest or seminarian vary with the personality traits present among the group under consideration (these would in turn vary with the recruiting and screening), and with the demands of the situation under which the individuals function.

Studies of changes occurring during the seminary training will be discussed in a later section of this review; they have generally found higher scores on the MMPI as training progresses (T. N. McCarthy, 1956; Murray, 1967; Carroll, 1970).

To summarize the results of research with personality inventories: numerous studies suggest that the priesthood is attracting more than its share of applicants with a low degree of masculine identification and a variety of emotional problems. The most frequently used inventory, the MMPI may be an inappropriate instrument for revealing more positive personality characteristics of seminarians and priests which studies using other inventories have suggested they also possess. Those who drop out often show poorer adjustment than those who persist, particularly in response to authority and in control of impulses; yet those who remain show signs of developing more problems as they progress in the training program. Such conclusions must be considered highly tentative, however, for the reasons discussed in this review. A number of studies have also reported differences between those seminarians and priests who are rated more and less effective, but little consistency is found in results of different groups.

Interest and Values

Studies of interests typical of priests and seminarians have been conducted using the Strong Vocational Interest Blank (SVIB), and to a lesser extent, the Kuder. D'Arcy (1962) has reviewed this research, reporting a dozen studies, including two describing development of special scales for priests on the SVIB: the diocesan priest scale by Lhota (1948), and his own missionary priest scale (D'Arcy, 1954; Kennedy, 1958). Lepak (1968) reviewed this research more briefly in conjunction with the report of his new scale for priests on the revised SVIB, while D'Arcy (1968b) added some comments on the role of research on clergy interests. Studies of the values of clergymen have been conducted with the Allport-Vernon Study of Values (or its revision, the Allport-Vernon-Lindzey) which measures the relative strength of six categories of values: theoretical, economic, aesthetic, social, political and religious.

In Lepak's study, in which he administered the 1966 revision of the SVIB to a representative sample of priests from one diocese, he found priests to score high (primary patterns) on Group V: Social Service and Group VI: Aesthetic-Cultural. They had reject patterns (a majority of scores lower than men in general) on Group II: Physical Science; Group IV: Technical and Skilled Trades; Group VII: CPA Owner; Group VIII: Business and Accounting; Group IX: Sales; and Group XI: President, Manufacturing Concern. These findings are consistent with the results of previous research with SVIB, although missionary priests and seminarians have normally scored fairly high in technical and outdoor interests.

Lepak's Priest Criterion Group scored highest on the SVIB Basic Interest Scales for Religious Activities, Social Service, Public Speaking, Teaching and Writing and lowest on Technical Supervision, Mechanical and Agriculture. The group scored relatively "feminine" on the Masculinity-Feminity Scale (as is common in occupational groups with cultural and altruistic interests) and higher than average on the Occupational Level Scale (indicating interests more similar to professional men and business executives than to blue collar workers). These results on the two non-occupational scales are consistent with previous research.

On the Kuder, seminarian groups typically have scored high in social service, literary and musical interest, and low in mechanical, scientific and clerical interests.

There are, of course, a number of variables which influence interest scores of religious personnel, at least to some extent, including age, educational level, socioeconomic background, geographical region, parental occupation and type of work to which particular religious communities are dedicated.

Most attempts to differentiate those who persevere in the seminary from those who drop out have been unable to do so on the basis of interests, although those who withdraw have often been found to possess more alternate areas of primary interests. Maffia (1954) developed a scale which discriminated ordained priests from seminary dropouts, but the reliability of the scale was rather low, and no additional studies using it have been reported in the literature.

Lee (1968), using the Kuder, found a group of 60 who persevered in a diocesan seminary to have higher musical and social service interests and lower literary and scientific interests than a matched group who voluntarily withdrew. This differs from Kenney's findings using 125 matched pairs of persisting and non-persisting seminarians studying to be foreign mission priests. Here no significant differences were detected on the Kuder, but the Strong showed the persisting group to have somewhat higher technical interests and lower verbal-linguistic interests than those who withdrew. Although the differences were not large, they were statistically significant (Kenney, 1959).

With increasing time in the seminary, groups become more homogeneous in tested interests. It is not clear whether this is caused by the departure of students whose interests differ from the group or by changes in interests of seminarians who remain.

Although priests as a group share considerable interests in common, there are a wide variety of interests present among them. There is also considerable diversity in the type of work which they perform. Whether those who are involved in tasks consistent with their interests are more satisfied or effective than those who are not has yet to be investigated. The interests of men leaving the priesthood or requesting change of assignment to a different type of work is also an area that is ripe for research.

The Allport-Vernon Study of Values has been used in a number of studies with samples of religious personnel since T. J. McCarthy (1942) used it in his research with seminarians. He found religious interests to be predominant in his sample, as was expected. Several other studies of clerical groups have been consistent with this, although small differences on other scales have been found with different groups.

The Allport-Vernon-Lindzey revision of the Study of Values has been used in studies of Catholic seminarians by Weisgerber (1969) and with Protestant seminarians by Maehr and Stake (1962). Both found seminarians significantly higher on religious and social values than control groups of non-seminary students, and significantly lower on theoretical, economic and political values. Weisgerber (1969) concluded on the basis of his research with the Study of Values that it was not a useful device for identifying potential dropouts since their scores were so similar to those of seminarians who persisted. He recommends it, however, as having potential value for counseling and guidance with students considering a career in the priesthood or religious life.

It is reasonable to assume that values play an important part in the lives of priests, particularly in view of the relationship between values, interests, attitudes and motives. Yet research on the values of priests has been sparse and limited to relatively simple studies using the one readily available test in this area.

Motivation

In addition to the research on traits measured by the MMPI, the SVIB and other standardized personality and interests inventories, several studies using a variety of procedures have emphasized the importance of motivational factors in predicting persistence and effectiveness in religious life.

Weisgerber (1969) found that 92% of the candidates for the seminary who were rated by the psychologist as having poor motivation dropped out. A similar high figure was found with applicants to a community of teaching sisters (Rooney, 1966). While such results point up a major area for investigation, they do not delineate the dynamics underlying the weak or inappropriate motivation. The assessment is typically a global one, using a number of tests and other devices including an interview.

Those rated as having poor motivation by such a diagnosis might include applicants who openly express doubt about the appropriateness of their choice as well as those who are convinced of the rightness of their choice, yet, reveal signs of deficits or conflicts in this area during the assessment. Potvin & Suziedelis (1969) in their national survey of seminarians show instances of open expression of doubts being a good predictor of withdrawal. Seminarians who withdraw within the year following the data collection were more likely than those remaining to agree to such questions as: "I am almost certain that I will give up the idea of becoming a priest," "I don't know why I want to become a priest," and "I am not absolutely certain that I want to be a priest." On the other hand, in the research of Lee (1968) those seminarians who were certain in 8th grade that they had a vocation to the priesthood were more likely to leave. Another finding of Potvin & Suziedelis (1969) involved those who responded on the questionnaire that they, as a priest, would seriously consider marrying if the Church would allow it. Three to four times as many of those who responded in this way left the seminary compared with those who indicated they would not marry even if it were permitted.

Sheridan and Kobler (1969) used the Loyola Seminarian Sentence Completion Test with a group of seminarians; although they found high concurrent validity for all subtests using psychologist's judgment as a criterion, the only subtest predicting persistence in the seminary was attitude toward the priesthood.

Perhaps the most striking studies of motivation of religious by means of a diagnostic device is the use of the Thematic Apperception Test (TAT) by Arnold (1962) and two of her students with teaching Sisters and student Brothers. These researchers used a Story Sequence Analysis and concentrated on the "motivational pattern" or "principles of action" revealed in the stories. In one study using this method, teaching Sisters rated high by their pupils were successfully differentiated from those ranking low (Burkard, 1958); in another with scholastics in a community of teaching Brothers, there was relatively high correlation between scores on the TAT and ratings of "promise for religious life" by peers (r = .59) and by superiors (r = .61) (Quinn, 1961).

A survey of the literature failed to turn up any similar studies on priests or seminarians, although the procedures used seem to hold considerable promise and the results are consistent with the more extensive research demonstrating convincingly that the TAT can be used successfully to assess motivation in a variety of groups (McClelland, Atkinson, Clark & Lowell, 1953).

Another instrument with considerable potential for research in this area is the Theological School Inventory (Dittes, 1964), designed to tap the various patterns of motivation found in theological students. Widely used in Protestant seminaries, particularly for counseling purposes, its worth has been demonstrated by a number of investigators. A modified form of this device for use with Catholic seminarians or a new inventory designed in a similar manner could make a significant contribution to research on motivation.

Effects of Seminary Training

Since Vatican II there have been an increasing number of questions raised about the nature of training for the priesthood and its impact on the seminarian. Wagoner (1966) reports a number of observations and suggestions after extensive visits to Catholic seminaries and discussions with officials and faculty. Compared with Protestant seminaries he found a heavier emphasis on spiritual formation, which he finds praiseworthy, but this was often accompanied by a failure to appreciate its essential relationship to the development of the total human personality, which he deems unfortunate; moreover, the need of the seminarian to accept responsibility for his choices and develop personal autonomy and initiative were often stifled by a fixed, rigid routine in which the student learned to passively follow the structure established by those in authority.

There have also been a number of studies reporting changes in personality test scores during training. In his review of such studies up to early 1966, T. N. McCarthy (1970) concluded that greater deviation in personality variables occurs with increased time in training, but that a reversion to a more normal pattern takes place after ordination; he urged caution in making these interpretations because of the relatively few studies and the fact that they were cross-sectional rather than longitudinal. Murray & Connolly (1966) and Carroll (1970) have since reported longitudinal studies which concur in the conclusion that greater deviation takes place as training progresses. Carroll observed that there is some partial evidence for the existence of critical periods where the students find "greater pressure, higher levels of anxiety, and deeper feelings of frustration at this time of their religious life than they had experienced or would later experience."

Differences in academic quality of seminaries are present, of course, and have been shown to be related to enrollment levels and matriculation rate (Potvin & Suziedelis, 1969). The relationship of such factors as quality of the faculty, adequacy of student personnel services, characteristics of the peer group, and other situational factors to the personality changes taking place during training must still be investigated.

Looking back at their own seminary training, the majority of the national sample of curates surveyed by Fichter (1968) agreed that it prepared them to lead a holy and intellectual life, but not to work with the laity nor to handle the practical problems of the parish work. Younger priests were generally less satisfied with their training than the older ones, perhaps reflecting a failure of improvements taking place in the seminary to keep pace with the rising tide of expectations.

Questions have also been raised concerning the desirability of the strict sexual segregation of seminarians, or whether dancing, dating and other such social activities should be permitted. Research in this area, though relatively limited, has been summarized by Kobler, Pizza and Doyle (1967).

Present day seminarians, as indicated in the survey of Potvin & Suziedelis (1969) are generally satisfied with the quality of seminary training, rating it good or excellent. They are not, however, equally pleased with all aspects of their training, for example, 65 to 70 per cent of those at the theological level rate the quality of instruction as most in need of reform — particularly with respect to its "relevancy." Students at the high school level report the highest degree of satisfaction with the seminary; as they progress through college and theological training they become more critical. In general, student personnel services and professional training programs have a greater influence on student evaluations of the seminary than does academic quality.

The influence of seminary training on the career development of priests is considered in a later part of this chapter.

Role and Work Environment of Priests

Characteristics found in any priest are determined not only by the traits he possessed when he entered the seminary and the influence of the training experience on his development, but also by the role or situation in which he functions after ordination. The role of the priest and the circumstances under which he lives and works will naturally influence his satisfaction, attitudes and effectiveness. All of these, in turn, will affect the image of the priest and the number and kinds of young men who will be attracted to this vocation.

Here research falls into the area where psychology and sociology overlap; sociology, starting with the structure of the organization within which the priest functions; psychology moving from the individual coping with the demands imposed on him by the situation.

In this area the work of Fichter (1968) and Schneider & Hall (1970) are particularly valuable. Fichter employed a questionnaire mailed to a one-third sample of all diocesan priests in the United States who were not pastors or monsignors and received replies from 51% of them. Previously, he had surveyed a nationwide sample of diocesan curates and pastors (Fichter, 1965). Schneider & Hall (1970) studied pastors, curates and diocesan priests on special assignments (high school teaching, hospital chaplain, newspaper work, etc.) in a single diocese, obtaining a 75% reply to the mailed questionnaire. As an aid in selecting the questions, 95 priests were first interviewed to help determine what issues they considered most important in their work life.

Both studies considered — among other things — working conditions, and in both cases, relationship to the pastor was an item considered highly significant by curates. In Fichter's survey, although most curates appraised rectory relationship as happy or fairly so, about one-third reported them as "fairly strained" or merely "formal and correct." Most curates are not consistently involved in joint planning of parish projects, although about one-half report free and open two-way communication in the rectory and a third indicate the relationship is such that they normally call the pastor by his first name. Whether or not curates feel their talents are being utilized is related to relationship with the pastor: where relations are poor, eight out of ten report that they are not working up to capacity; where relations are good, this figure drops to four out of ten.

Schneider & Hall found marked differences in work functioning, perceptions and satisfaction among priests based on whether they were pastors, curates or specials. There were also individual differences cutting across all groups in ideas of the role of the priest and the Church in today's society.

The type of activities that priests perform were divided, based on factor analysis, into four categories: Parochial, Community Involvement, Administration and Personal Development. Parochial activities included saying Mass in church, administering the sacraments and visiting the sick; community involvement incorporated such activities as saying Mass in homes, attending community meetings and participating in ecumenical work; administration involved supervising lay employees, administering the school and parish and raising funds; personal development included private prayer, reading and taking training designed for self-improvement. Aside from parochial duties, which are identical for both groups, curates report significantly less activity in each of the other dimensions than do pastors. At the same time, curates feel that community involvement and personal development are more important to them than do pastors who, in turn, put more emphasis on administrative work. In general, both groups see the job of parish priest as a meaningful one where there is important work to be done, and prefer it to a special assignment. Curates, however, often feel that even though they are kept busy their talents are underutilized and they are not able to do the type of work in the parish which they believe should be done. Responses similar to the Fichter study were obtained in that more than 8 out of 10 of the pastors and specials reported their most important skills and abilities being utilized either "a great deal" or "fairly much," but fewer than 4 out of 10 of the curates responded in this way. Here too, the situation under which the priest is working in his present assignment emerges as the most important factor influencing his work satisfaction, self-image and use of skills and abilities. Compared with pastors and priests on special assignments, curates find this work climate to be relatively poorer and their work less challenging and satisfying. The superior-subordinate relationship shows up as a key one in influencing the attitude of the curate. Commonly, there was dissatisfaction when little autonomy or responsibility was given and, at the other extreme, where the assistant was left entirely on his own with little or no consultation or support. A type of supervision which permitted autonomy and responsibility, yet provided for assistance when needed, seemed most effective.

Pastors rated their assignments significantly higher than curates on all dimensions of work climate, but differences present among pastors are more related to whether or not they have been assigned to a "good" parish and to their evaluation of their superior rather than to the work climate or activities performed.

Priests on special assignment rated their work climate higher than pastors, indicating that they find more challenge and meaning and personal acceptance in their work.

For all three types of assignment, however, superior effectiveness was given a lower relative ranking than the other three dimensions of work climate found in the study (work challenge and meaning, personal acceptance and supportive autonomy).

Returning to Fichter's nationwide research, he also investigated relationships between priest and bishop, finding that more than half of the curates expressed a negative opinion on three related items: personal interest of the bishop, his communication with them and the free and open communication existing in the diocese. Pastors have a less negative view of relations with the bishop, with a third of them indicating that the bishop had quite a bit of personal interest in pastors and curates, and priests on special assignments outside the parish tend to have the closest communication with the bishop. Fichter (1968) found strong support among his sample for a diocesan senate of clergy, a personnel committee and an elected grievance committee.

The image that priests and religious project to young people was examined in a survey in the New Orleans Archdiocese (Louis, Bowles & Grace, 1967). The subjects of the study were 79 priests (33 pastors and 46 assistants), 31 Brothers and 246 Sisters. Those priests and religious who were in a position to associate with young people reported that the image which priests projected to them was a relatively unattractive one. A large part of that image seemed related to inadequate interpersonal relations existing among priests and religious and between them and the laity. The survey reported a feeling that if priests and religious would relate to one another in a more warm and personal way it would improve the general spirit and effectiveness of the Church as well as foster more vocations. Differences of opinion about the work of the priest were also indicated — particularly between pastors and curates. The authors summarized this as follows:

> As a group, pastors are found to be somewhat differently oriented than their assistants but they concur in the general need for improvement of interpersonal relationships. Assistants are more inclined to express need for greater opportunities to work with people on a personal level and help them with individual problems. Pastors are disposed to look for ways to make their assistants more under-

standing of over-all parish problems and more cooperative in matters of administration. Pastors particularly, but others also, complain of the burdens of administration. Many pastors point out they could be of greater service to people if there were ways of lightening the burden of parish administration, hopefully by sharing more of it with competent and interested laymen.

The marked turmoil presently taking place in the Church and the weakening of the social structure supporting the traditional role of the priest is bound to affect his life and work. A discussion of role conflict among the clergy and a number of suggestions for research in this area is contained in the Proceedings of the Research Conference on Ministry (Mills, 1968) and in the work of Kinnane (1970). The traditional view sees the priest in a sacred state: set apart; performing routinized duties; practicing self-denial; dedicated to the institution; relating to the laity in a formal manner primarily as a spiritual authority; measuring success by a code which emphasized following the rule; a priest 24 hours a day, every day. Set against this view are those who by their words and actions opt for a change to a professional role: living a more secular life in the world; emphasizing innovation and creativity; developing skills and abilities; operating outside the typical structure; relating to the laity on a personal, social and professional level in cooperative action; serving as an agent of social change; having a personal life apart from work as a priest.

Career Development in the Priesthood

Such controversy over the proper role of the priest and the related issues emerging from the re-examination of the Church and its institutions may generate major changes in the nature of this career. For the present, however, research is available only on the career development of today's priests and the various stages they have undergone. These empirical findings may also shed some light on the paths future priests will follow.

Some aspects of career development were touched on earlier in this paper in reviewing studies of the personality of seminarians and priests as well as in the section on role and work climate. In this section, research relating to the career development of priests is reviewed starting with childhood interest and moving through the various stages to retirement.

The seeds of a vocation are planted at an early age. Potvin & Suziedelis (1969) indicate that 86% of all seminarians first thought of a vocation to the priesthood in elementary school; Hall and Schneider (1969) report one-third of their respondents made the decision to enter by this time. Boys thinking of the priesthood are often encouraged to serve as altar boys or to become members of some parish club or other organization where such interests may be examined or fostered. Why some boys are attracted to this vocation and others are not, how those expressing such interests differ from those who do not, and what impact participating in various prevocational activities has, are some examples of possible research questions at this early stage of career development. The influence of parents and personal contacts with priests and religious are worth examining. Many with such early interests quickly decide against this career, but in others it persists to the point where they enter the seminary. Potvin & Suziedelis (1969) report that seminarians come mostly from middle income families. Few have fathers who are college graduates. Most come from larger families where the parents attend Mass regularly and receive Holy Communion frequently. They are likely to have attended Catholic schools. Most of this is consistent with Fichter's earlier report of the background of seminarians. But his observation that most were from urban areas differs from the more recent finding that more are from the suburbs and smaller cities. This may simply be a reflection of the shifts in population that have taken place as revealed in the 1970 census data. Fichter (1961) also noted that the seminarian is more likely than the non-seminarian to have one or more close relatives in the religious life. In Fichter's later survey, although the majority of priests indicate that they did not enter seminary training until after high school (and one out of six not until after college), nearly three out of ten entered a minor seminary directly from elementary school (Fichter, 1968). Many students apparently enter at this age with the idea of "trying it out," and Potvin & Suziedelis (1969) suggest that some parents see it as an inexpensive private boarding school.

Fichter (1961), discussing the relative influence of various individuals in encouraging the choice of a vocation to the priesthood, comments:

> A general stereotype has existed among Catholics to the effect that the strongest influence and encouragement to the religious career comes from the candidate's mother. Professional religious functionaries seem to have a greater attachment to their mother than to their fathers, and in the past they have often been quoted as saying that they 'owe everything,' especially their vocation, to their mothers. Current research surveys, however, show consistently that the greatest encouragement to the seminary comes from priests. . . .

He goes on to indicate, however, that for those entering the minor seminary immediately after elementary school the order of influence is: mother, religious Sister, priest, father; further, he cautions that the results, based as they are on surveys, are dependent on the respondents' awareness and memory. Potvin & Suziedelis (1969) found results that emphasize the role of the mother. In an attempt to ascertain how vocations are fostered, they studied the relationship of perceived parental environment to vocational choice. Commenting on previous studies of family influence they state:

> What has been lacking, with but a rare exception, are studies of the more dynamic psychological dimensions of the parental environment, and of the relevance of such dimensions to the vocational choice. The human role of the priest has some easily specifiable attributes, which, taken together, are unique among vocations: a life of celibacy, a greater or lesser degree of required submission to authority, a mission to work with and among people, assumptions of one or another form of leadership, a long apprenticeship in community living, acceptance of some lifelong rules of discipline and of prescribed activities. It seems logical to assume that whatever prepares a person to 'fit' such requirements deserves study.

To assess this parental environment the investigators used a newly developed instrument consisting of several brief scales, and administered it to the seminary sample at the high school, college and theologate level. For comparison groups, high school and college students from eight Catholic institutions were used. Analyses of the data were made based on differences between the responses of the comparison group and a sample of seminarians matched with them on a number of appropriate background variables. Although the non-seminary samples may not be representative of Catholic high school and college students, they are probably a reasonable approximation. Additional samples of students at these levels can be surveyed with this instrument in the future; a comparison group for the theologate level might also be sought.

In interpreting the results, the authors emphasize the key role of the mother in encouraging her son to aspire to this vocation and in sustaining this interest. Both parents, though strict, are seen as affectionate and supportive, but there is a special closeness between the mother and the seminarian — especially the religious seminarian. This relationship with the mother is also related to the tendency to define the priesthood in sacred terms and the willingness to accept celibacy, as well as to perseverance in the seminary. Further studies may want to focus on the dynamics of maternal relationship to see when it fosters a type of maturity required to meet the demands of the priesthood and when it encourages a dependency, passivity or sex-role identification which is maladaptive. In any case, surveys such as Fichter's which report a priest as being more influential than the seminarian's mother in encouraging him to consider a vocation to the religious life seem to greatly underestimate the role of the mother.

Barry & Bordin (1967), based on an analysis of the ministerial career, developed a number of hypotheses about the kinds of gratifications those attracted to this vocation might expect to achieve and therefore the characteristics we might find in its members. Assuming that the priest is seen as speaking for a distant, all-powerful master and taking on some of his authority without displacing him, they hypothesize that a certain kind of relationship is likely to be found between boys attracted to this vocation and their parents. They speculate that the child's relationship is to an idealized father held up as a model by the mother, particularly when the real father is absent or inadequate. The mother, then, would be particularly important, and the son would develop a mixed masculine and feminine sex role by identifying in part with the mother, because of her closeness and influence, and in part with the idealized father in whose name she speaks. These authors find some support for this and a number of other hypotheses from a collection of biographical and autobiographical material on clergymen and from a review of empirical studies. While the Potvin & Suziedelis (1969) study supports the special significance of the mother, it does not show the father as typically absent or inadequate; rather he is seen by the seminarians as more affectionate and accepting compared with the way the average non-seminarian views his father. The role of the father's personality and his relationship to his wife and son deserves further study.

Hall & Schneider (1969) have expressed concern over the relatively early age at which the tentative career choice to the priesthood is made, the indications that the decision is often greatly influenced by someone else and the relatively passive part the individual seems to play in the choosing. A related problem worth investigation is the opportunity present in the seminary to realistically explore alternate vocational choices. Where this opportunity is absent or greatly limited, some individuals who are unsuited for this career may drift along passively, lacking the initiative to leave yet not so obviously unqualified as to be dismissed. The degree to which the seminary presents a realistic picture of even the priestly vocation cannot be taken for granted. Kinnane's (1970) comment on the observation of another investigator is worth noting:

> William F. Tageson (1960), in his role of scientist-practitioner, has concluded on the basis of empirical research that seminary faculties, even on the minor seminary level, are very consistent in their decidedly Spartan concept of the 'ideal seminarian' which is impressed quite early on the boys under their charge. It is highly significant that this Spartan ideal was found to bear no empirical relationship to the faculty's concept of the 'average seminarian.' It must be concluded that the uncritical presentation of such a demanding ideal at this level of immature development can hardly be effective, and may indeed be damaging in light of modern psychological knowledge of maturation and learning.

No doubt seminarians have changed during the decade since this observation was made. Keef's study of high school seniors in boarding seminaries, Catholic boys' schools and Catholic coed schools did not find any evidence of great differences in psychological maturity in the four groups, and would tend to refute the position that minor seminary training retards the development of psychological maturity (Keefe, 1968).

There is still the continued need to study the extent to which seminaries provide students with the opportunity to explore and modify a tentative vocational choice on the basis of realistic information about the priesthood, about alternative choices and about the possibilities for implementing their self-concept through this career in the light of their present level of development.

A study by Lavoie (1968) suggests that seminaries are not providing a desirable kind of environment for helping young people achieve a sound identity. He compared students in the relatively restricted environment of the seminary with Catholic students in the relatively freer environment of the non-seminary high school and college. Analysis of the tapes of interviews with the participants led to the conclusion that a restricted environment produces an identity foreclosure, i.e., a premature acceptance of an identity from others, whereas a free environment promotes a facing of the identity crisis and a resolution of it into an achieved identity.

Many who enter the seminary decide not to continue in this career. Fichter (1961) reports that fewer than one-sixth of those entering the freshmen year of high school in diocesan minor seminaries reach ordination. Potvin & Suziedelis (1969) give figures that suggest the present rate of withdrawal is even higher: one year after their survey 25% of the high school students, 21.2% of the college group and 11.7% of those at the theologate level were no longer enrolled in the seminary. The loss is greatest at the point of transition from high school to college: 34% do not go on in the seminary. Those who leave at the high school and college level were found, in this study, to have a stronger identification with the father than those remaining. They were inclined to be more dogmatic and less likely to define the role of the clergy primarily in sacred terms or to accept celibacy as a requirement.

Kinnane (1970) reports the major reason young adults give for leaving the seminary involves the struggle for autonomy in choice. He comments that the normal course of development in adolescence is from a dependence and outer-directedness to an increasing independence and self-direction, and he emphasizes the need for seminaries to foster psychological self-support.

The research of Lee (1968) mentioned in an earlier section of this review is consistent with this position in that it found those withdrawing from the seminary to be less submissive or conforming and higher in self-esteem than those perserving. Studies with the MMPI, however, more frequently find those who leave to be less well adjusted than those remaining. The Pd score, which is commonly higher, may reflect greater independence or less control.

Seminary training is the first critical career experience, according to Schneider & Hall (1970), followed by ordination, first assignment, later assignments and pastorate. These investigators see the process as one in which the steps in the answer are influenced less by the priest's own initiative than by seniority within the system. This makes it difficult for him to learn to make decisions about his future and to experience the psychological success and growth that occurs when a person accomplishes goals through his own efforts.

They comment:

> We conceive of the general dependence of priests on the system to be the result of two interacting factors: 1) a tendency for immature decision-makers who are passive, non-choosing individuals to enter the system, and 2) the tendency for the organization to create and reinforce acquiescence and non-choosing. The combination of some individuals with a tendency toward passivity and a system rewarding passivity creates a potent climate inhibiting psychological success.

After completing his seminary training and being ordained, the new priest receives his first assignment. This step in his career development shows up as affecting his attitudes throughout his career (Schneider & Hall, 1970). Fichter (1968) found in his survey that the typical curate feels that the seminary has not prepared him for many of the realities of the work or the interpersonal relations involved. If he is fortunate enough to have an excellent pastor or other supervisor who provides him with a desirable model of the life and work of a priest and who gives him responsibility and support, his self-perception and degree of satisfaction will tend to be higher throughout his career than if he is first assigned to a situation where the superior is a source of frustration or confusion.

The need for some type of parish internship as part of the priest's training, the care required in making first assignments and the importance of helping pastors learn to be more effective in supervising and training new assistants are all suggested by these findings.

Schneider & Hall (1970) in the diocese they studied found that the typical curate believed that his abilities were being under-utilized particularly in his early years as a priest. They found that it took twenty-two years before the average curate was given the opportunity to take on the challenge and responsibility of the pastorate. In this survey curates reported some increase in responsibility from the sixth to the sixteenth year after ordination, followed by a decline in the five years preceding appointment as a pastor.

There are, of course, wide differences from one diocese to the next in the length of time the average priest serves as a curate before being made a pastor, from as little as five years in one of the least populous dioceses to as many as thirty in one of the most populous (Fichter, 1968). During the years he spends as a curate he will usually change assignments several times. Among Fichter's respondents between 35 and 49 years of age, 15% were still on their first assignment, 47% on their second or third, 27% on their fourth or fifth and 11% on their sixth or more. As for the manner of making the change, the great majority (84%) stated that they were simply told to report to their new assignment, typically on very short notice. Considerable dissatisfaction with the method of making assignments was indicated by the strong support expressed for 1) the establishment of a personnel office to work out clergy assignments (86%), 2) interviewing curates before making assignments (83%) and 3) giving curates ample notice to prepare for a new appointment (89%). Some diversity exists in the type of assignments available in most dioceses. Although over half of the diocesan priests in Fichter's sample were serving as full-time curates, one-fourth were in non-parish assignments and another fifth were part-time curates. These non-parish assignments chiefly involve high school teaching, but also include a variety of other kinds of duties. This would indicate that, at least in many dioceses, a priest stands a good chance of service in a position outside of parish work for some time during his career. The impact of this interim assignment on career development has been only slightly explored. So far the evidence indicates that curates do not aspire to this type position, but that those who are involved in it find their work more challenging and satisfying than do curates (Hall & Schneider, 1969). A large majority of priests (87%) believe that "curates who want to prepare for specialized work should be encouraged to do so"; moreover, the majority of those in this type assignment have, or intend to obtain, graduate academic degrees, while the large majority of curates do not intend to go beyond the Bachelor's degree (Fichter, 1968). The overwhelming majority (86%) of Fichter's respondents endorse the statement that "diocesan priests should have periodical sabbatical leaves to take refresher courses in the work and problems of the ministry." When asked if they themselves had attended summer institutes or study weeks in the preceding year, 48% of the men in specialized work replied that they had, compared to only 30% of the curates; however, more than twice as many of the non-curates (33%) were table to attend outside their vacation time as compared with those in parishes (17%). The availability and impact of various kinds of continuing educational programs on the career development, satisfaction and effectiveness of priests is a topic worth investigation.

Although a priest may change assignments several times throughout his career, the first promotion is usually considered the long-delayed promotion to pastor. Fichter (1961) indicates other possibilities to consider:

> Career-wise, there are other positions and honors in the diocese. A diocesan priest may be an assistant in the Chancery office, a teacher in the seminary, active in the parochial school system. Other positions, like head of Catholic Charities, superintendent of schools, editor of the diocesan newspaper, are sometimes held by men who are already pastors, and often by monsignors. Similarly the various committees that function under the bishops are most frequently composed of pastors.

There has been even less research published in the literature on the career development of priests who are members of religious communities. Here two avenues of progress are normally provided. One is within the community structure as superior or one of several intermediate positions;

these are usually held for a limited time after which the individual must be replaced. The second is within the institution with which the community is affiliated, i.e., school, college, university, hospital, etc. The opportunity to move into positions of responsibility would seem likely to come more rapidly for priests in religious communities than for diocesan priests. Studies similar to those of Fichter (1968) and Schneider & Hall (1970) would contribute greatly toward a better understanding of career development in religious.

A trend toward moving out of large communities into smaller groups or more personal apostolic and professional work is also evident among religious, producing some marked changes in the nature of this career.

Returning to the diocesan priest, the promotion to pastor makes a major change in his career. As far as the basis of promotion to this position is concerned, 78% of curates across the nation agree with the opinion that it should be based on ability rather than seniority (Fichter, 1968), but in actual practice seniority seems to be the major consideration. Although they have been preparing for the pastorate for many years, most pastors studied by Hall & Schneider (1969) reported that they did not feel that this experience provided them with the training needed to meet the demands of the job. Many of them, in fact, felt overwhelmed by their new responsibilities and experienced a decline in their own self-image. The new pastor reported spending considerable time in administrative activities and indicated a lack of training for this, but pastors in this survey by Hall & Schneider (1969) also saw themselves as more involved in community activity and personal development than did curates. The need for in-service training for those priests who are soon to be assigned to the pastorate is clearly indicated by these findings. So, too, is the importance of giving curates greater responsibilities in the administration of the parish.

In this study, the degree of satisfaction reported by pastors increased rapidly in the first years of their new position so that the average pastor had a much more positive attitude toward his work and a higher degree of satisfaction than the average curate; he was still not as satisfied, however, as the average professional man according to the national norms used by the authors. Fichter (1968) reports differences in degree of satisfaction among pastors to be related to the type of parish they are in, with the more satisfied pastors being in a large parish with few debts. As for their manner of assignment and transfer, the 1960 survey of Fichter showed that one-half of the pastors were "simply told to report to their present assignment," while some degree of consultation was reported by the other half. In the diocese studied by Schneider & Hall (1970), pastors were usually given the opportunity to refuse a reassignment.

Relatively little information is available about the characteristics of pastors and the effect of various background and situational factors in influencing their effectiveness and satisfaction, but this important step in the priest's career deserves the attention of researchers. This is true to an even greater extent of bishops and others in high administrative posts in the Church. Social and behavioral scientists who conduct research on organizations emphasize the advantage of studying administrators at the highest possible level since their influence extends throughout the system. Empirical research by psychologists and sociologists on bishops and other administrators is apparently non-existent. Yet information of this kind could be invaluable to such officials in assessing their role in the contemporary Church and in helping them to supply the leadership needed in facing the challenges of our time.

Although few priests reach this stage in their career, all who survive long enough reach the stage of retirement. Hall & Schneider (1969) conclude from their observations that the transition from active priest to retirement is often as great as those from seminary to first assignment and from curate to pastor. The newly retired priest is probably equally unprepared for this new status. Research on this career stage could help clarify problems involved and pave the way for a more serene retirement.

Summary and Conclusions

Psychological studies of the priesthood are a part of the rapidly growing body of research in the social and behavioral sciences on religious careers.

The empirical information emerging from these studies has potential value for anyone who is concerned with helping present and future priests be more effective and find greater fulfillment in their work.

Yet there has been no grand design for the research. Instead, as is common in behavioral science, investigators have selected questions that were convenient or interesting at the time and supplied partial answers to them; new researchers have moved on to new questions in preference to wrestling with the traditional ones until they were clarified and answered definitively.

Starting with the concern of Moore that an excessive number of priests might be developing serious emotional illness, the focus of research effort moved first to the characteristics of seminarians which were revealed by interest and personality inventories and then to the influence of seminary training on personality development.

More recently, research inquiry has expanded its scope to include the various stages that the priest goes through, sometimes smoothly, sometimes stressfully, and the situations he experiences as he progresses in his career.

It has been common knowledge that vocations to the priesthood come more frequently from certain types of family background; it is only recently, however, that the personality dynamics existing in the family have been disclosed — particularly the special closeness existing between the mother and the future priest. The dominant role of the mother (along with an affectionate and supporting father) appears to be a crucial element in influencing a youngster to project himself into an idealized role at an early stage of career development, rather than to identify with the father and model his behavior after him. Later, in adolescence, the presence of a priest who can provide an appealing real-life image seems also to be significant.

The characteristics of seminarians and priests that are revealed by tests of personality and interest are compatible with the above observations. Typically those entering the seminary are found to be interested in people and desirous of helping them, emotionally sensitive, cooperative (often to the point of being passive), dependent, serious-minded (perhaps even perfectionistic) and interested in aesthetic and cultural activities. These traits are labelled "feminine" ones in the nomenclature of interest and personality inventories, since in our society they are present to a greater degree in the average woman than the average man. They are more likely to develop in boys whose mothers are overprotective, dominant and ambitious. Test results do not agree on a number of other facets of personality, including the degree of introversion-extraversion and emotional stability present in priests and seminarians.

The most frequently used test, the MMPI, has been useful in pointing out the number of young people with emotional problems who are attracted to the priesthood and in showing that seminary training can exacerbate these difficulties. Studies using this test have a number of limitations, however, particularly since it was designed to detect clinical problems rather than to identify positive personality traits.

Although seminarians as a group have much in common, there is still considerable variety among young men attracted to this life. As they progress in training, with many dropping out, those remaining become a more homogeneous group. There are many reasons why students withdraw from the seminary and we would expect that, at this level of development, many would do so.

Yet many apparently leave because they have interests and attitudes which differ from the typical member of their peer group and, therefore, fail to receive their support; included among them are some who are more independent and creative than the average seminarian who persists.

What might be done to salvage this lost potential? It is probably neither practical nor desirable to develop separate seminaries for small groups of students with special interests or other traits — particularly since size and quality of seminaries have been found to be related to persistence. But the program within a seminary of good quality can be planned so that students with diverse interests could have the opportunity to associate with other seminarians who have similar traits. A need is also indicated for an open atmosphere, so that students at this stage of career development can form a realistic picture of the life and work of priests in a variety of assignments (and of other career possibilities) and explore these to test their suitability.

Following seminary training the newly ordained priest normally finds himself unprepared for the realities of his first assignment — particularly for the interpersonal relations involved. Since the experience here is something that affects his attitudes and satisfaction throughout his career, the following recommendations would seem appropriate: 1) modify the seminarian's training to help him to understand and relate to people in a more effective way; 2) provide for a well supervised internship in parish work (or other assignments where appropriate); 3) select initial assignment with care; and 4) provide training for pastors and others who supervise newly ordained priests.

The system of assignment and promotion and the nature of continuing education programs for priests would benefit from a re-examination. The nature of the work of the curate, the long delay often found before he can take on the responsibility of challenging and meaningful tasks, the relationship between curate and pastor and the preparation of curates for promotion to the pastorate, seem particularly in need of change. The opportunity for priests to take a more active role in choosing their goals and planning their lives would seem to be in order. The present system apparently encourages passivity and conformity rather than planning and initiative.

The continued improvement of interpersonal relationships existing among priests and between priests, religious and laity is essential. The priest has chosen a life of love and service. But the situation under which he functions, and his background and training, often encourages him to relate to others in a formal manner rather than with the personal warmth that is needed to be effective.

There are a number of aspects of the priestly life that have not yet been studied by empirical methods. There is also a need for continuing study of the priest's career as it is influenced by the many changes taking place in the contemporary Church.

APPENDIX B

PILOT STUDY

A pilot study is a kind of test run. The aims are to see if the men and instruments function in the manner in which they are, in theory, expected to, and to make revisions as needed. Our pilot study, which took place during June and July of 1969 in Chicago, Illinois, involved a number of people: 15 interviewers; 125 priest volunteers, the large majority of whom were enrolled in Loyola's Pastoral Institute at the time; several consultants drawn from the hierarchy and clergy and from the fields of psychiatry, sociology and psychology; and numerous graduate students and assistants. Many techniques, tests and procedures were tried, evaluated and revised. The details of this process are beyond the scope and purposes of this report. However, highlights of this piloting will be discussed. These may be grouped into four major areas; personnel, interview techniques, evaluation format and psychological tests.

Personnel. Since much in the study was to rely upon the professional judgment of the psychologists, careful screening, instruction and field training were undertaken. As noted earlier, potential interviewers were selected on the basis of their personal and professional abilities. Those who were willing to devote a considerable amount of time to the study attended several meetings where they were introduced to the history, aims and specific methodology of the project. They observed practice interviews in a group and were encouraged to comment on, criticize and question the methodology. The next major step was a series of practice interviews and evaluations. Later, other meetings were held at which problems were discussed.

The permanent staff of the study had ample opportunity to observe the potential interviewer in action. The level of their skill and the suitability of their demeanor became manifest upon observing their participation in the discussions, by listening to their practice tapes and by reading their evaluations. Those interviewers who were not willing to make the necessary commitment to the study and/or who were not suited to a research

221

project of this type were dropped. Those who were retained comprised a skilled and cooperative research team.

Interview Techniques. Clinical interviews, that is, interviews designed to be therapeutic for the interviewee, are characterized by a relatively small amount of structuring on the part of the interviewer. The interviewee usually selects the content, sets the pace and sequence of topics and determines the level of emotional involvement. Hence, clinical interviews differ along these dimensions from interviewee to interviewee, interviewer to interviewer, and day to day given the same interviewee and interviewer. Research interviewing, on the other hand, most often provides rigid controls on just what is to take place during the interview. For example, as in polling studies, the interviewer is provided with a list of preset questions and the interviewee is allowed to choose among a relatively small number of possible answers. Clinical interviewing tends to forsake objectivity and organization for richness and personal meaning. The priorities are reversed in research interviewing. The interview schedule prepared for the present study was a compromise between these two extremes.

The pilot study provided an opportunity for the interviewers to acclimate themselves to the technique. In addition, data on style, physical location, form of address and other interview dimensions were collected, analyzed and considered in determining the nature of the later field work. For example, it was found that the priests were less prone to defensiveness when interviewed in a neutral setting, a university, than in the more affectively charged settings of a psychologist's private office or seminary office (Pierre, 1971). Hence, an early plan to conduct the interviews in Church-affiliated settings such as seminaries for the sake of convenience and low cost was abandoned and the great majority of interviews were scheduled for hotel settings.

Evaluation Format. The final form which the evaluation procedure took was the result of several revisions arising out of 60 practice interviews and evaluations. The major revisions will be discusssed here.

It became clear after the pilot study that there was a need to homogenize the evaluations. In the pilot study psychologists were allowed a free hand in the form of their evaluations. The interviewers differed among themselves in the sheer number of words used and in emphases placed on different aspects of the "Functioning" section of the report as described in Chapter III. Hence, for the actual field evaluations, the psychologists were required to make five "dynamic" statements for each of the six areas of functioning. A dynamic statement is an interpretation which sheds light upon the nature of the subject's personality. In order to illustrate to the interviewers what was required of them in making these dynamic statements, the authors read all of the pilot evaluations and selected those sentences which they judged to be dynamic. From this pool of sentences was constructed a manual of sample dynamic statements illustrative of the six areas of functioning. The manual was discussed at a meeting of the interviewers where it was pointed out that the field evaluations were to be comprised of statements similar in level of abstraction to those in the manual, but should not, of course, merely parrot these statements.

In addition to writing the five dynamic statements in each of the six areas, the interviewer was required to rank order each set of statements twice: once for the salience in describing the subject and then again for his confidence in the statement. These two rankings were done in order to guard against the possibility that some minor point about the man would be given emphasis equal to some major characteristic. This same structure was imposed on the section of the report dealing with "Future Outlook" for the priest. Added to this latter section was a five-point scale on the probability of the man leaving the active ministry.

Another refinement of the evaluation format was the specific inclusion of developmental sketches. Many pilot evaluations intertwined developmental dynamics with current dynamics. The revised format included specific sections which dealt with developmental dynamics.

It also became clear that a more wholistic evaluation of the subject was needed in addition to the analytic sections which dealt with development and functioning. Hence, in the field the interviewers were required to write integrative summaries which tied together their own personal observations of the subject, his developmental history and current functioning.

Since the interviewer had the benefit of first-hand observation of the subject, he was asked to formalize these observations in a special section of the report. Here the interviewers typically described the way the subject looked, his reactions to being interviewed and other clues which might relate to his personality. In addition, the interviewer was asked to describe how he felt about the subject personally (friendly, angry, fearful, etc.) and how he believed the subject felt toward him. By this means, the interviewer might bring into his awareness emotional reactions which could contribute, on the one hand, to a more vivid understanding of the subject or, on the other, to distortions or biases.

The revisions mentioned so far have dealt with efforts to provide a measure of organization to the discursive accounts of the subjects written by the psychologists. In addition to these discursive accounts, several formalized ratings were piloted. These were dropped, retained or revised. Three scales were dropped: one (Grinker, Grinker, and Timberlake, 1966) dealt with behavioral manifestations characteristic of neurotics; another, a specially constructed scale, dealt with "self-disclosure" during the interview; and a third, another specially designed scale, with feelings of the subject during the interview. A rating scale of Erik Erikson's Psycho-social Modalities (Prelinger and Zimet, 1964) was extended to take into account the eighth modality, "integrity vs. despair." This rating schema was retained because it was closely linked with the theoretical underpinnings of the study. After the pilot study a "scale of adjustment" was expanded from four to twelve points. This scale was retained because it offered the possibility of comparing the distribution of ratings of the priest sample with that of other normal male samples (Westley and Epstein, 1969; Golden, Mandel, Glueck, and Feder, 1962).

Psychological Tests. Psychological tests were to be included in the overall plan for several reasons. Such tests provide a source of information about the priest which is independent from the evaluations based upon interview data. They provide the possibility of comparing the results of this study with those of other studies of priests and other populations. And, from another point of view, the study provided rich opportunity for a better understanding of the tests themselves and how they might be applied more effectively in subsequent studies.

Out of the huge number of psychological tests available, the Minnesota Multiphasic Personality Inventory (MMPI), was selected for use in the pilot study. As pointed out in the technical review by Rooney which is found in Appendix A, the MMPI is the instrument which has been used most widely in the evaluations of the seminarian and priest populations and, indeed, very widely in general psychological evaluative work. This test, however, is oriented to the detection of psychopathology. Since the focus of the present study was psychological health and growth, the test had quite limited utility. Another drawback is that this test contains items which a priest may be hesitant to answer in a research study. Hence, the MMPI was used only in the pilot study. The purposes for its use were to aid in the development of another test (sentence completion) which was custom tailored for this study and to serve as a check for certain ratings made by the psychologists during the pilot study.

A sentence completion test was constructed during the pilot study for use in the field. This type of test requires that the subject finish in his own words a series of sentences, each of which has only a beginning. His responses may be scored quantitatively for the level of adjustment indicated by the responses. The sentence completion is one of a variety of projective techniques. Projective techniques are so labeled because the subject "projects" his personality into his responses to ambiguous stimuli. According to Murstein (1965), "The Sentence Completion Method is a valid test, generally speaking, and probably the most valid of all the projective techniques reported in the literature [p. 777]." The Psychology Department of Loyola University of Chicago has a history of research with and application of the sentence completion technique, especially as it has been adapted for use with the religious population (Gorman and Kobler, 1963; Heinrich, 1967; McLaughlin, 1969; Sheridan and Kobler, 1969). The present research team adapted the Loyola Sentence Completion Test for Seminarians for use with the priest population during the pilot study. Mary Agnes Sheehan (1971) was primarily responsible for this phase of the pilot study, the development of the Loyola Sentence Completion Blank for Clergymen (LSCBC).

The development of the LSCBC will be outlined briefly. In the overall plan of the study it was decided to investigate the adjustment of the priests in six major areas of functioning: interpersonal relations; psychosexual maturity; self-perception; job-satisfaction; Church, faith, religion; priesthood. These comprise the six areas the psychologist writes about in his evaluation of the priest's functioning. They are described in Chapter III. It was also decided that the sentence completion test should be designed so as to tap the subject's adjustment in each of these six areas. At least twenty "stems" per category were compiled from existing similar tests. Four clinical psychologists then judged the suitability of the stems for the population of priests. On the bases of these judgments and subsequent additions and deletions, the total number of stems eventually used in the pilot study was 84, that is, 14 per category. The LSCBC in this early form was administered to priests in attendance at Loyola's Pastoral Institute in the summer of 1969. One hundred and seven useable protocols were obtained. Forty of these protocols were used in the construction of a scoring manual. Four additional clinical psychologists rated the 3,360 responses on a seven-point rating scale, ranging from most positive affect to most negative affect. These responses which were rated the same by at least three of the four psychologists were utilized in the scoring manual as examples of various points along the scale.

Two graduate students in psychology then independently scored 32 additional protocols according to the rules and examples in the manual.

The co-efficient of correlation, a measure of relationship ranging from −1.00 (perfect negative correlation) through 0.00 (no correlation) to +1.00 (perfect positive correlation), was computed between the scores for each of the six subscales (a subscale score is derived by adding the scores for the individual stems comprising the subscale) and for the total LSCBC score. The correlations ranged from .84 to .92 for the subscales and was .96 for the total score. All these correlations were "significant," that is, not due merely to chance. Hence, the LSCBC is a "reliable" test in that reasonably sophisticated judges can agree very well on what a person's score is.

"Validity" refers to the utility of a test. A test is "valid" if it actually does what it is intended to do. The LSCBC is intended to indicate adjustment. As noted above, the MMPI is a widely used, if not perfect, indicator of adjustment. The validity of the LSCBC was estimated, in part, by correlating it with MMPI scores. The MMPI had been administered to the priest volunteers during the same session as the LSCBC. A further index of the validity of the LSCBC was to be found in the correlations between it and the ratings of the adjustment of the volunteers made by the psychologists at the time of the pilot interviews. Several ways of defining adjustment on the bases of the MMPI scores and psychologists' ratings singly and in combination were explored. In each case, the total LSCBC score and, in almost all cases, the subscale scores, correlated with the criterion well beyond chance levels. For example, the correlation between the LSCBC with the MMPI criterion was .62; with the psychologist criterion, .66; with the two criteria in combination, .86. Hence, the LSCBC is thought to be a valid index of adjustment.

In addition to the psychological tests described above, other instruments were employed during the pilot study. Since these were included in order to test out certain fairly limited hypotheses, they were not used in the field work. These were the following: an adaptation of Jourard's Self-Disclosure Questionnaire (Jourard, 1969), Edwards' Social Desirability Scale (Edwards, 1957) which was administered separately from the MMPI, and two specially constructed measures of the subject's feelings and degree of self-disclosure during the interview.

APPENDIX C

LIFE AND MINISTRY OF ROMAN CATHOLIC PRIESTS

INTERVIEW GUIDE

Loyola University

1969–1970

I. *Beginning the Interview*

  A. Greetings and introductions
  B. Assurance of anonymity
    1. Coding system
    2. Use of recording device
  C. Turn on recording device
  D. Standard introductory stimulus: "As you may already know, the study for which you have volunteered is aimed at obtaining a comprehensive view of the life and ministry of American Catholic priests. Could you tell me your reactions to this study?" (Allow and encourage approximately five minutes of free responding.)
  E. Communicate that interview will cover a range of topics, including both developmental history and current life situation.

II. *Developmental History*

  A. Family life and relationships
    1. Parents: Father/Mother
      — what kind of person, disposition, occupation, health, religion
      — alive or when deceased
      — relationship to wife (husband), other children

227

— relationship to him: warm-distant; permissive-authoritarian
— traits he admired most in parents — weaknesses
— parent he is most like
— which parent made most of the decisions about him
— quality of discipline; father/mother: harsh-kind; consistent—erratic
— what was he punished for
— what was he rewarded for

2. Siblings:
— who, how many, where was he in line of siblings
— who was he closest to
— with whom did he have most difficulty — why

3. Family values:
— what were the dominant values and concerns for his family
— education, religious practices, other people, money
— was his family closely knit or not
— what were some of the important crises in the life of his family

4. Other important people:
— did anyone else live with his family
— who visited his family
— who did his family visit
— his favorite people besides family

5. Changes in family:
— as the years went on how has his family changed: attitudes, ambitions, goals, etc.
— how does he feel about his family *now*

B. Illness and accident history
— what kind of illness or accidents did he have
— what kind of illness or accidents did family members have
— was he frequently sick
— how did family (father, mother) react to his illness
— was he separated from family for any length of time due to illness
— any history of him having minor and recurrent illness
— any history of repeated accidents — what parts of body injured

— what were his attitudes towards accidents, i.e.: punishment due to hostility, neglect of others, own shortcomings, etc.
— present state of his health

C. School career
    — what kinds of schools did he attend — how long
    — academic success or failure
    — what areas, courses were preferred/disliked by him
    — parental attitudes toward school and his performance
    — school careers of parents and siblings
    — what kinds of relationships did he establish with teachers
    — what kinds of sports, clubs, other extra-curricular activities did he enjoy
    — is he satisfied with his education

D. Relationship with peers
    — was there ample opportunity for him to have social interactions with other children
    — was he popular — why
    — was he respected — why
    — what kinds of relationship did he establish: bully, hanger-on, detached observer, intellectual leader, etc.
    — any close friends — boys — girls:
    definition of a close friend; what did he value in a friendship; what kinds of people became his friends: intellectuals, religiously orientated, social misfits, handicapped and underprivileged, rebels, thrill seekers, party goers, etc.; quality of friendship: was he only a "giver" or did he receive too
    — did the pattern of his social relationships and social values change as he grew up: how — why

E. Psychosexual development
    — what were the sources of sexual information — how adequate were they
    — parental attitudes toward sex
    — early experience with sex
    — how did he feel about sexual development at puberty
    — what types of sexual exploration occurred
    — was there any over-concern about masturbation/sexual adequacy

— what kind of relationships with girls — dating, etc.

— any specific problems with sexuality during seminary — solutions

— were there any changes in his attitudes, problems, behavior patterns as he grew up

— what was his conception of the masculine role

— what was his conception of the feminine role

F. Self-concept at present time

— how does he feel about himself — like, dislike

— how does he feel others see and evaluate him

— what does he think his strong points and weaknesses are

— what gives him security

— does he see himself as: creative, flexible, daring or rather ordinary, rigid, safety oriented

— does he see himself as warm and affectionate or rather distant

— does he feel any power or influence — where — how

— what are his plans — what would he like to do in ten or twenty years — how does he see the future

III. *Core Areas of Priesthood*

A. Development of vocation

— at what age did he start thinking of the priesthood

— at what age did he definitely decide to become a priest

— what were the most influential factors that determined his initial interest and ultimate choice of the priesthood: i.e., people, values

— what was his family's attitude toward his decision

— what was the most attractive part of becoming a priest

— what was the most difficult part of becoming a priest

— how would he evaluate the favorable and unfavorable aspects of his high school, college and theology careers re: personal formation, intellectual development, relations to peers and authorities

— vocational crises: when, nature of: i.e., faith, celibacy, authority, etc.

— how did he resolve it

B. Priestly assignments

— describe the type of assignments he has received as a priest and his reactions to each

— what has proven to be of most satisfaction to him in the priesthood

— what has been the most difficult part of the priesthood for him

— does he feel adequate to his job — supported, challenged by it

— does he feel needed by others and respected by them as a priest

— how does he see his role of priest

— what is preventing him from doing what he wants to do in his priesthood

— what is the present status of his vocation: why does he remain a priest — what would make him consider leaving the priesthood — what other occupation can he see himself in

— how does he view the changes in the priesthood: i.e., greater freedom of thought, different ministries, etc.

C. Interpersonal relations

— describe his ordinary relations with parishioners and friends: warm-distant; personal-task oriented

— what kind of personal relations does he have with family

— what kind of personal relations does he have with clerical friends

— what kind of personal relations does he have with lay friends — men — women

— who is his closest friend (friends)

— why is this person valuable to him

— describe other personal relationships he has had in his life

— who does he worry about, really care for, sacrifice self for

— how does he feel others care about him — who

— who does he feel really knows and understands him

— has the pattern of personal friendship changed since his ordination: how — why

— how would he describe his relationship to superiors and those over whom he exercises authority

D. Faith and Church

— what are the basic values he believes in, sacrifices for, lives for

— how would he describe his faith life: i.e., strong, weak, confused, etc.

— what *means* does he use to strengthen and support his faith life: i.e., prayer, reading, discussions, liturgy, serving people

— how effective does he feel these means are

— how does he feel about the present turmoil of the Church

— what does it mean for him personally

— what is the most difficult part of this turmoil for him

— what is the most exciting, challenging part

— what are his hopes for the Church

— what are his fears for the Church

E. Priesthood

— describe his life as a priest now: happy, challenging, frustrating, depressing — why

— what is the most satisfying aspect of his priesthood

— what is the most painful aspect of his priesthood

— what is the most hopeful aspect of his priesthood

— does he feel supported, encouraged, rewarded by his priesthood

— does he feel he is operating at a level commensurate with his potential — if not, what changes would he like to see in his life

— how does he feel about priests leaving the active ministry

— has he ever thought of leaving — if so, what would prompt him to leave — how would his life be different if he left the priesthood

F. Celibacy

— what kind of relationships does he have now with women: family, married women, single women, nuns

— what is his definition of celibacy

— has his definition changed since ordination — how

— does he feel celibacy is an aid or burden to his priesthood — why

— how does he handle the loneliness of not being married

— does he feel celibacy should be optional — why

— if celibacy were optional, would he marry

— if celibacy were optional and he married, would he continue in the priestly ministry

G. Future

— if he had his way, what would he want his life to be in: five years — ten years — twenty years

IV. *Ending the Interview*

As the interview comes to an end the Interviewer should:

A. Handle any anxiety that may have been aroused during the interview.

B. Communicate clearly to the Interviewee that there is no follow-up from this interview, i.e., no opportunity with the present team for counseling, etc.

C. Thank the person for the time and interest he has shown in the interview, for example, "I enjoyed discussing these topics with you. I hope you found it interesting also."

V. *Hand Over and Explain Test Packet*

APPENDIX D

NOTES ON INTERVIEW EVALUATION

I. *Interview Process*

In Part A, note those behavioral observations which you would normally mention in a psychological report. In Part B, focus on the feelings which you had toward *S* and the feelings you infer he had toward you.

II. *Development: Childhood, Adolescence, Adulthood*

In Parts A and B, briefly characterize *S*'s relationships to those persons listed and the ways in which these may have changed. In section C list significant happenings which may have influenced *S*'s development.

III. *Functioning*

Parts A through F require five statements each which describe *S*'s functioning in each area. After you have made the five statements for a given area, rank order these five statements in the following manner. First, rank order on the basis of importance in describing the person with that statement having the greatest importance as number one, that having the least importance as number five. Enter these rankings on the first set of horizontal lines. Second, rank order on the basis of your confidence in the statement with that statement meriting the greatest confidence as number one, that meriting the least confidence number five. Enter these rankings on the second set of horizontal lines.

IV. *Report*

Write a personality evaluation of approximately 300 words. This evaluation should be more synthetic than those discrete statements in the previous section.

V. *Future Outlook*

Make five statements regarding S's future. These could include such areas as prognosis, need for treatment, growth factors, possibility of leaving the priesthood, etc. Rank order these according to the two criteria in Section III.

RATING SYSTEM FOR
PSYCHOSOCIAL MODALITIES

The following variables concern complex phenomena and are not intended to be independent from one another. Since they represent issues arising at subsequent stages of development, it follows that the successful solution of later developmental crises is dependent to a considerable degree on a successful solution of the earlier ones. Thus, evidence for those ratings should be drawn from several levels.

There are two parts to the rating system. In Part A, rate the subject's standing on each modality. In Part B, rank order the eight modalities according to the directions provided. Enter the ratings and rankings on page 8–9 of the *Interview Evaluation*.

A. *Subject's Standing on Each Modality*

1. *Trust vs. basic mistrust*

Trust may be defined as a deeply ingrained conviction that one's needs, material and emotional, will be satisfied, that the world and the people in it are basically good, abundant in their supplies and well-meaning. But it also implies a personal feeling of "being all right" oneself, and of being considered all right by significant others; a feeling that one can cope with the world and with oneself, and that one is at home in one's body. Finally, it implies a confident feeling that requirements and even frustrations coming from the outside generally make sense.

Basic Mistrust may be defined as a sense of always living precariously, that good things never last, that one does not know if one's needs will be satisfied tomorrow and rather doubts that they will be. That the world contains many hidden dangers, that people are out to exploit or even "get" you; that oneself is bad and empty, can't cope and is doomed to suffer failure and injury; that the world is an unsafe, unpredictable, threatening cold place.

The trust *vs.* mistrust issue is also considered to be an acute one if there appears in the record a marked emphasis on orality as ex-

237

pressed in concerns over such matters as food, nourishment, dependence, nourishing persons, etc. These concerns may appear in a benevolent form, indicating a more passive and naive form of trust or denial or frustration of dependency. If these oral concerns appear in a more aggressive and destructive context (demandingness, greediness, teeth, devouring, gnawing, etc.), mistrust would seem implied.

A more successful solution of this developmental issue would be indicated by some not extreme and not too primitively expressed or too conflicted manifestations of oral concerns. Ratings would then tend towards 2 or 3.

Scale:

1. The subject is entirely trusting in a naive, childish and unrealistic, if benevolent way; is a kind of guileless fool.
2. Trust predominates markedly, but there are some realistic limitations, some cautiousness; occasional, moderate, relatively brief crises in significant relationships.
3. Trust and mistrust keep an approximate balance in their frequency and intensity; there may be vacillation between instances of predominating trust or mistrust.
4. Mistrust predominates markedly, but some concessions are made at times. The world and people are given an occasional chance.
5. Pathological mistrust entirely dominates the picture; it may assume delusional proportions.

X. Cannot say.

Comments:

2. *Autonomy vs. shame and doubt*

Autonomy can be defined as a sense that one is capable of being and may be the originator of one's own actions; that one has a will of one's own and can exercise it; that one "stands on his own feet"; that one is in control of oneself and exercises this control comfortably; it includes a sense of pride and independence, and of being able to hold one's ground in the face of others.

Shame and doubt refers to a sense of being easily exposed as powerless, incapable, weak and bad. It includes a wish to hide from others, to cover up one's despicability and worthlessness. One's own plans and actions are surrounded by doubts concerning their justification, value and efficacy. Self-consciousness and a lack of self-confidence are present; inability to make up one's mind.

If this issue is prominent, there may be a marked emphasis on anality as expressed in concerns with the following, or their opposites: orderliness, cleanliness, regulation and scheduling of things, balance, tenderness, utility, parsimony and efficiency, authority and compliance. Also emphasis on hiding, covering-up, being seen, exposed. Representation of and concern with the excretory organs and their products, with retention and elimination. Refined, deliberate, and controlled forms of sadism or masochism. Stubbornness, dutifulness.

Scale:

1. An exaggerated sense of autonomy, self-importance and omnipotence is present. Realistic limitations are disregarded, social maladaptation may result.
2. A strong sense of autonomy is present, but some of its limitations are recognized and occasional self-doubting occurs. An "independent" personality.
3. The proportion of autonomy and doubt or shame is about even. One or the other predominates on different occasions, but the crises are not extreme enough to cause maladaptation.
4. Doubt and shame predominate; a self-conscious, indecisive person tending to apologize for his existence, but sufficient autonomy is present to deal marginally and very effortfully with normal life situations. Possible rebelliousness against own insignificant status and against authority.
5. Extreme degree of shame and doubtfulness. Continuous wish to sink into the ground and disappear, no sense of capability for any self-originated action. Sense of being worth nothing and doing everything badly. Possibly marked rebelliousness against authority.

X. Cannot say.

Comments:

3. *Initiative vs. guilt*

Initiative refers to evidence of ambition, energetic driving in pursuit of accomplishment, a tendency to solve problems by attack, pleasure in attack and conquest, striving towards goals lying in the future, but also to active, curious exploration and active, expansive movement; rivalrous and jealous competition.

Guilt is here understood specifically as guilt over enjoyment derived from acts of "making," and over the aggressive components of active competition. Excessive guilt would be manifested by self-restriction, overconscientiousness in planning enterprises and paralysis of action.

This issue would also be reflected in emphasis on representations of sexual organs, their adequacy and intactness, as well as of the body in general, especially in terms of showing and showing off.

With *men* the accent would lie on intrusion of a physical, intellectual and social sort, on "making" by invading, monopolizing and manipulating of people and things.

In *women* the emphasis would lie on "making" by inception, maternal inclusion or creation. Also on seductive, bitchy, bodily-narcissistic demandingness for attention to her as a physical being.

Negatively, in both sexes may be found: fear of damage, confinement, weakness, losing out to rivals, or a sense that all these should occur or have already occurred. In women also: being found unattractive, unlovable, repulsive.

Scale:

1. Exaggerated initiative, constantly striving for new goals, full of plans, hard-driving, unscrupulously forging ahead, "big operator."
2. Initiative predominates, is in general moderated, guided or influenced by considerations of conscience, but the latter are not inhibiting in an unrealistic way.
3. Initiative and guilt are in approximate balance. At times initiative has the upper hand and new goals are striven for; at times pursuits are inhibited by somewhat unrealistic considerations of conscience or are laden with guilt.
4. Guilt predominates, inhibiting the choice and active pursuit of new goals considerably. There is marked restriction and paralysis of initiative.
5. Excessive guilt. Almost completely blocked in all forms of enterprise to the degree of actual, symbolic or symptomatic self-injury.
X. Cannot say.

Comments:

4. *Industry vs. inferiority*

Industry refers to an active orientation towards producing things and thus to win recognition. There is eager absorption in the productive situation and determined striving towards the completion of things; "stick-to-itiveness." There are sincere attempts to be useful and to do useful things. Skills are acquired, practiced and valued. There is marked interest in learning how things are done in the surrounding culture from the points of view of know-how and/or rules.

Inferiority refers to a despairing of one's tools and skills, leading to a sense of being unable to be like others, of being doomed to mediocrity or of being crippled, multilated and isolated.

Scale:

1. Excessive industry; use of production and persevering work as exclusive means towards achievement of a place in society at the cost of direct human contact and leading to impoverishment in other areas of life. Feels that everything can be accomplished with sufficient persistence and energy.
2. Industry predominates. Engages persistently in energetic production but admits that he cannot do everything and has certain limitations.
3. Industry and inferiority in about equal proportions. There are skills and productive drive in some areas, while lack of ability and interest for other areas are perceived by the subject; or the drive may be coupled with a sense of inferiority.
4. Inferiority predominates. A general sense of inability and lack of skill is present, but there are exceptions. In certain relatively narrow areas or at certain times production does occur with some degree of proficiency.
5. A sense of overwhelming inferiority in all areas predominates. The subject feels generally incapable, poorly equipped and thus isolated.

X. Cannot say.

Comments:

5. *Identity vs. identity diffusion*

Identity refers to a sense of inner sameness and continuity in time and of inner homogeneity at any given point in time. Specifically it implies a sense of being at home in one's body, of "knowing where one is going," and of an assuredness of recognition by others. All this is based on good integration between inner drives and wishes and social conditions, specifically in terms of work, sex, relationships to peers and the community.

Identity diffusion implies a sense of discrepancy between one's appearance and being, doubts concerning one's sexual identity and inability to choose a career because of conflicting interests and doubts, an inability to relate to others as an equal partner or to compete with them, a feeling of emptiness, lack of a coherent philosophy of life and of a goal for one's existence. No commitments are made and a state of paralysis with regard to the making of choices exists.

Scale:

1. Rigidly developed identity with a maximum of internal homogeneity; nearly all psychological structures and functions are forcibly integrated with and attuned to limited aspects of the present environment. Implied is an arrest of development at this stage which leaves little possibility for future change; there are no dormant potentials left.
2. Well developed identity and good social integration. However, some unintegrated capacities, wishes, etc., remain.
3. Moderately developed identity. Some of the time or in some major areas there is fairly good integration between personal factors and the social surroundings; at other times or in some areas it is lacking. Occasional crises.
4. Identity diffusion predominates. Only occasional or partial integration of personal factors with surrounding society; internal conflict and indecision or presence of a moderately negative (autistic, oppositional) identity.
5. General identity diffusion. No integrated picture of the self, its qualities, purposes and goals at all. Much internal contradiction and conflict, and lacking or very poor integration of personal wishes, capabilities, etc., with the surrounding society; or presence of markedly negative identity.

X. Cannot say.

Comments:

6. *Intimacy vs. isolation*

Intimacy refers to a capacity for full mutuality with a loved partner. This includes ability to achieve full orgasms, but also to share mutual trust and to regulate together the "cycles of work, procreation and recreation." All this is based on an ability to face "ego loss" with others as well as within oneself (in the form of orgasm, abandon, giving oneself up to inspiration, intuition, etc.).

Isolation refers to a sense of having to remain alone and of being self-absorbed, on the basis of the fear of ego loss. Social relations remain formal or abortive, sexual relations lack emotional mutuality.

Scale:

1. Full capacity for intimacy as shown by the fact that the subject has achieved it.
2. Capacity for intimacy appears to be definitely present; no lasting intimate relationship is as yet achieved, but successful experimentation with such relationships is being undertaken.
3. Intimacy and isolation are present in about equal degrees; there is vacillation between these two poles.
4. Isolation is predominant. Occasional attempts at intimacy remain absortive or are of short duration.
5. The subject is fully isolated, self-absorbed and is not able to or refuses to share anything close to his self with anybody.
X. Cannot say.
Comments:

7. *Generativity vs. stagnation*

Generativity refers to a deeply sensed interest and involvement in establishing and guiding the next generation; or, in the absence of actual parental responsibilities, to other concerns of an altruistic and creative quality.

Stagnation on the other hand represents an absence of such generative involvement; it may result in an obsessive need for pseudo-intimacy, in self-indulgence and be represented in a subjective sense of impoverishment and lack of genuine purpose.

Scale:

1. There is full absorption in child care and rearing as the major item of involvement; or a sense of cumulative and creative activity, of building or developing something of major proportions.
2. Considerable absorption in generativity but with some doubts and mildly interfering egocentric concerns.
3. Generativity is present to some degree but it is absent at times or sensed as a pressing responsibility, and it is conflict-laden.
4. Stagnation predominates. The issue of generativity has, in general, been avoided or approached only tentatively. There is no marked involvement in it.

5. Over-all stagnation. Complete absence of powerful, reproductive, caring and creative interest. No purpose, one lives for the moment and his own short-term gratification.

X. Cannot say.

Comments:

8. *Ego integrity vs. despair*

Ego integrity refers to a sense of satisfaction with self and accomplishments. This satisfaction is had despite a life marked by disappointment and failure as well as success. Integrity implies a transcendence over the particular happenings of one's own life and the belief of there being a harmony or order of which one's own life is but a part. It also implies a transcendence over the physical difficulties of growing old.

Despair refers to a sense of dissatisfaction with self and accomplishments. The focus is on the past, especially failure. There may be feelings that time is now too short to "wipe the slate clean" and start again. Preoccupation with discomforts, both small and large. Death seems near and is feared.

Scale:

1. Satisfaction with life and work. Emphasis is on positive aspects of life, both present and past. Conviction that own life is part of a larger order. Aging and its difficulties are recognized and accepted.
2. Major emphasis is on satisfactions and positive evaluations. Mild and passing periods of despair.
3. Integrity and despair are present in about equal degree. Vacillation between the two poles.
4. Despair predominates, many regrets. Occasional temporary periods of positive evaluations of past and present.
5. Past does not support, but rather is cause for despair and regret. Feels isolated and that life has been pointless. Feels time is now too short to start afresh. Process of aging is either denied or recognized and negative evaluated. Fears death.

X. Cannot say.

Comments:

B. *Degree of Emphasis of Each Modality*

Here the degree of emphasis is rated with which each psychosocial issue appears in the material regardless of which of its two poles is the more prominent one. Rank order the eight modalities with that modality having the greatest emphasis as number one, that having the least emphasis as number eight.

_____ Trust vs. basic mistrust
_____ Autonomy vs. shame and doubt
_____ Initiative vs. guilt
_____ Industry vs. inferiority
_____ Identity vs. identity diffusion
_____ Intimacy vs. isolation
_____ Generativity vs. stagnation
_____ Ego integrity vs. despair

SCALE OF ADJUSTMENT

Enter rating on Page 10 of *Interview Evaluation*

I. The Scale.

A	B	C	D
1 2 3	1 2 3	1 2 3	1 2 3

A. Absence of structured psychiatric symptoms; social and occupational adaptation; dynamic integration.

B. Absence of structured psychiatric symptoms; social and occupational adaptation; mild impairment of dynamic integration with mild anxiety.

C. Absence of structured psychiatric symptoms; social or occupational maladaptation; moderate impairment of dynamic integration with moderate psychopathology and moderate anxiety.

D. Presence of structured psychiatric symptoms; social and occupational maladaptation; severe psychopathology and severe anxiety.

II. Directions for Use of the Scale: To Be Followed in Sequence

A. Between Category Rating.
  1. If structured psychiatric symptoms are present, place the individual in category *D*.
  2. If structured psychiatric symptoms are absent, evaluate the individual's social and occupational adaptation. If maladaptation is present, place the individual in category *C*.
  3. If social and occupational adaptation is present, evaluate the individual's dynamic integration. If mild impairment of

        dynamic integration is present, place the individual in category *B*.

    4. If dynamic integration is present, place the individual in category *A*.

B. Within Category Rating.

    1. After the individual's Between Category Rating is determined, the individual is to be rated either *1, 2,* or *3* within that category.

    2. A rating of *1* is given when the individual tends toward the *more* healthy pole of the scale.

    3. A rating of *3* is given when the individual tends towards the less healthy pole of the scale.

    4. A rating of *2* is an intermediate rating.

INTERVIEW EVALUATION

I. Interview Process

   A. Behavioral Observations

   B. Affective Tones
     (Feelings between interviewer and interviewee)

II. Development: Childhood, Adolescence, Adulthood

   A. Parents and Other Significant Adults

   B. Relationship Between Parents

   C. Siblings, Peers, Group Identifications

   D. Notable Events

III. Functioning

   A. Interpersonal Relations

     ————   ————

     ————   ————

     ————   ————

     ————   ————

     ————   ————

   B. Psychosexual Maturity

     ————   ————

     ————   ————

     ————   ————

     ————   ————

     ————   ————

C. Self-perception

___ ___

___ ___

___ ___

___ ___

___ ___

D. Job Satisfaction

___ ___

___ ___

___ ___

___ ___

___ ___

E. Church, Faith, Religion

___ ___

___ ___

___ ___

___ ___

___ ___

F. Priesthood

___ ___

___ ___

___ ___

___ ___

___ ___

IV. Report (300 words)

V. Future Outlook

——————   ——————

——————   ——————

——————   ——————

——————   ——————

——————   ——————   Circle most appropriate item:

    1. *S* definitely will not leave.
    2. *S* probably will not leave.
    3. *S* is uncertain about his future.
    4. *S* will probably leave.
    5. *S* has definitely decided to leave.

VI. Psychosocial Modalities

    A. Subject's Standing on Each Modality (Circle)

        1. Trust vs. basic mistrust

            1 2 3 4 5 X

            Comment:

        2. Autonomy vs. shame and doubt

            1 2 3 4 5 X

            Comment:

        3. Initiative vs. guilt

            1 2 3 4 5 X

            Comment:

        4. Industry vs. inferiority

            1 2 3 4 5 X

            Comment:

        5. Identity vs. identity diffusion

            1 2 3 4 5 X

            Comment:

6. Intimacy vs. isolation

1 2 3 4 5 X

Comment:

7. Generativity vs. stagnation

1 2 3 4 5 X

Comment:

8. Ego integrity vs. despair

1 2 3 4 5 X

Comment:

B. *Degree of Emphasis of Each Modality*

Here the degree of emphasis is rated with which each psycho-social issue appears in the material regardless of which of its two poles is the more predominant one. Rank order the eight modalities with that modality having the greatest emphasis as number one, that having the least emphasis as number eight.

_____ Trust vs. basic mistrust
_____ Autonomy vs. shame and doubt
_____ Initiative vs. guilt
_____ Industry vs. inferiority
_____ Identity vs. identity diffusion
_____ Intimacy vs. isolation
_____ Generativity vs. stagnation
_____ Ego integrity vs. despair

VII. Diagnosis

(CIRCLE A OR B)

A. Normal

B. Abnormal (If S is abnormal, specify diagnostic category.)

1. mild   2. moderate   3. severe

VIII. Scale of Adjustment

A	B	C	D
1 2 3	1 2 3	1 2 3	1 2 3

APPENDIX E

PSYCHOLOGICAL TESTS

Instructions

1. Please do not write your name on any sheets. Your code number is already recorded.
2. Please respond freely and frankly.
3. A blank sheet is attached to this packet. Any other reactions (e.g., the way the study was conducted, the test used, etc.) would be welcome. Please note them on the final blank sheet when you have completed the rest of the packet.

Thank you for your cooperation.

FAITH

Everybody has some idea of what having a mature faith means. Some people, we say, have a mature faith. Others, we claim, have an immature faith. From your point of view, what are the essential characteristics of the most mature kind of faith? (Take your time in answering; such things aren't easy to put into words.)

Now, again from your point of view, what are the essential characteristics of the most immature kind of faith? (Again, take your time in answering.)

Below is a picture of a ladder. Suppose we say that at the top of the ladder (step number 10) is the most mature kind of faith you have just described; at the bottom of the ladder (step number 0) is the most immature kind of faith you have described.

1. Where on the ladder do you feel you stand *as you really are?*
   Step Number _____.
2. Where on the ladder would you *like to* stand?
   Step Number _____.
3. Where on the ladder do you feel your closest friends believe you stand?
   Step Number _____.

251

| 10 |
| 9 |
| 8 |
| 7 |
| 6 |
| 5 |
| 4 |
| 3 |
| 2 |
| 1 |
| 0 |

4. Where on the ladder would you say you stood *five years ago?*
   Step Number _____.
5. And where do you think you will be on the ladder *five years from now?*
   Step Number _____.

Instructions: On the next few pages are pairs of words or phrases arranged in the following way:

```
     tall   O  o  .    .  o  O   short
      sad   O  o  .    .  o  O   happy
excitable   O  o  .    .  o  O   calm
```

We'd like you to judge *YOURSELF AS YOU REALLY ARE* by marking these pairs according to these directions:

First, decide which side (word or phrase) is more appropriate; after deciding on which word or phrase you are going to mark:

Then, decide how much or to what degree you feel this way and—

Circle: O—when you feel *very* much this way
         o—when you feel *somewhat* this way
         . —when you feel only *slightly* this way

There are no right answers. Your own opinion is what matters. Even where you find it difficult to make up your mind, *BE SURE* TO MAKE A CHOICE, and ONLY *ONE* CHOICE. Otherwise, your opinion can't be counted. Don't be disturbed if some of the word pairs are not exact opposites. Simply decide which of the two is *most* applicable and then decide to what degree you feel this way. Below is an example.

tall	O	o	.	.	o	O	short
sad	O	o	.	.	o	O	happy
excitable	O	o	.	.	o	O	calm

CIRCLE O—when you feel *very* much this way
o—when you feel *somewhat* this way
. —when you feel only *slightly* this way

1.	sense of well-being	O	o	.	.	o	O	sense of emptiness
2.	emotionally disorganized	O	o	.	.	o	O	emotionally integrated
3.	anxious	O	o	.	.	o	O	secure
4.	sexually attractive	O	o	.	.	o	O	sexually unattractive
5.	keeping	O	o	.	.	o	O	giving
6.	unprepared	O	o	.	.	o	O	ready
7.	feminine	O	o	.	.	o	O	not feminine
8.	sharing	O	o	.	.	o	O	jealous
9.	sexually inactive	O	o	.	.	o	O	sexually active
10.	contributing	O	o	.	.	o	O	conserving
11.	willing to be a leader	O	o	.	.	o	O	unwilling to be a leader
12.	foolhardy	O	o	.	.	o	O	careful
13.	difficulty in showing feelings	O	o	.	.	o	O	usually expresses feelings easily
14.	powerful	O	o	.	.	o	O	ineffective
15.	unproductive	O	o	.	.	o	O	productive
16.	unskilled	O	o	.	.	o	O	skilled
17.	giving	O	o	.	.	o	O	demanding
18.	clean	O	o	.	.	o	O	dirty
19.	fuzzy	O	o	.	.	o	O	clear
20.	willing to be a follower	O	o	.	.	o	O	unwilling to be a follower
21.	contemptuous	O	o	.	.	o	O	accepting
22.	justified	O	o	.	.	o	O	guilty
23.	exposed and vulnerable	O	o	.	.	o	O	covered and defended
24.	consistent feelings about myself	O	o	.	.	o	O	inconsistent feelings about myself
25.	sufficient progress	O	o	.	.	o	O	life is getting away from me
26.	people know what to expect of me	O	o	.	.	o	O	people don't know what to expect of me
27.	bored	O	o	.	.	o	O	ecstatic
28.	people can trust me	O	o	.	.	o	O	sometimes I let people down
29.	not masculine	O	o	.	.	o	O	masculine

30.	moderate	O o . . o O	overdo things
31.	enriched	O o . . o O	barren
32.	worthy	O o . . o O	unworthy
33.	unloved	O o . . o O	loved
34.	stubborn	O o . . o O	cooperative
35.	short-lived relationships	O o . . o O	enduring relationships
36.	self-doubting	O o . . o O	self-assured
37.	relaxed	O o . . o O	tense
38.	sluggish	O o . . o O	quick
39.	a sense of loneliness	O o . . o O	a sense of belonging
40.	usually nonconforming	O o . . o O	usually conforming
41.	on my guard with others	O o . . o O	trusting of other people
42.	growing	O o . . o O	stagnant
43.	frustration	O o . . o O	rapture
44.	acceptance of death	O o . . o O	fear of death
45.	undemonstrative	O o . . o O	affectionate
46.	safe	O o . . o O	apprehensive
47.	self-condemning	O o . . o O	accepting of myself
48.	know what I want to be	O o . . o O	unsure as to what I want to be
49.	able to concentrate	O o . . o O	easily distracted
50.	despairing	O o . . o O	hoping
51.	inhibited	O o . . o O	spontaneous
52.	on time	O o . . o O	late
53.	cynical	O o . . o O	believing
54.	in control	O o . . o O	overwhelmed
55.	manipulated by others	O o . . o O	self-directed
56.	sharing	O o . . o O	lonely

On the following pairs of words—you are to judge *YOURSELF AS YOU WOULD LIKE TO BE* by following the previous instructions:

First, decide which side (word or phrase) is most appropriate; after deciding on which word or phrase you are going to mark;

Then, decide how much or to what degree you feel this way and—

CIRCLE   O—when you feel *very* much this way

o—when you feel *somewhat* this way

. —when you feel only *slightly* this way

Remember, please be sure to make a choice and only one choice for each word pair.

1.	relaxed	O o . . o O	tense
2.	on my guard with others	O o . . o O	trusting of other people
3.	usually conforming	O o . . o O	usually nonconforming
4.	believing	O o . . o O	cynical
5.	contributing	O o . . o O	conserving
6.	giving	O o . . o O	demanding
7.	usually expresses feelings easily	O o . . o O	difficulty in showing feelings

8.	anxious	O	o	.		.	o	O	secure
9.	sometimes I let people down	O	o	.		.	o	O	people can trust me
10.	life is getting away from me	O	o	.		.	o	O	sufficient progress
11.	spontaneous	O	o	.		.	o	O	inhibited
12.	self-condemning	O	o	.		.	o	O	accepting of myself
13.	stubborn	O	o	.		.	o	O	cooperative
14.	unsure as to what								know what
	I want to be	O	o	.		.	o	O	I want to be

On the following pairs of words you are to judge:
THE CHURCH, as you experience it.
Follow the same instructions stated previously.

CIRCLE O—when you feel *very* much this way
　　　　o—when you feel *somewhat* this way
　　　　. —when you feel only *slightly* this way

1.	inhibited	O	o	.		.	o	O	spontaneous
2.	cooperative	O	o	.		.	o	O	stubborn
3.	giving	O	o	.		.	o	O	demanding
4.	tense	O	o	.		.	o	O	relaxed
5.	believing	O	o	.		.	o	O	cynical
6.	knows what								unsure as to what
	it wants to be	O	o	.		.	o	O	it wants to be
7.	usually nonconforming	O	o	.		.	o	O	usually conforming
8.	usually expresses								difficulty
	feelings easily	O	o	.		.	o	O	in showing feelings
9.	sufficient progress	O	o	.		.	o	O	life is getting away from it
10.	secure	O	o	.		.	o	O	anxious
11.	people can trust it	O	o	.		.	o	O	sometimes it lets people down
12.	trusting of other people	O	o	.		.	o	O	on its guard with others
13.	conserving	O	o	.		.	o	O	contributing
14.	accepting of itself	O	o	.		.	o	O	self-condemning

INCOMPLETE SENTENCES BLANK

Please complete the following statements as quickly as possible. Express your real feelings.

1. I wish my fellow priests
2. Being loved
3. For me, being a priest at this time
4. Counseling women
5. Preaching the Gospel
6. Sexual relations
7. My greatest strength

8. The woman I most like
9. My most difficult obligation as a priest
10. When I have trouble with someone
11. People who work with me usually
12. The most serious crisis of my life
13. To me, prayer
14. The sacrifice of the Mass
15. The thought of getting married
16. The most important element of my faith
17. The greatest pressure in my work
18. My deepest feeling about the Church
19. Working as part of a large organization
20. Earning my living
21. I feel powerful when
22. The bishop
23. When the odds are against me
24. Working as a priest gives me
25. Feelings of loneliness
26. Trusting other people
27. Physical contact with others
28. The children that I know
29. I am apt to get discouraged when
30. My work as a priest
31. When I meet an attractive woman
32. To me, the afterlife
33. Sexual tension
34. I
35. Taking off my collar means
36. The people I tend to go around with
37. To the laity, the priest
38. To me, religion
39. My mother
40. My greatest worry is
41. I became a priest because
42. Christ's presence
43. Celibacy
44. My present assignment
45. My first assignment
46. At ordination, I
47. When I administer the sacraments

48. God
49. I feel that romantic love
50. On my own initiative
51. What really bugs me
52. If someone gets in my way
53. The social status of my work
54. My father
55. My body
56. The future of the Church
57. What I like most about my work as a priest
58. When people work for me
59. Sex
60. My experience of love
61. The Christian life
62. I am best able to
63. On my job, initiative
64. My deepest feeling about the priesthood
65. When I see a man and a woman together
66. I wonder if a priest ever
67. The most satisfying work
68. My most intimate personal relationship
69. The training I've had for my work
70. I am happiest when
71. The ideal of the priest as "a man set apart"
72. Selecting my own work

REFERENCES

Allport, G. W. *The individual and his religion.* New York: Macmillan, 1950.

Allport, G. W. *The person in psychology.* Boston: Beacon Press, 1968.

Arnold, M. B. A screening test for candidates for religious life. In V. V. Herr, (Ed.), *Screening candidates for the priesthood and religious life.* Chicago: Loyola University Press, 1962.

Ashbrook, J. B. Evaluating seminary students as potential ministers. Unpublished master's thesis, Ohio State University, 1962. Cited by R. J. Menges & J. E. Dittes, *Psychological studies of clergymen: Abstracts of research.* New York: Nelson, 1965.

Barry, W. A. An MMPI scale for seminary candidates. Unpublished master's thesis, Fordham University, 1960.

Barry, W. A. & Bordin, E. S. Personality development and the vocational choice of the ministry. *Journal of Counseling Psychology,* 1967, 14, 395-403.

Bier, W. C. A comparative study of the seminary group and four other groups on the MMPI. *Studies in Psychology and Psychiatry from the Catholic University of America,* 1948, 7, 107.

Blos, P. *On adolescence.* New York: Free Press, 1962.

Bolgar, H. The case study method. In B. B. Wolman (Ed.), *Handbook of clinical psychology.* New York: McGraw-Hill, 1965.

Bowers, M. K. *Conflicts of the clergy.* New York: Nelson, 1963.

Brammer, L. M., & Shostrom, E. L. *Therapeutic psychology.* New Jersey: Prentice-Hall, 1960.

Burkard, M. I. Characteristic differences determined by TAT sequential analysis between teachers rated by their pupils at the extremes of teaching efficiency. Unpublished doctoral dissertation, Loyola University of Chicago, 1958.

Caffrey, C. B. Behavior patterns and personality characteristics as related to prevalence rates of coronary heart disease in Trappist and Benedictine monks. Unpublished doctoral dissertation, Catholic University, 1966.

Cardwell, S. W. The MMPI as a predictor of success among seminary students. *Ministry Studies,* 1967, 1, 3-20.

Carroll, D. W. A follow-up study of psychological assessment. In W. C. Bier (Ed.), *Psychological testing for ministerial selection.* New York: Fordham University Press, 1970.

Cattell, R. B., Eber, H. W., & Tatsuoka, M. M. *Handbook for the sixteen personality factor questionnaire.* Champaign, Illinois: Institute for Personality and Ability Testing, 1970.

Coelho, V. A personality scale for candidates to the priesthood. Unpublished master's thesis, University of Detroit, 1963.

Coville, W. J. Psychologists and the assessment of candidates for religious life. *American Catholic Psychological Association Newsletter Supplement,* 1962, No. 59 & 60.

Dahlstrom, W. G., & Welsh, G. S. *An MMPI handbook: A guide to use in clinical practice and research.* Minneapolis: University of Minnesota Press, 1960.

D'Arcy, P. F. Constancy of interest factor patterns within a specific vocation of foreign missioner. *Studies in Psychology and Psychiatry from the Catholic University of America,* 1954, 9, 54.

D'Arcy, P. F. Review of research on the vocational interests of priests, brothers and sisters. In V. V. Herr (Ed.), *Screening candidates for the priesthood and religious life.* Chicago: Loyola University, 1962.

D'Arcy, P. F. Bibliography of psychological, sociological and related studies on the Catholic priesthood and the religious life. In W. J. Coville, P. F. D'Arcy, T. N. McCarthy, & J. J. Rooney, *Assessment of candidates for the religious life.* Washington, D.C.: CARA, 1968a.

D'Arcy, P. F. The role of research on clergy interests. *Ministry Studies,* 1968b, 2, 3-5.

D'Arcy, P. F., & Kennedy, E. C. *The genius of the apostolate.* New York: Sheed and Ward, 1965.

de Hueck, M. *Dear seminarian.* Milwaukee: Bruce, 1950.

Demerath, M. J. Converging lines of research interest. *Ministry Studies,* 1968, 2, 55-61.

Dittes, J. E. *Vocational guidance of theological students: A manual for the use of the theological school inventory.* Dayton, Ohio: Ministry Studies Board, 1964, 128.

Dittes, J. E. The usefulness of the MMPI. *Ministry Studies,* 1967, 1, 25-28.

Dondero, E. A. *No borrowed light.* Milwaukee: Bruce, 1965.

Dunn, R. F. Personality patterns among religious personnel: A review. *Catholic Psychological Record,* 1965, 3, 125-137.

Engel, G. L. *Psychological development in health and disease.* Philadelphia: Saunders, 1962.

Erickson, E. H. *Childhood and society.* New York: Norton, 1963.

Erickson, E. H. *Identity, youth, and crisis.* New York: Norton, 1968.

Erickson, E. H. The problem of ego identity. *Psychological Issues,* 1959, 1.

Fehr, R. An inventory and a projective personality study of a religious and lay groups. Unpublished doctoral dissertation, Fordham University, 1958.

Fichter, J. H. *Religion as an occupation.* Notre Dame: University of Notre Dame Press, 1961.

Fichter, J. H. *Priest and people.* New York: Sheed & Ward, 1965.

Fichter, J. H. *America's forgotten priests, what they are saying.* New York: Harper & Row, 1968.

Freud, A. *The ego and the mechanisms of defense.* London: Hogarth Press, 1937.

Godfrey, R. J. Predictive value of the MMPI with candidates for the religious brotherhood. Unpublished master's thesis, Marquette University, 1955.

Gorman, J.R. Adjustment and interests of fourth year minor seminarians studying for the diocesan priesthood. Unpublished master's thesis, Loyola University of Chicago, 1961.

Hall, D. T., & Schneider, B. A study of work experiences and career growth of Roman Catholic diocesan priests. Unpublished manuscript, Yale University, 1969.

Henry, W. E., Sims, J., & Spray, S. L. Mental health professionals in Chicago: Some preliminary observations on origins and practice. *Research in Psychotherapy,* 1968, 3, 547-572.

Hispanicus, P. Selecting seminarians. In V. V. Herr (Ed.), *Screening candidates for the priesthood and religious life.* Chicago: Loyola University Press, 1962.

Horney, K. *Neurosis and human growth.* New York: Norton, 1950.

Hunt, P. A. An exploratory study of some relationships between personality variables and achievement in seminary. Unpublished mimeographed paper, Christian University, Texas, 1963. Cited by R. J. Menges, & J. E. Dittes, *Psychological studies of clergymen: Abstracts of research.* New York: Nelson, 1965.

Ingram, O. K. Student recruitment. *Duke Divinity School Bulletin,* 1963, 28, 188-198. Cited by R. J. Menges, & J. E. Dittes. *Psychological studies of clergymen: Abstracts of research.* New York, Nelson, 1965.

Jourard, S. M. *Disclosing man to himself.* Princeton: Van Nostrand, 1968.

Kania, W. Healthy defensiveness in theological students. *Ministry Studies,* 1967, 1, 3-20.

Keefe, J. Maturity in the high school seminarian: An empirical approach. *The Catholic Psychological Record,* 1968, 6, 15-29.

Kennedy, C. E. A comparison of the psychological test scores of successful and unsuccessful major seminarians in a foreign mission seminary. Unpublished master's thesis, Catholic University of America, 1958.

Kennedy, C. E. *Comfort my people.* New York: Sheed and Ward, 1968.

Kennedy, C. E. Differential vocational interest patterns of successful and unsuccessful foreign mission seminarians. Unpublished doctoral dissertation, Loyola University of Chicago, 1959.

Kennedy, C. E. *Fashion me a people: Man, woman and the church.* New York: Sheed and Ward, 1967.

Kennedy, C. E. *The people are the church.* New York: Doubleday, 1969.

Kennedy, C. E. The relationship of self-perception to express motivation for occupational choice. Unpublished doctoral dissertation, Catholic University of America, 1962.

King, H., & Bailar, J. C. The health of the clergy: A review of demographic literature. *Demography,* 1969, 6, 27-43.

Kinnane, J. F. *Career development for priests and religious.* Washington, D. C.: CARA, 1970.

Kobler, F. J., Rizzo, J., & Doyle, E. Dating and formation of religious. *Journal of Religion and Health.* 1967, 6, 2.

Lavoie, P. E. Identity formation in Catholic seminarians as a function of adolescent environment. Unpublished doctoral dissertation, Boston University, 1968.

Lee, J. L. An exploratory search for characteristic patterns and clusters of seminary persisters and leavers. Unpublished doctoral dissertation, University of Michigan, 1968.

Lepak, R. C. Research in clergy vocational interests. *Ministry Studies,* 1968, 2, 6-24.

Levine, M. *Psychotherapy in medical practice.* New York: Macmillian, 1942.

Lhota, B. Vocational interests of Catholic priests. *Studies in Psychology and Psychiatry from the Catholic University of America,* 1948.

Lidz, T. *The person.* New York: Basic Books, 1968.

Lonsway, F. A. Background characteristics and personality traits of Catholic first year theological students. Unpublished doctoral dissertation, University of Minnesota, 1967.

Louis, A., Bowles, W., & Grace, R. Attitude study among priests and religious in New Orleans Archdiocese. Unpublished paper, *Project 560,* May, 1967.

McAllister, R. J., & VanderVeldt, R. J. Psychiatric illness in hospitalized Catholic religious. *American Journal of Psychiatry,* 1965, 121, 881-884.

McCarthy, T. J. Personality traits of seminarians. *Studies in Psychology and Psychiatry from the Catholic University of America,* 1942, 5.

McCarthy, T. N. Personality trait consistency during the training period for a Roman Catholic congregation of teaching brothers. Unpublished doctoral dissertation, University of Ottawa, 1956.

McCarthy, T. N. Evaluation of the present scientific status of screening for religious vocation. In W. C. Bier, & A. A. Schneiders (Eds.), *Selected papers from the ACPA meeting of 1957, 1958, 1959.* New York: American Catholic Psychological Association, 1960, 35-43.

McCarthy, T. N. Testing for the Roman Catholic priesthood. In W. C. Bier (Ed.), *Psychological testing for ministerial selection.* New York: Fordham University Press, 1970.

McClelland, D. C., Atkinson, J. W., Clark, R. A., & Lowell, E. L. *The achievement motive.* New York: Appleton-Century, 1953.

McDonagh, A. J. A study of adjustments and interests of first year college seminarians for the diocesan priesthood. Unpublished master's thesis, Loyola University of Chicago, 1961.

McNemar, Q. *Psychological statistics.* New York: Wiley, 1962.

Madigan, F. C. Role satisfactions and length of life in a closed population. *American Journal of Sociology,* 1962, 67, 640-49.

Maehr, M. L., & Stake, R. E. The value patterns of men who voluntarily quit seminary training. *Personnel and Guidance Journal,* 1962, 40, 537-540.

Maffia, L. A. Measured interests of priests, seminarians and former seminarians in the selection of seminary applicants. Unpublished doctoral dissertation, St. John's University, 1954.

Meissner, W. W. *Annotated bibliography of religion and psychology.* New York: ARMH, 1961.

Menges, R. J., & Dittes, J. E. *Psychological studies of clergymen: Abstracts of research.* New York: Nelson, 1965.

Menges, R. J. Studies of clergymen: Abstracts of research supplement I. *Ministry Studies,* 1967, 1, 5-67.

Mills, E. W. (Ed.) Types of role conflict among clergymen. *Ministry Studies,* 1968, 2.

Moore, T. V. Insanity in priests and religious. I. The rate of insanity in priests and religious. II. The detection of prepsychotics who apply for admission to the priesthood or religious communities. *American Ecclesiastical Review,* 1936, 95, 485-498, 601-613.

Murray, J. B. Training for the priesthood and personality and interest test manifestations. Unpublished doctoral dissertation, Fordham University, 1957.

Nunnally, J. *Psychometric theory.* New York: McGraw-Hill, 1967.

Pittel, S. M., & Mendelsohn, G. A. Measurement of moral values: A review and critique. *Psychological Bulletin,* 1966, 66, 22-35.

Potvin, R., & Suziedelis, A. *Seminarians of the sixties.* Washington, D.C.: CARA, 1969.

Quinn, T. L. Differences in motivational patterns of college student brothers revealed in the TAT, the ratings of their peers, and the ratings of their superiors: A validation study. Unpublished doctoral dissertation, Loyola University of Chicago, 1961.

Rogers, C. *On becoming a person.* Boston: Houghton-Mifflin, 1961.

Rooney, J. J. Psychological assessment in a community of teaching sisters. *The Catholic Psychological Record,* 1966, 4, 56-62.

Rooney, J. J. Problems of interpretation: A commentary. *Ministry Studies,* 1967, 1, 21-24.

Rooney, J. J. Needed research on the psychological assessment of religious personnel. In W. J. Coville, P. F. D'Arcy, T. N. McCarthy, & J. J. Rooney, *Assessment of candidates for the religious life.* Washington, D.C.: CARA, 1968.

Saul, L. J. *Emotional maturity: The development and dynamics of personality.* Philadelphia: Lippincott, 1960.

Scheffe, H. *The analysis of variance.* New York: Wiley, 1959.

Schneider, B., & Hall, D. T. The role of assignment characteristics in the career experiences of diocesan priests. In W. E. Bartlett (Ed.), *Vocational Development of Religious Careers.* Washington, D.C.: CARA, 1970, in press.

Sheehan, S. M. The Loyola sentence completion blank for clergymen: Construction and validation. Unpublished master's thesis, Loyola University of Chicago, 1970.

Sheridan, E., & Kobler, F. J. Loyola seminarian sentence completion test. *Journal of Projective Techniques and Personality Assessment,* 1969, 33, 507-512.

Shostrom, E. L. *Manual, Personal Orientation Inventory.* San Diego: Educational and Industrial Testing Service, 1966.

Shostrom, E. L. *Personal orientation inventory.* San Diego: Educational & Industrial Testing Service, 1963.

Simons, J. B. Congruence between self and religious percepts: A descriptive study of satisfaction with the religious life among seminarians in different stages of preparation for the priesthood. Unpublished doctoral dissertation, University of Notre Dame, 1966.

Sims, J. Identity and identity diffusion: The professional actor. Unpublished monograph, University of Chicago, 1962.

Skrincosky, P. A comparative study of the standard form of the Minnesota Multiphasic Personality Inventory and a modified form of the same adapted for a seminary group. Unpublished master's thesis, Forham University, 1953.

Strunk, O. Self-anchoring scaling for study of perceptions of religious maturity. *Perceptual and Motor Skills,* 1967, 25, 471-472.

Super, D. Vocational development theory. *The Counseling Psychologist,* 1969, 1. 2-14.

Sutter, C. R. A comparative study of the interest and personality patterns of major seminarians. Unpublished doctoral dissertation, Fordham University, 1961.

Sward, K. Temperament and religious experience. *Journal of Social Psychology,* 1931, 2, 374-396.

Sweeney, R. H. Testing seminarians with the MMPI and Kuder: A report of ten years of testing. Unpublished master's thesis, Loyola University of Chicago, 1964.

Tageson, C. Relationship of self-perception to realism of vocational choice among minor seminarians, Washington: Catholic University of America, 1960. Cited by J. F. Kinnane, *Career development for priests and religious.* Washington, D.C.: CARA, 1970.

Thompson, J. S. A study of the relationships between certain measured psychological variables and achievement in the first year of theological seminary work. Unpublished doctoral dissertation, University of Minnesota, 1956.

VanderVeldt, A. J., & McAllister, R. J. Psychiatric illness in hospitalized clergy: Alcoholism. *Quarterly Journal of Studies in Alcoholism,* 1962, 23, 124-130.

Vaughan, R. P. A psychological assessment program for candidates to the religious life: Validation study. *Catholic Psychological Record,* 1963, 1, 65-70.

Wagoner, W. D. *The seminary: Protestant and Catholic.* New York: Sheed and Ward, 1966.

Walker, R. E., Davis, W. E., & Firetto, A. An experimenter variable: The psychologist-clergyman. *Psychological Reports,* 1968, 22, 709-714.

Walker, R. E., & Firetto, A. The clergyman as a variable in psychological testing. *Journal for the Scientific Study of Religion,* 1965, 4, 234-236.

Wauck, L. A. An investigation into the use of psychological tests as an aid in the selection of candidates for the diocesan priesthood. Unpublished doctoral dissertation, Loyola University of Chicago, 1956.

Webb, S. C., Goodling, P. A., & Shepherd, I. L. The prediction of field work ratings in a theological school. *Religious Education,* 1958, 53, 534-538.

Weisgerber, C. A. *Psychological assessment of candidates for a religious order.* Chicago: Loyola University Press, 1969.

Welsh, G. S., & Dahlstrom, W. G. (Ed.) *Basic readings on the MMPI in Psychology and Medicine.* Minneapolis: University of Minnesota Press, 1956.

Wright, H. W. Memorandum for the Chief of Chaplains: Predicting the success of army chaplains. Unpublished paper, University of Minnesota Counseling Bureau, 1951. Cited in R. J. Menges, & J. E. Dittes. *Psychological studies of clergymen: Abstracts of research.* New York: Nelson, 1965.

INDEX